American Urbanization: A Comparative History

American Urbanization:
A Comparative History

BLAKE McKELVEY
City Historian of Rochester, New York

SCOTT, FORESMAN AND COMPANY
Glenview, Illinois   Brighton, England

Library of Congress Catalog Card Number: 72-90733
ISBN: 0-673-07616-4

Copyright © 1973 Scott, Foresman and Company, Glenview, Illinois.
Philippines Copyright 1973 Scott, Foresman and Company.
All Rights Reserved. Printed in the United States of America.

Regional offices of Scott, Foresman and Company are located in Dallas, Texas; Glenview, Illinois; Oakland, New Jersey; Palo Alto, California; Tucker, Georgia; and Brighton, England.

Preface

The mounting flood of books on cities published during the last three decades has filled many shelves in the history and social science divisions of our public and university libraries, and overflowed the bookcases of an increasing number of students of urban affairs. This outpouring of volumes from many fields has explored all the civic, economic, and cultural aspects of our urban-metropolitan society. Many books have contributed to our factual knowledge, and some to our understanding, of the internal structures, the growth processes, and the external relationships of individual cities or of urban societies in different time periods. Some have sought to distill the vital essence of urbanization, to convey the inherent character of the urban experience, while others have discussed books already and yet to be written. These works have all revealed wide contrasts between the urban patterns and urbanizing trends of different societies. And while our knowledge of the cities and their growth processes in some parts of the world is still incomplete, it seems desirable at this point to make a preliminary effort at least to view urban developments in America in comparison with what is known of developments in other urban societies.

American Urbanization: A Comparative History aims to place our knowledge of the history of American cities in better perspective for both college students and general readers, and to open new research vistas for graduate students. I am grateful to Scott, Foresman and Company for the opportunity to undertake this study, and to the following academic editors for their constructive criticism during the preparation of this book: Frederick Kershner, Columbia Teachers College, David B. Bien, the University of Michigan, Merle Curti, the University of Wisconsin, and Kai T. Erickson, Yale University. Their encouragement, and that of Michael S. Werthman and the late George Vlach of Scott, Foresman, has been greatly appreciated. I am indebted to Diane Culhane for her painstaking editorial assistance, and to Faye Geldin for her care in the preparation of the successive typescripts. Of course I am myself responsible for the shortcomings that must remain in this pioneer effort to treat urban history from a comparative viewpoint.

Blake McKelvey
Rochester, New York

Introduction

The rapid and pulsating growth of American cities over the past three hundred years has been one of the most striking but least understood aspects of the nation's development. Only in the last few decades have increasing numbers of scholars—sociologists, political scientists, geographers, economists, as well as some historians—become aware of the crucial importance of the urbanization process. Indeed, it was in 1953 that a small band of historians formed the Urban History Group to assure an audience for their pioneer studies. To avoid the parochialism of local history, some undertook comparative studies of two or more cities, while others borrowed the techniques and drew upon the findings of urban scholars in other disciplines. Soon an outpouring of books on the city began to appear, and program chairmen at annual conferences, as well as department chairmen at the leading universities, began frantically to seek lecturers and instructors for urban history programs that increasingly commanded top priority.

That priority was less a product of scholarly stirrings, however, than of the mounting problems of urban congestion and disorder that were thrusting the crisis of the cities into the headlines of every daily paper, and into the chambers of state and federal legislatures and judicial tribunals. The parochial aspect of urban studies has disappeared as the problems of the cities have become nationwide. Unfortunately, the overpowering sense of the crisis has tended to obscure rather than illuminate the complex character of the urbanization process. The city's traditional role as the cradle of civilization has been challenged, and its subsidiary roles as the birthplace of technology, the home of industry, the citadel of law and order, and the temple of learning are almost forgotten. Predictions of doom have multiplied and they have not been confined to American cities.

But as studies of cities in other lands have also increased in number, some interesting comparisons have come to light. A number of social and political scientists, as well as economists and geographers, after wide studies of other societies stimulated in several instances by UNESCO assignments to seek solutions for the problems of underdeveloped countries, have come to recognize the great potential of urbanization (as experienced in the West) as a creative process in social development. Perhaps a review of the history of urbanization in America, viewed comparatively in relation to the sometimes similar but frequently quite different growth of cities in other lands, will help bring our own urban situation and the historical role of our cities back into focus.

First we must clarify our understanding of the urbanization process. It is, of course, a dynamic phenomenon, and has many complex aspects. Various social scientists have highlighted different features in their interpretations. Thus the human ecologists have stressed the increasing size and proportion of the urban population, together with changing age and family patterns, and other human characteristics, as the dominant factors. Other sociologists have focused attention on the degree of heterogeneity in the urban population, the appearance and differentiation of specialized groups, classes, and neighborhoods within growing cities, and the developing networks of other social relationships. Most of these scholars have been keenly interested in measuring, and some in explaining, demographic trends—the migration of newcomers to the cities from nearby and distant hinterlands, the changing fertility of the resident population at various stages, and the internal redistribution that growth produces. Some sociologists have insisted that these are the only aspects of the development of cities that properly belong to a study of urbanization. That approach has, however, proved to be too narrow.

While urging the primary importance of the demographic interpretation of urbanization, Eric E. Lampard, our most exacting theorist, has significantly broadened that conception of the process. "For cities to increase in number and size," he has declared, "there must be not merely population and a spatial environment, but relevant social and cultural capacities as well."[1] In his study of the "functional-structural differentiation" of cities as economic centers, he postulates an "ecosystem" to encompass the growth of urban economic regions and the evolving system of cities. Wilbur R. Thompson, in an intensive analysis of urban economic growth, fills in the details of such an ecosystem for a hypothetical city by constructing a model showing fourteen possible factor linkages. Some economists rely more heavily on input and output ratios and on internal and external economies to account for the vitality of individual cities, while others stress various economic and geographic variables as the determinants influencing the location and expansion of specific centers. Still other economists give major attention to such physical phenomena as technological innovations, local building practices, housing programs, and planning.

Urban geographers view the economic and structural aspects of cities from their own special perspectives. They, too, are interested in demographic trends, particularly in the concentration and distribution of people and the effects of their various patterns of settlement on the larger society. They are concerned also with the larger constellations of cities and with the internal patterns of land use and their relation to urban functions. Although most of their early studies were empirical and endeavored to increase the substantive knowledge of urban forms, in recent years they have sought by building models to test hypotheses and develop concepts to aid in the planning of future cities.

Political scientists are concerned not only with the developing governmental structure of cities, but also with the internal alignment of political forces. Their analyses overlap and sometimes conflict with those of the sociologists in the study of power groups and political cultures, and they impinge on the field of the economists in planning and welfare. They anticipated the historians in noting the development of new urban-federal relationships. With most historians, they have generally been content with an empirical approach to the cities, defining urbanization as the process of their development in

1. "The Evolving Systems of Cities in the United States: Urbanization and Economic Development," in *Issues in Urban Economics,* ed. Harvey S. Perloff and Lowdon Wingo (Baltimore: The Johns Hopkins Press, 1968), p. 109.

social, political, and economic respects as circumstances and the available leadership dictate. A few, such as Daniel Elazar, have recently endeavored to identify socioeconomic variables to assist in political analysis.

The historian brings to the study of urbanism the dimension of time, which is, of course, an essential aspect of urbanization as a process. His second basic contribution is the empirical evidence he provides of man's experience with cities. But this evidence is so rich and varied that the urban historian has a wider choice of approaches to the city than do any of the social scientists. He can focus on the history of one city and study its internal development and external relationships to the larger society, much as one would write the biography of a man, always mindful, of course, that his subject is a social organism, not a biological one. He can make a comparative study of two or more cities over a number of years, or attempt a comprehensive review of urban developments in one or more nations within a certain time period. Or, with Corinne Gilb, he can undertake an urban systems analysis, viewing the growth of cities in a four-dimensional time and space relationship. Whatever the extent of his topic, he has the challenging opportunity to apply and test the various conceptual approaches of the social sciences, including the data-processing methods that scholars trained in the use of statistics have employed to extract aggregative insights from bulky records often neglected in documentary research.

The historian has the additional (some would say the primary) task of determining the extent and character of the urban influence on the broader course of a nation's history. This certainly is our major interest, but since we have elected to view America's urbanization comparatively, as well as in historical depth, the insights of several of the social sciences will prove useful. We will accept the demographic view of urbanization as its basic element, but in addition to recognizing the increasing concentration of the population in cities as the chief criterion in determining the rate of urbanization, we will look for other factors to determine the level or dimension of urbanization. Thus, as additional growth brought some cities new functions that increased not only the rate but also the scope and direction of their development, the urbanization process achieved new economic, social, and political dimensions. Urbanization as a meaningful historical process envisages not only a progressive concentration of the population into cities, but also the development of increasingly complex patterns of urbanism. Historically this dynamic quality has produced in the modern period in Europe and America several successive stages of urbanization. Various scholars have described different periods of growth, and several can profitably be studied, but we will follow the lead of Lampard and Patrick Geddes and divide America's urban history into three parts: the age of commercial expansion, the era of the rapid growth of industrial cities, and the modern period of the nation's metropolitan reorganization.

To improve our understanding of the urbanizing forces active in these several periods, we will view them in relation to contemporary and comparable developments in other urban societies. Although the comparative approach does not supply a perfect control device, and does not produce scientific knowledge, it will help assure an objective selection of relevant data. It will also serve to highlight the special quality of America's urbanization.

Thus in Part One, Urbanization in an Age of Commercial Expansion, we will note significant contrasts between the colonial ports of British and Latin America and between the later frontier towns of these and other expanding societies. We will be especially interested in determining the respective sources and qualities of their populations—natives, colonial adventurers or yeomen, immigrant minorities, slaves—and in observing the varied roles each played in the development of the cities. And as we review the spreading development of commercial cities in the States, occasional glances at contrasting urban trends in Britain and on the Continent, as well as in Latin America, will help define the special character of America's cities. The greater heterogeneity experienced by cities in the States will command special attention.

For Part Two, Urbanization in an Age of Industrialism, frequent comparisons with trends in Britain and on the Continent will be illuminating. We will be interested in observing the contrasting effects of relatively homogeneous as against heterogeneous populations, of local as opposed to centralized authority, of private or corporate as distinguished from public enterprise, and of traditional as opposed to innovative social and cultural patterns. Of course, no one of these dichotomies alone holds the secret that explains the remarkable transformation of America in the late nineteenth century. Yet the combination of a heterogeneous population free to develop private and corporate enterprise on a local urban scale, and forced because of the diversity of its origins to be innovative, proved sufficient to infuse the emerging system of cities with unprecedented productive energies. The vast geographic setting and the broader horizons available to Americans have been a constant influence on the development of their industrial cities.

The influence of these geographic factors on the development of metropolitan regionalism will be even more apparent in Part Three, Urbanization in an Age of Metropolitanism. The effects of the automobile and other technological advances, and the impact of wars and depressions, have considerably dominated urban developments in this period. New organizational achievements and new sources of power, both natural and human, finally raised metropolitan America to first place not only in production, but also in world leadership. And if a new population movement, with blacks from southern plantations displacing immigrants from Europe in inner-city slums and creating a new heterogeneity, provides a tragic unity to the historical drama of America's urbanization, as viewed in the 1970s, the historian's expectation that a fourth and less dismal act is still in the making is supported by a few comparisons noted in Chapter 10.

BIBLIOGRAPHY

Beaujeu-Garnier, N., and G. Clobot. *Urban Geography.* New York: John Wiley & Sons, Inc., 1967.

Dyos, H. J., ed. *The Study of Urban History.* New York: St. Martin's Press, Inc., 1968.

Gilb, Corinne L. "Urban History and Comparative National History: Some Common Questions and Points of Congruence." Paper delivered to the American Historical Association in Boston, December 1970.

Hauser, Philip M., ed. *Urbanization in Asia and the Far East.* Calcutta: UNES-
CO Research Center on the the Social Implications of Industrialization in
Southern Asia, 1957.

Hauser, Philip M., and Leo F. Schnore, eds. *The Study of Urbanization.* New
York: John Wiley & Sons, Inc., 1965.

Lampard, Eric E. "The Evolving Systems of Cities in the United States: Urbanization and Economic Development." In *Issues in Urban Economics,* ed.
Harvey S. Perloff and Lowdon Wingo. Baltimore: The John Hopkins Press,
1968.

McKelvey, Blake. *The Emergence of Metropolitan America.* New Brunswick,
N.J.: Rutgers University Press, 1968.

Schlesinger, Arthur M. "The City in American History." *Mississippi Valley
Historical Review,* 27 (June 1940), 43–66.

Thernstrom, Stephan. "Reflections on the New Urban History." *Daedalus,*
Spring 1971, 359–75.

Thompson, Wilbur R. *A Preface to Urban Economics.* Baltimore: The John
Hopkins Press, 1965.

Weber, Adna F. *The Growth of Cities in the Nineteenth Century.* New York: The
Macmillan Co., 1899.

Contents

PART ONE

Urbanization in an Age of Commercial Expansion, to 1860

America's urbanization commenced with the founding of New Amsterdam, Boston, and the other colonial ports in the early 1600s. We call them colonial and so they were, but not in the modern sense of that term, nor did they closely resemble the cities established in the previous century in the West Indies, Mexico, or South America. The mainland ports in North America were commercial outposts of an advanced and expanding mercantile nation, not imperial fortresses in an occupied land. Moreover, unlike the older towns and cities of Great Britain and western Europe, they started at an advanced stage of urban development as the frontier settlements of an existing system of cities centered in London. They escaped the medieval restraints that still curbed most of their contemporaries in Europe, and displayed urbanizing trends similar in character though not in rate to those of the frontier towns of the early 1800s. Unlike the primordial cities, which as Eric Lampard tells us had slowly emerged from their agrarian environment several millennia earlier, they were generators and promoters, not products, of their rural hinterlands. And although they were in some respects comparable to the colonial towns planted by Greek and other thriving Hellenic cities in their age of expansion, vividly described by Lewis Mumford in *The City in History,* the two colonial movements were as far apart in urban style and traditions as each was from the South American and Southeast Asian developments. Thus the urbanization of North America, particularly in the eras of settlement and commercial expansion, was in many respects unique, and some of the distinctive characteristics of America's urban society were acquired in the course of these formative centuries.

To document these generalizations and appraise the influence of the cities of America on its history, in Chapter 1 we will review their establishment in comparison with that of other colonial cities. We will want to see to what extent these respective groups of cities were planned in advance and controlled from the outside, and to what extent they developed naturally and indigenously. We will want to consider the source and character of their populations, the extent of their homogeneity or heterogeneity, the breadth of their urban linkages, and the degree of freedom they enjoyed. Finally, we will want to identify their intended functions and observe the development of new ones, and we will want to evaluate their respective roles in the history of these colonies.

With the achievement of independence cities in the United States acquired new roles, and Chapter 2 will compare the new frontier towns with their colonial predecessors and with frontier towns elsewhere. In our search for the implications of a diffusion of urban sites, an acceleration of urban growth, and an increased diversity of population, we will contrast city developments in the States with those in Britain and its new colonies, as well as in Latin America. We will note some comparable trends in the cities of both South America and the southern States because of their mutual involvement with slavery, and we will consider some of the contrasting effects of popularly based as against autocratically structured urban trends.

Of course the predominant force in the urbanization of pre-Civil War America was its commercial development and expansion. But similar forces were active in Britain and on the Continent, and in order to understand the special character of urbanization in the States we will attempt in Chapters 3 and 4 to identify the diverging population and spatial trends. We will also observe their varied reliance on technology, natural resources, and entrepreneurial and corporate as distinguished from bureaucratic enterprise; and we will consider the relationships of rates of urbanization to productivity, degrees of well-being, and the recurrent outcroppings of antiurban sentiments. Although these developments were most easily and most frequently described and evaluated in economic terms, they also had civic, social, and cultural aspects, and the contrasts displayed here will shed light on urbanizing trends in the States.

1

Urbanization and Mercantilism

Expanding mercantile empires, each centered in a dynamic metropolis—
Madrid, Lisbon, Amsterdam, Paris, London—were establishing rival colonial
outposts in North and South America, and in Southeast Asia as well, in the
sixteenth and seventeenth centuries. Each of these outposts, several score in
number, represented an advanced stage in the urbanization of its mother country, and each had provincial ties with its metropolitan progenitor. The new
urban centers, like the old cities in Europe, were all preindustrial, but the
contrasts with the provincial towns at home were almost as striking as those
among the mercantile outposts themselves. These latter differences sprang in
part from varied geographic settings, but chiefly from divergent cultural traditions and the urban functions they fostered.

URBAN BEGINNINGS IN LATIN AMERICA

Most of the Central and South American cities date from the sixteenth century and an early and crude stage of mercantilism. They were established in
the wake of the Conquistadores, by officials and adventurers from the Spanish
Court, as imperial outposts to control the native inhabitants of the newly
conquered lands and to supervise the extraction and shipment of precious
metals. Some, notably Mexico City in 1521 and Lima in 1535, were erected on
or near the ruins of pre-Columbian cities and quickly acquired large native as
well as Spanish populations. Others, such as Bogotá in 1538 and La Paz in
1539, were planted at strategic points to control the exploitation of nearby
mines. These and most of the other Spanish towns were built in the Spanish
Renaissance style, in accordance with the Laws of the Indies. First issued by
Charles V in 1523, these laws provided a standardized plan calling for broad
streets with spacious residential blocks adjoining a central plaza and surrounded by a wall for defense against possible native uprisings. The cities
were in effect stylized products of sixteenth-century Spanish planners.

Several of the early Spanish American cities quickly acquired major proportions. Planted in the midst of the populous Incas, Mayas, and Aztecs,
whose well-established communities had been subjugated, they drew many

refugees from the native towns. Missionary priests, military governors, tax collectors, and adventurous merchants occupied the Spanish quarters of these administrative strongholds, with the Indians residing in nearby streets and in more populous settlements clustered beyond the walls. The economy of these cities depended on their ability to maintain a flow of precious metals from nearby or distant mines and a steady return of taxes exacted from Indians in the remaining pre-Columbian towns and the new mining camps in the mountains beyond.

Products of an early stage of mercantilism, the Latin American capitals were the precursors of the "parasitic" cities established by later intruders into Southeast Asia. Defined by Professor Bert F. Hoselitz of Chicago as places whose growth tended to check rather than stimulate the economic development of their hinterlands, these cities exploited the human and the natural resources of their subject regions. Even Santiago (1541) and Buenos Aires (1570), founded as ports in fertile regions where the sparsely settled Indians were chiefly engaged in agriculture, developed as strongholds for the control of distant trade routes from which they exacted their tribute. They served, as the years advanced, as market centers for the Spanish-owned and operated plantations and cattle ranches that absorbed an increasing portion of the fertile lands. Except for the missionaries they sent out to Christianize the Indians who worked the mines and plantations, the Spanish American ports and capital cities contributed little to the numerous inhabitants of the broad colonies they dominated.

The Portuguese, who had explored and conquered Brazil, shared the Spaniards' thirst for treasure, penchant for large plantations, and loyalty to the Church. They established Rio de Janeiro in 1566 as an ocean port and stronghold for the defense of their settlers and traders, and São Paulo in 1555, on a walled hilltop, as a nucleus for missionaries. Lacking a master plan, the Brazilian cities grew, like many North American cities in a later century, as their local builders determined. In other respects, however, they followed the lead of their Spanish neighbors by erecting walls for defense and permitting the natives to cluster in crowded settlements on the outskirts. Of all South American capital cities, only Buenos Aires, and a century later Montevideo, developed slowly and almost exclusively as European, at first chiefly Spanish, settlements, but both relied heavily on fortifications to protect their commerce.

URBANIZATION IN THE BRITISH COLONIES

In contrast with the urban beginnings in South and Central America, the mainland ports to the north were at the start bridgeheads through which adventurous British and other migrants passed enroute to their nearby village or rural settlements. Although some Englishmen, like many Spaniards a century before them, came in search of gold or other treasure, others—tradesmen, artisans, and yeomen—hoped to acquire homes and freedom in a new land. Their first contacts with the Indians were for the most part conciliatory, though the impact of strange customs and new diseases proved disastrous for many natives. Since neither the widely scattered and generally nomadic Indian tribes in these northern districts nor the small parties of British settlers were very numerous, there seemed more than ample space for all. The new-comers negotiated one-sided agreements for permission to establish the various ports and virtually hoodwinked the natives out of the surrounding lands. Some of the more adventurous engaged in the fur trade and endeavored to enlist the aid of the Indians, who were skilled as hunters and trappers, in developing that wide-ranging activity. Less domesticated than their brothers in Central and South America, where urban societies, as J. M. Houston tells us, had already developed, few of the still nomadic North American Indians adopted the ways of the white man, and fewer still gravitated to the cities. As the colonists increased, the outnumbered Indians gradually withdrew from the coastal territories. Their withdrawal was not always peaceful, but it was so complete that by 1790, when the first federal census counted nearly 4,000,000 inhabitants east of the Mississippi, only an estimated 33,000 were Indians.

Meanwhile the widely spaced mainland ports, as transplanted European, predominantly English, towns, supplied commercial and cultural as well as administrative links between the scattered settlers and the home country. Populated in large part by middle-class migrants from London or the provincial ports, and sometimes, as at New Haven, lead by a Puritan minister, these towns grew in size and importance as their provinces filled up, calling for added services, but their major function was to serve as a merchandizing and administrative center, not to establish military control over the settlers they distributed. They were located at the best natural harbors and they performed from the beginning the functions the provincial towns of Britain had acquired after many centuries of development as administrative and trading centers. Because of their prior settlement, they assumed in addition the role of promotional or, as Hoselitz describes it, "generative" leadership in their expanding hinterlands.

A major source of that leadership was the entrepreneurial vitality of many residents of these ports. Thus merchants took the lead in promoting shipbuilding and commercial fishing in New England, and grain farming and the fur trade in the middle colonies. Recruited from the skilled artisans and ambitious tradesmen who migrated to America, they developed a culture of "privatism," as Sam Bass Warner describes it. The well-known career of Benjamin Franklin, destined to become Philadelphia's most famous citizen, was a prime example. His settlement there as a fugitive apprentice from Boston, and his rapid advance based on enterprise and skill, set a pattern for aspiring youths and newcomers which his talents as a writer, publisher, and founder of volunteer citizen associations helped promote.

Thus the British ports, in contrast with the stylized administrative cities of Latin America, had both a historic and a natural quality. Founded at different stages of Britain's imperial expansion, they had varied origins, but each based its growth after the first few seasons on the energies of its residents rather than on the resources and plans of distant promoters. Even the most carefully planned of the British ports, Philadelphia, unlike the cities of Latin America and many in Europe, was a community of entrepreneurs, each man eager to exploit every opportunity within the town and its province to get ahead. In Boston, where maritime opportunities favored a limited group to the disadvantage of an increasing number of the less fortunate, and in Charleston, where the plantation economy had a similar effect, a wealthy upper class made its appearance, as well as a depressed stratum of unattached workers and (in Charleston) slaves. Yet in Boston and Charleston, as in Philadelphia and New York, a sturdy middle class also emerged and assumed a major role in the economic development of the city and its hinterland.

The history of the colonial ports of North America has been brilliantly recaptured by Carl Bridenbaugh and ably reviewed by other scholars, yet several aspects of their urbanization merit elaboration. In spite of the progressive development of the five ports, studied by Bridenbaugh in *Cities in the Wilderness* and *Cities in Revolt,* their combined populations, which increased from 21,000 in 1700 to 72,500 in 1760, failed to keep pace with the total colonial growth from 275,000 to 1,610,000 in these six decades. The urban proportion at the start was, however, surprisingly high (7.7 percent in 1700), and although the sum of the five cities represented only 4.5 percent of the colonial total in 1760, if the fifteen other colonial towns that exceeded 2,500 each by 1775 are included, the urban total for that date reaches 180,000, or 7.2 percent of the population. If the accuracy of these statistics is somewhat questionable, as are all population estimates before the advent of regular censuses, the best evidence reveals that the urban proportion in the colonies was slightly over half that of Great Britain in 1700 and only slightly under half of it in 1775. The colonial ports, in other words, were an integral part of an expanding British system of cities. Moreover, London, the great metropolis of the entire empire, benefited from and contributed to development abroad as well as at home. Its growth from 500,000 to 700,000 in this period accounted for a major portion of the English advance, while two or three of the colonial ports outpaced, and Philadelphia actually surpassed, all but two of the provincial cities in Britain.

The five colonial ports in North America had not only become twenty within a century and a half, but they had also spawned a host of lesser towns and created a vibrant society. Most of the lesser towns were agricultural hamlets, tightly clustered, particularly in New England. Many were "covenanted" settlements founded by like-minded settlers who feared diversity, but practically all hastened to produce a surplus, which they dispatched to the larger market towns in exchange for household supplies and other imports. The agricultural settlements as well as the market towns—the latter peopled by migrants from the commercial towns and districts of Great Britain, with increasing numbers from similar districts in western Europe—were market oriented. As Professor Julius Rubin of Pittsburgh has recently observed, "Colonial America, though certainly 90 percent agricultural in an occupational sense, may also be described as 90 percent urban in a cultural sense."[1] The proportion living in cities was not as large as in England or in Holland, and it was not increasing. But if the urbanization process, as defined by the ecologists, was at a stand in the British colonies, the stage of urbanization was well advanced, and the cities were progressively increasing their internal functions and improving their urban services to the surrounding colonists.

The urbanization achieved by the thirteen British colonies contrasted even more sharply with that in Latin America. After an extended tour of the New

---

1. "Urban Growth and Regional Development," in *The Growth of Seaport Cities: 1790–1825* (Charlottesville, Va.: University Press of Virginia, 1967), pp. 5–6.

World in 1755 and a diligent use of all available reports on South as well as North America, Edmund Burke concluded that no city in the north could rival either Lima or Mexico City in size or in the splendor of their churches and public buildings. Lima in particular, rebuilt after an earthquake and tidal wave that destroyed its port in 1746, was a decade later an impressive imperial capital, boasting 54,000 residents, where the officials and leading merchants of all the Spanish colonies gathered for gala festivities. Its cathedral and numerous churches, many of them richly decorated with precious metals, demonstrated the wealth of its religious orders. But these colonial capitals, each comprising a few thousand Spanish American residents surrounded by vast throngs of natives, had drawn all the administrative, religious, commercial, and other urban functions of populous colonies into their hands and had become the first American examples of the "primate" city type, first identified by Mark Jefferson in the 1940s. These monolithic urban centers contrasted not only with the multiple urban pattern in British North America, but also with the native communities in their own hinterlands. Almost the only hold they had over the production of the Indian inhabitants of the surrounding territories was based on taxes and other impositions, including now tithes for the construction and maintenance of churches and monasteries in the capitals.

SOCIAL AND ETHNIC DIFFERENCES

The cities of Central and South America, as vividly described by Professor William L. Schurz, had sharply divided dual societies, with the minority dependent for its safety as well as for its dominance on the strength of its imperial ties with Madrid or Lisbon and, in some West Indian cities, with Paris and London as well. In the islands and increasingly in the Atlantic coast cities in South America, the colonists had early found the Indian natives too intractable or too few to man the plantations. To replace or supplement the Indians, the colonists imported thousands of black slaves from Africa. By the late 1700s the blacks comprised the largest group in several of these cities, or stood second to the Indians, with whom they in some colonies intermixed. The dual society of peons or slaves and masters left no room for intruding third parties. Thus the Sephardic Jews, who in the still fluid circumstances of the sixteenth century had migrated in considerable numbers from Spain and Holland to Brazil and Peru, were forced by the hostility of the Church and the rivalry of Christian merchants to migrate again, some to New York and Charleston in the north.

The British ports in North America had attracted other minority groups as well. Many of the Hollanders who had established New Amsterdam maintained active roles in the more dynamic New York that superseded it. Philadelphia and New York attracted many German, Scottish, and Irish migrants who, with some Swedes and the Dutch, rivaled in number the English in their midst. A shipload of French Huguenots settled at Charleston, but that port received many more shipments of black slaves. While most of the blacks spread inland, both to the north and the south, to man the rice, tobacco, and cotton plantations, a sufficient number found lodgement in Charleston to equal its white inhabitants. Merchants and other householders in several of the other mainland ports acquired slaves, too, but only in New York did they approach 20 percent of the total in 1750. Meanwhile, a motley assortment of traders from many ports added to the diversity of the chief mainland cities. This heterogeneity, contrasting with the pervasive uniformity that character-ized the agricultural towns that surrounded them, intensified the en-trepreneurial struggles and enhanced the leadership of the cities by making them the indispensable agents of the country's unification.

More significant than the increased ethnic diversity was the development in most of the mainland ports of an urban middle class. In contrast with the cities of Latin America, which continued to rely on imports for handicrafts not of native origin, the British ports attracted a host of artisans who quickly vied with the shopkeeping merchants in supplying the domestic needs and eventu-ally dispatched their products to neighboring and distant markets. This devel-opment soon stirred the hostility of the British king, who was chiefly inter-ested in promoting the handicrafts of his London metropolis. Local enterprise was more spontaneous and dramatic in Boston, Philadelphia, and New York than in many provincial cities in Britain or on the Continent, partly because those old towns, imbedded in a feudal society, experienced many restraints unknown in the New World. The cities of Latin America had a medieval or pre-Columbian heritage of their own to contend with, and failed to develop an enterprising middle class comparable to that which increasingly animated the mainland ports to the north.

It was, moreover, the middle class that took the lead in the development of new civic functions. Its members were heirs to the British tradition of local self-government, in contrast to the French and Spanish traditions of central-ized administration that prevailed in Latin America. They were the property-holding residents who crowded the town meetings in New England and pres-sured the town councils elsewhere to provide more adequate community ser-vices. Small shopkeepers and artisans demanded fire protection and were ready to serve in volunteer companies to get it. They formed the mutual benefit societies, the craftsmen's relief and marine self-help associations, that supplied private assistance, and they promoted the establishment of municipal almshouses and workhouses in the leading cities. In every port, even in Charleston, they protested the intrusion of untrained workers into their jour-neymen's associations. To facilitate internal travel and the transport of goods, the tradesmen wanted paved streets and adequate drainage sewers, and Boston by 1720 provided such facilities of a quality that only London could match.

Because of the varying attitudes of successive regimes at home, the British colonial towns, founded at widely spaced dates, received quite dissimilar char-ters. As Professor Griffith has shown, the early charter granted by King Charles II to New York City (1665) was generously democratic, permitting local election of the councilmen, but as Charles and his successors subse-quently became embroiled with Parliament, they generally granted only close corporation charters, in both England and America, naming the members themselves or delegating that privilege to the governors. In some colonies the proprietor or governor received authority to grant municipal charters and ex-ercised it in accordance with his views of the situation. The governors in New York, New Jersey, and Pennsylvania, faced with the need to harmonize various ethnic groups, generally granted elective councils but named the mayors themselves. All, however, granted fairly general powers checked by narrowly limited taxing privileges. The emerging cities managed nevertheless to provide numerous services. Boston's excellent public market and docks were eventually matched, if not surpassed, by both New York and Philadelphia.

RELIGIOUS AND CULTURAL ASPECTS OF URBANIZATION

The ethnic and functional diversity helped nurture a religious and cultural diversity as well. In contrast with the cities of Latin America, where the Catholic churches maintained exclusive religious control, the Puritans in Boston, who soon split into Congregational and Unitarian branches, found themselves surrounded by Baptist, Methodist, and Episcopal churches, as well as some Catholic and Jewish groups. In Philadelphia, the Quakers early made their peace with the Scotch Presbyterians and the German Lutherans, as well as with most of the denominations active in Boston and New York. Although each of these cities soon had several modest and a few elegant church buildings, none could match the size and wealth of the cathedrals that arose in Lima, Mexico City, and other Catholic capitals to the south, or in French Quebec to the north. None of the British cities, predominantly Protestant, had institutions to rival the thirteen monasteries and twelve convents of Lima, or those of Mexico City and other Spanish and Portuguese capitals.

Among the five British ports, only Charleston approached the high culture of some of the Latin American cities. With its planter aristocracy and large slave population, it resembled the dual-society pattern to the south, and nurtured the theater, dancing, and other high-society diversions popular in the imperial centers of South America. Lima and Mexico City had their own colleges long before Boston saw the establishment of Harvard in nearby Cambridge, but none of the Latin American cities could match the output of pamphlets and books produced by ambitious printers in Boston, New York, and Philadelphia, where struggling weekly papers had made their appearance before the midcentury.

Because of their separate colonial origins, the British ports on the American mainland had at the start fewer similarities and contacts than existed among the Spanish cities to the south. Urban growth, however, fostered the development of intercity ties that ultimately gave them the lead in the struggle for independence. Unlike the Spanish American cities, they had no standard plans, but that lack gave their founders a measure of freedom in the application of current urban designs to the requirements of their settings, as the original street plans of Boston, New York, and Philadelphia, recently assembled by John Reps, demonstrate.

Not only were the plans of the British ports less standardized than those of Spanish America, but their development was increasingly determined by the free play of market forces and by the deliberate efforts of their inhabitants, rather than by the decisions of imperial governors or church dignitaries. By the late 1600s most of the British backers of colonial ventures had abandoned their early hopes of reaping mercantile advantages from their investments and had become content in large part with the normal profits of trade monopolies. In this respect, as in many others, the mainland ports followed the lead of

London, which likewise grew in response to the play of the market and achieved a freer design than that of any of the great Continental cities. Medieval London, with its gabled roofs and Tudor moldings and paneling, had its influence on early Boston. After the great London fire of 1666 created an opportunity for a new beginning there, efforts to replan the city failed. However, new styles did creep in, the Queen Anne briefly and then the more pervasive Georgian designs, both of which quickly made their appearance in the colonies—in each of the five mainland ports and in several of the new towns as well. Moreover, the London pattern of row or attached houses, three or more stories high, provided the model for many in Boston and New York. Philadelphians were inclined to build lower but deeper houses, and Charleston favored separate, free-standing homes. As Professor Bridenbaugh tells us, some wealthy merchants and other affluent residents in the three northern ports followed the example of many rich Londoners and in the mid-1700s acquired rural estates where they erected summer homes to escape the heat and congestion of the city. Others built more substantial urban mansions on favored streets in each of the four principal cities.

A few architects arrived from London in the Georgian period to assist in the rapid construction of new buildings. But the American cities offered few opportunities similar to the estate projects in London, as described by Sir John Summerson, for most of the houses even when attached were individually constructed, and generally by a master carpenter or mason who shared the direction of the other craftsmen with the owner or speculator who had launched the venture. Builder's manuals imported from London supplied ample guides for most structures, although British-trained architects sometimes received charge of the construction of churches, markets, and other public buildings, some of which, by the late 1700s, began to rival those of the more ornate Spanish American cities.

The flexibility in planning and construction was matched by a diversity of functions, which soon saw the merchants and shipbuilders of Boston challenging the British monopoly over the intercolonial carrying trade, while merchants and civil leaders of Philadelphia and New York established intercity communications and other links, and artists and theatrical performers from Charleston visited the northern cities for extended seasons. Printers, publishers, and numerous other craftsmen, following Benjamin Franklin's example, journeyed from city to city in search of new opportunities. Wealthy merchants in the northern cities and wealthy planters in Charleston exchanged visits and frequently sent their children to American rather than British academies and colleges.

Thus a community of English-speaking cities was developing which shared an increasing number of interests divergent from those of the British Empire. They had achieved by the 1770s a sufficient sense of unity with their hinterlands and a sufficient measure of confidence in each other to assert and maintain their independence. The revolt of the thirteen colonies did not attract the support of British settlements in the West Indies, or of the newly acquired British colony in the St. Lawrence Valley to the north, for the British residents of Kingston, Spanish Town, and St. John in the islands, and of Quebec and Montreal in Canada, were too dependent on the Royal Navy for the maintenance of their control over subject blacks, Indians, and Frenchmen to risk a revolt. Only those mainland colonies that had achieved a sufficient measure of urban-rural integration to acquire a sense of unity could engage in the struggle for independence and participate on an equal basis in the establishment of a new republic. And the plural urban nuclei, like the thirteen colonies, fostered the development of a federated rather than tightly centered nation.

Table 1.   EARLY POPULATIONS OF SELECTED WORLD CITIES.

Cities	1700	1750	1800	1830
London	500,000[1]	650,000	888,000[3]	1,508,000[3]
Edinburgh	35,000[1]	50,000	83,000[2]	162,000[2]
Glasgow	15,000[1]	25,000[1]	77,000[2]	202,000[2]
Liverpool	10,000[1]	35,000[1]	82,000[2]	202,000[2]
Birmingham	15,000[1]	35,000[1]	71,000[2]	144,000[2]
Manchester		20,000[1]	75,000[2]	182,000[2]
Paris		500,000	550,000	912,000[3]
Constantinople		450,000	500,000[3]	600,000
Cairo		250,000	263,000[3]	260,000
Moscow		200,000	250,000	305,000[3]
Vienna		175,000	232,000	319,000[3]
Berlin		100,000	155,000	236,000[3]
Mexico City	30,000[4]	70,000	120,000	175,000[4]
Lima	30,000[4]	60,000	80,000	70,000
Panama		30,000	20,000	30,000
Havana		10,000	50,000	50,000
Buenos Aires		15,000	40,000	50,000
Quebec		8,000	15,000	27,000[3]
Boston	6,700[5]	16,000[5]	24,900[3]	61,400[3]
New York	5,000[5]	15,000[5]	60,500[3]	202,500[3]
Philadelphia	5,000[5]	20,000[5]	41,200[3]	80,400[3]
Charleston	2,000[5]	8,000[5]	18,900[3]	30,000[3]

1. Phyllis Deane and W. A. Cole, *British Economic Growth: 1688–1959* (Cambridge: Cambridge University Press, 1962), pp. 7–8.
2. B. R. Mitchell, *Abstract of British Historical Statistics* (Cambridge: Cambridge University Press, 1962), pp. 24–26.
3. U.S. Census Office, *Seventh Census: 1850* (Washington, D.C.: U.S. Government Printing Office, 1851), p. liii; U.S. Bureau of the Census, *Thirteenth Census: 1910* (Washington, D.C.: U.S. Government Printing Office, 1911), I, p. 80.
4. B. W. Diffie, *Latin American Civilization: Colonial Period* (Harrisburg, Pa.: Stackpole & Heck, Inc., 1945).
5. Carl Bridenbaugh, *Cities in the Wilderness* (New York: Alfred A. Knopf, Inc., 1938).
Note: Statistics not specifically credited are based on varied estimates.

BIBLIOGRAPHY

Bridenbaugh, Carl. *Cities in the Wilderness: The First Century of Urban Life in America: 1625–1742.* New York: Alfred A. Knopf, Inc., 1938.

Bridenbaugh, Carl. *Cities in Revolt: Urban Life in America: 1743–1776.* New York: Alfred A. Knopf, Inc., 1955.

Burke, Edmund. *An Account of European Settlements in America.* Dublin: Wilson, 1762.

Griffith, Ernest S. *History of American City Government: The Colonial Period.* New York: Oxford University Press, 1938.

Hoselitz, Bert F. "Generative and Parasitic Cities." *Economic Development and Cultural Change,* 3 (April 1955), 278–94.

Houston, J. M. "The Foundation of Colonial Towns in Hispanic America." In *Urbanization and Its Problems,* ed. R. P. Beckinsale and J. M. Houston. New York: Barnes & Noble, Inc., 1968.

Jefferson, Mark. "The Law of the Primate City." *Geographical Review,* 29 (April 1939), 226–32.

McKelvey, Blake. *The City in American History.* New York: Barnes & Noble, Inc., 1969.

Mumford, Lewis. *The City in History.* New York: Harcourt Brace Jovanovich, Inc., 1961.

Reps, John W. *The Making of Urban America.* Princeton, N.J.: Princeton University Press, 1965.

Rubin, Julius. "Urban Growth and Regional Development." In *The Growth of the Seaport Cities: 1790–1825,* ed. D. T. Gilchrist. Charlottesville, Va.: University Press of Virginia, 1967.

Schurz, William L. *This New World: The Civilization of Latin America.* New York: E. P. Dutton & Co., 1954. Chapter IX.

Sjoberg, Gideon. *The Preindustrial City.* New York: Free Press, 1960.

Summerson, John. *Georgian London.* New York: Praeger Publishers, 1946.

Warner, Sam Bass. *The Private City: Philadelphia in Three Periods of Its Growth.* Philadelphia: University of Pennsylvania Press, 1968.

2

Urbanization
on the Frontier

The urbanizing services rendered to the British colonies by their ports, and redoubled after independence to the states, were performed for the western territories by new towns planted on the frontier. These "spearheads" of the frontier, as Richard C. Wade has described them, assumed from the start an active leadership in the settlement and development of the new states that soon appeared in the interior. Unlike most of the cities of western Europe, Asia, and Latin America, they antedated, and in fact promoted, generated, and equipped, the rural settlements that grew up about them. The new western cities depended in turn on the links they maintained with the eastern cities, from which many of their leaders had come. It was to Philadelphia, Baltimore, New York, and Boston that the western towns looked for guidance and support, as the eastern ports had formerly looked to London. But since, unlike London, none of the Atlantic cities exercised political authority over their frontier outposts, the rapid growth of the western cities as the urban leaders of new states and regions was unhindered, and contributed not only to the development of a wider union of states, but also to the early emergence of a unique and remarkably dynamic system of cities. As municipalities, however, the new towns acquired their charters from the state legislatures and remained subject to their control, rather than to that of the nation.

THE GROWTH OF THE CITIES

The urbanization of the frontier, like the urbanization of the colonies, cannot easily be measured. The primary demographic formula of an increasing ratio of urban to rural growth scarcely applies when the original settlements are on the site of the future urban centers. Thus, although the statistics fail to separate the town promoters—the rural nonfarm inhabitants of the day—from the rural farm population, every contemporary account of the westward migration notes their importance. If that dynamic element could have been measured and added to the population of the growing towns, the urban percentage would have been much higher from the start than the statistics suggest, as we will demonstrate below. Even the census statistics, as George R. Taylor has shown, need to be juggled a bit, for the cities of the early 1800s, like those of the present, had a suburban overflow in adjoining hamlets whose later annexation distorted the record of their urban growth. Thus, the development of the four leading Atlantic Coast ports between 1790 and 1830 appears rapid (rather than slow, as generally described) when their suburbs are included, for the rate of their combined growth was more than double that of the total population. Although the growth ratio of urban settlements (over 2,500 in size) dipped a tenth of one percent between 1810 and 1820, the overall advance in those four decades from 5.1 to 8.8 percent was impressive and restored the urbanization process to the course attained in the late colonial period.

The temporary drop in the size of American cities during the Revolution (and probably again in the War of 1812) did not represent a real decline in urban leadership. Boston's drop from 15,520 in 1770 to 10,000 in 1780, and New York's from 21,000 to 18,000, as reported in Rossiter's probing study for the Census Bureau, was a statistical loss comparable to that suffered by many European cities during World War II. Many Tory residents fled permanently to England or Canada, but the major losses suffered at the time in these and other ports were of merchants and craftsmen who sought and found safer locations where they could continue their productive efforts during the hostilities. This diffusion of urban functions, as well as of the urban population, supports the contention of Julius Rubin that the colonists as a whole were predominantly urban in a cultural sense.

Few if any of the former colonists lost their urban characteristics as they migrated in increasing numbers to the frontier to establish new towns or to develop more productive farm holdings. Even the perennial frontiersmen, who repeatedly pulled up stakes and pushed farther into the wilderness whenever neighbors approached too close, were in effect specialists in clearing the land, and generally reaped modest profits from the sale of their squatter's rights. Their successors, who frequently laid claim on their titles with a first down payment, had to produce a surplus to meet later payments on the land and to buy the equipment their ambitious holdings called for. Their frequent trips to market supported the rapid growth of the interior towns, a few of which dramatically outpaced the healthy increases of the older cities to the east.

Several of the new towns achieved growth rates that none of their predecessors could match. Pittsburgh, the first west of the mountains to experience a boom, increased fivefold in the first fifteen years of the century, reaching 8,000 by 1815; with its suburbs it topped 22,000 in 1830, but by that date Cincinnati, some 300 miles down the Ohio, had bounded ahead. The Ohio city, with a 26,800 total, all but 2,000 within its corporate limits, had enjoyed a tenfold growth in two decades, a rate that Louisville had also experienced, though it had started from a smaller base. Even Washington, the new national capital, which grew from 3,200 to 13,000 in these two decades, could not equal that rate, and only Rochester, on New York's new frontier opened by the building of the Erie Canal, slightly exceeded the Ohio Valley rates by achieving a tenfold increase in fifteen years. European travelers marveled at the rapid growth of these western towns which, in contrast with their ancient cities, had "sprung up overnight in the midst of a forest," as many exclaimed in their journals.

Most of the rapidly growing new cities soon exhausted their first boom, though each of those mentioned above would increase threefold in the next two decades. More remarkable was the fivefold growth in four decades of New York and Baltimore, despite the substantial proportions they had previously attained. Among the leading ports only newly acquired New Orleans, at the mouth of the Mississippi River, exceeded that rate with a tenfold growth in the same period. Its sudden rise won it fifth place by 1830 and gave promise of further triumphs. No city in Britain, with the possible exception of suburban Brighton, could match its rate, although three emerging industrial cities, Birmingham, Manchester, and Glasgow, and the rising port of Liverpool, rivaled New York's gains and exceeded all but that metropolis in size. New York, numbering with its suburbs included 242,278, now surpassed Mexico City and all other American rivals and ranked twenty-first among the world's great cities. London with 1,471,941 in 1831 held undisputed leadership; its great size dwarfed all subordinates within the empire and emphasized its status as the world's first city.

Of course the statistics tell only part of the story. To see the full picture in America we must have not only the total urban growth on the frontier, but also a record of the numerous unsuccessful town promotions, and a measure of the progress made at new town sites that had not yet reached the 2,500 size. A hint of this urban activity can be found in the early censuses. The 1810 census records the town or borough population within each county for a few states. In Pennsylvania, for example, in addition to Philadelphia, its suburbs, and interior Lancaster and Pittsburgh, the census takers recognized twenty boroughs, all but three under 2,500 in population, but with urban aspirations soon in most cases to be realized. If the ten whose population had reached 500 (and which would shortly become urban centers) are added to the total for the cities, the state's urban percentage is increased from 12.6 to 16.8. Similarly in Kentucky, a frontier state, the modest urban total for Lexington and Louisville would be more than doubled by adding those resident in eight towns falling between 500 and 2,500. There were, in other words, many citizens in these pioneer times who, though not resident in cities, were engaged in the urbanization process. A further check of Pennsylvania in the 1820 census reveals an increase of 20,000 in the number of these subcity urbanites, sufficient to boost that state's urban ratio to 17.3 percent. Unfortunately that census does not list the Kentucky towns separately, but the evidence for Pennsylvania suggests that the retarded rate of urbanization generally attributed to the period from 1810 to 1820 possibly masked a wider diffusion of the urbanizing efforts, which would in due course contribute to the character and strength of America's urban society.

ECONOMIC DIFFUSION

Despite difficulties in measurement, the upward course of the country's urban ratios was clearly evident even in these Jeffersonian years. And, as Professor George R. Taylor has shown, the rate of urbanization compared favorably with that of Great Britain and probably exceeded that of any other nation in this period. Moreover, the contributions the cities made to the unity and stability of the young republic were not only historically important but also conceptually significant in that they helped determine the pluralistic character of America's urbanization. These contributions, which were economic, social, and cultural, helped lay the foundations for a unique and independent urban nation.

The diffusion that characterized America's urban population developments was matched and partially explained by a diffusion of economic efforts. The predominant position held by exports and imports in the economy of the colonial ports had left them virtually prostrate when the Revolution drastically reduced their flow. Baltimore and Boston prospered with the revival of the West Indian trade, and New York developed an increasing commerce with Europe, but, deprived of their favored position in the British Empire, the American ports began for the first time to face inland. Some of their residents, and many vigorous men who might have located there, turned instead to the development of old and new urban centers on the fall line, and to the establishment of new towns on the frontier. Freed of British restraints, they exploited every opportunity their talents and the local situation presented.

With the ties of empire severed by independence, each of London's old American satellites assumed some of its metropolitan functions. Philadelphia secured the lead for a time in banking and produced many kinds of craftsmen. Baltimore expanded its trade with the West Indies and endeavored to capture that of the South and the West. Boston, unable because of its isolation to compete in the West and handicapped by distance in the South, joined Salem and other New England ports in opening a new trade with the Far East; its leaders also turned, as we shall see in a later chapter, to the promotion of new industrial towns in its vicinity. New York, with the most central and most adequate harbor and with the most rapidly growing hinterland, not only became the chief entrepôt and largest exporter, but soon captured the lead in banking and insurance, and in the expanding trade with the South and the West.

New York's increasing leadership enabled it to surpass both Philadelphia and Boston in population by 1800 and to equal the total of these plus Baltimore by 1830, but it never compared to the position held by London in the empire. Not only were the governmental functions far removed and securely planted in Washington, but the reduced importance of foreign trade, which was New York's chief specialty, reflected the increased reliance on local production in the ports and their hinterlands and throughout the expanding country. Although New York's more rapid growth enabled it to outstrip Philadelphia even in handicraft production, and although it secured the lead in most metropolitan functions, it made no claim to predominance such as that held by London, Paris, or the newly independent capitals of South America, which continued to monopolize most urban functions. New York was but the first in a system of cities and, despite its rapid growth, saw its share of the nation's urban total fall from 24.4 to 21.5 percent in these four decades.

Urbanization in America was in this period essentially a regional phenomenon. Thus a major factor in New York City's growth, as Robert G. Albion so ably describes it, was the rapid settlement of the state, whose population likewise quadrupled in these four decades. In the process Brooklyn, a close suburb, also quadrupled, while Albany, the state's new capital, increased eightfold, and six other upstate cities made their appearance, each with important urban specialties. Pennsylvania's growth, like that of Philadelphia, was less dramatic, yet it saw the rise not only of populous suburbs around that burgeoning metropolis, but also of four new regional cities, including Pittsburgh west of the mountains. Massachusetts, more completely settled in colonial days, increased only 62 percent, yet it also saw the emergence of five new urban centers, which, with old Salem and six other New England cities, two in rapidly settling Maine and New Hampshire, strengthened Boston's regional position. Although four of the twelve were potential rivals for that port's trade, the changing course of international commerce and the building of larger ships requiring deeper harbors turned them increasingly to other productive activities that complemented the industrial specialization of the new fall-line centers. A similar diversity marked the urban satellites of New York and Philadelphia. Only Baltimore failed to nurture diversified urban outposts in this period, although Richmond and Norfolk in Virginia, Washington, and Hagerstown in Maryland each developed specialized though by no means tributary functions within its broader region.

The still more rapid growth of a dozen frontier cities resulted from the successful assumption by their leaders of numerous regional functions. Established originally in most cases as provisioning centers to accommodate the flood of settlers moving west, they soon became industrial processors and exporters of the region's products. Moreover, because of the difficult overland haul from the east, both Pittsburgh and Lexington, the pioneer western outposts of the 1790s, also developed handicraft industries to produce needed supplies on the spot. That productive activity assured their leadership until the introduction of steamboats able to ascend the Mississippi and Ohio rivers facilitated the importation of cheap goods over that route and gave urban priority to Cincinnati and Louisville by the 1820s.

The rapid settlement of the western territories and states, which saw their totals increase eightfold in the first three decades of the century to reach 3,400,000 by 1830, maintained a lively demand for imports. The output of western farms and mines was, however, even more abundant and taxed the energies of the urban centers to prepare it for market. Pittsburgh developed iron foundries, blacksmith shops, and glass factories to supply frontier needs, and built rafts and boats to accommodate the westward migrants and to market regional products. Cincinnati processed the mounting flood of grain and livestock from its fertile hinterland. Lexington manufactured hemp sacks and rope, while Louisville cured and marketed tobacco. Each of these cities became the banking as well as the trade center for its region and in many ways supplied the indispensable economic leadership. Although their leaders looked at the start chiefly to Philadelphia and Baltimore for guidance and support, the rapid development of steamboat traffic after 1815 established new contacts with New Orleans at the mouth of the Mississippi and thus enhanced the independence of the Ohio Valley towns.

New Orleans, a thriving port of 10,000 at the time of the Louisiana Purchase in 1803, became the nation's second largest exporter by 1830 and, with 46,000 inhabitants, its fifth city in population. Such rapid growth enabled it to overshadow other southern towns, such as Savannah, Mobile, and even old Charleston, with which it shared two important characteristics—a basic dependence on the cotton trade and a major reliance on slave labor. New Orleans shared with Mobile its French origins and traditions, but they were much more firmly imbedded in the Mississippi port, which still retained active trade contacts with the West Indian islands and with far-off Paris as well. Yet its French character, dominant until Andrew Jackson's successful defeat of an invading British army on its outskirts in 1815 enhanced the prestige of American frontiermen, was beginning to change as the western trade and its New York contacts increased. These northern and western influences were held in check, however, by the city's increasing population of blacks, more than half of them slaves.

Because of the dual character of their populations, the four southern ports compared more closely to the cities of Latin America than did any in the North. They were, however, comparable only to a degree, for the differences were even more significant. Approximately half the residents of each of these southern towns were blacks, the great majority of them, throughout these decades, slaves. The proportion of bondsmen was greater in Charleston than in New Orleans, where indeed nearly half the blacks were free, but the presence of such large numbers of slaves in each town sharply reduced the proportion of its citizens and limited the range of their enterprise. Moreover, the high percentage of slaves absorbed a large share of the local capital in what proved in the city, as Professor Richard Wade has shown, to be relatively unproductive investments. As a result, the southern ports permitted the New York merchants to assume almost completely the operation of their carrying trade, thus surrendering to the northern metropolis much of the profit as well as full control over the marketing of their chief export, cotton.

The West Indian cities, preoccupied with the control of their slave populations, had previously abandoned their trading activities to the Americans— first to merchantmen from Boston and later to Baltimore shippers. But the black population in the islands was so predominant that despite many precautions the whites could not forestall occasional riots and insurrections, most of which were harshly suppressed. As reports of these conflicts and refugees from their violence reached the southern cities, the States too suffered spasms of terror. The most appalling was the hysterical reaction in Charleston in 1822 to the alleged Vesey conspiracy. Despite the absence of any overt acts, the confessions of several fearful blacks led to the arrest and execution of thirty-five suspected plotters, the expulsion of thirty-one more, and the detention and trial of sixty others who were ultimately discharged. Although no other North American city experienced such an ordeal, the constant fear of slave outbreaks prompted the major southern towns to institute paid nightwatches and to hold local militia units in constant readiness.

The liberation of Central and South America brought a different response. Except for the prospecting visits of enterprising merchantmen from Boston or New York, few contacts had developed between the cities of North and South America, but when news of the southern drive for independence reached the States it was greeted and applauded as a revolt against imperial Spain. Little if any thought was given to the status of the peons and slaves, who remained largely unaffected by the achievement of independence. Controlled as in the past, but by new masters, the great mass of the population, as Professor R. A. Humphreys tells us, remained lethargic. Although a surge of patriotism among the victorious Spanish American elites brought fresh adornments to several of the capitals, notably to Buenos Aires, which now began to prosper, the ports permitted the British and North Americans, many from Boston and New York, to take over much of the reduced flow of trade. Most of the Latin American cities turned inward for a period of uneasy transition, over several decades, from their earlier parasitic stage to one of increased cultural integration which would eventually develop generative capabilities.

The Black Belt cities in the States experienced a similar though less dramatic withdrawal. Despite their fear and distrust of free blacks and the failure of all except Richmond to find industrial uses for the numerous slaves in the cities, they avoided the development of a peon class and the dampening effect was not so great. Moreover, the invention of the cotton gin by Eli Whitney of New Haven and its widespread introduction in the early 1800s had given the South an increasingly profitable plantation crop, and the mounting price of prime fieldhands enhanced the value of urban slaves as a form of investment. The southern cities developed as a result a languorous way of life that contrasted sharply with the more restless and enterprising activity in northern and western cities.

Only New Orleans, despite its Latin origins, Creole traditions, and large slave population, escaped this stagnation. The incessant flow of trade up and down the Mississippi attracted newcomers as well as capital from the North and started a migration of poor refugees from Ireland whose competition with free blacks as well as slaves for unskilled jobs created an animated and bustling trade on the docks. This influx had only commenced in the late twenties in New Orleans, but already it had created a new affinity between that port and both New York and Boston, where early migrants from Ireland were likewise arriving. New Orleans had by 1830 a more diversified mix of residents than any American city except New York, to which it was now bound by close trade ties as well.

ETHNIC DIVERSITY AND INTELLECTUAL GROWTH

A slowly mounting stream of newcomers from abroad was bringing increased diversity to several other northern cities. Most of the over 200,000 aliens who had come to America before 1820 and many of the 10,000 or more who arrived in each subsequent year headed for rural settlements, but many others, particularly among the Irish and the Jews, found homes in the cities. New York City, where more than half the immigrants landed, retained a sufficient number of various groups to enable their members to establish churches and benefit societies in great profusion. Many Irish newcomers journeyed up the Hudson to locate at Albany, where they became a major part of its mounting population; others, after helping with the construction in the early twenties of the Erie Canal, found lodgment in the mushrooming cities along its route, Troy, Utica, Rochester, and Buffalo. Other streams of Irishmen were landing at Boston and scattering to its industrial satellites, and at New Orleans, from which many journeyed north to the frontier settlement at St. Louis or up the Ohio to Louisville and Cincinnati. A new influx of Germans was beginning to follow these routes, too, while Philadelphia's older German and Scotch-Irish settlements attracted congenial newcomers from abroad. Baltimore, with its strong ties to the South and the West Indies, drew an influx of blacks which reduced its demand for immigrants; the census of 1830 credited it with 15,354 slaves and 2,107 free blacks, who comprised together almost a fourth of its total. New York's 14,000 Negroes, all but seventeen of them free, represented almost 7 percent of its population, while Philadelphia's 9,800 amounted to 12 percent. No other northern city approached these proportions.

Although the diversity that characterized the leading ports—New York, New Orleans, Boston, Philadelphia, and Baltimore—was less evident in the smaller cities of the North and West, the contrast most of these cities presented to the rural settlements and "covenanted" towns was striking. A New England settlement pattern under which groups of families, often clustered around a young pastor, moved in a body to a new site to establish a congenial community, "covenanted" towns had spread into the Ohio Valley, where hundreds of such communities, as described by Page Smith, appeared in these decades. Numerous groups of foreign migrants planted similar colonies, some in rural settings like Caledonia in western New York, settled by a group of Scottish Presbyterians, others in the vicinity of growing towns. The conformity generally expected of all participants in such settlements long remained undisturbed in the rural areas, but in the cities every effort to maintain it added to the tensions that increased diversity had created.

In addition to the array of Protestant and Catholic churches that graced the cities of the North, several Jewish synagogues made their appearance, and the fourteen denominational colleges of 1790 had increased to fifty by 1830. A few of these colleges represented a cooperative attempt by leaders of several groups to work together for the benefit of the larger community, as in Lexington, Kentucky, where Transylvania College became in the 1820s the town's chief hope of becoming the "Athens of the West." Since most of the colleges located in modest towns, only a dozen cities had such institutions; all, however, had their boys' academies and young ladies' seminaries, and many had athenaeums patterned after Benjamin Franklin's Junta, or young men's associations that maintained modest libraries and served as debating societies affording educational opportunities for clerks and mechanics as well as young and aspiring professionals.

The children presented a major concern in every city. The dame schools, conducted by respected widows for modest fees, no longer appeared adequate and failed to attract the many poor youngsters who thronged the streets of growing towns. Church leaders in most cities organized Sunday schools and established charity schools to serve as a "powerful lever for reformation," as John Griscom put it in 1823 in his *Discourse on the Importance and Character of Education in the United States.* The object, as the Free School Society of New York saw it in 1805, was to counteract "ignorance and vice and all those manifold evils resulting from every species of immorality" that seemed to abound in the cities. Repeated efforts in New York and several other cities to secure authority to operate free public schools proved unavailing in these decades, though New York State authorized the creation in 1812 of district schools and voted modest funds to assist local parents in maintaining them. Except in Boston and a few other New England cities, the chief reliance throughout these decades was on the Sabbath schools and the charity schools, of which New York City, for example, had more than a score in 1824.

Even more important in the intellectual life of the emerging cities was the increasing number of weekly and even daily newspapers. Sixty towns scattered from Portland, Maine, to Savannah, Georgia, had at least one of the ninety-five weeklies or monthlies published in 1790. New York City already had three, Charleston one, and Philadelphia four daily papers at that date, and twenty-three other cities would produce one or more of the sixty-five dailies launched during the next four decades, while printers in these and many smaller towns increased the number of weeklies to 650. Most of these early papers were small four-page issues filled with two- and three-line advertisements, official legal announcements, and brief reports of local fires and crimes or more distant catastrophes, plus occasional editorials or excerpts from a sermon, political address, or book. Despite their brevity, these papers, unmatched in numbers and enterprise, effectively performed their promotional function and helped create and maintain a sense of community in the growing towns. Practically every urban center also produced a local directory before it reached eight thousand inhabitants, the early "threshold" size for this type of urban self-consciousness, and nine saw the publication during the twenties of two or more of these books, some with informative data on the town's growth. Some printers published other books, most of them reprints, but a few by local authors, such as Daniel Drake's on Cincinnati and its environs. The local output supplemented but did not supplant the flood of books made available at local book stores by a book trade that was becoming another distinguishing feature of America's emerging urban society.

CIVIC LIFE

The cities generally supplied leadership in the early adoption of manhood suffrage. Restrictions of the franchise to male property holders and those who paid specified taxes were difficult to enforce and unpopular in new towns eager to attract settlers, even men of limited means. Thus Colonel Rochester protested in 1817 when some merchants and other property owners in his newly chartered village tried to exclude the mechanics from participation in its government. Moreover, the demands of New York State's workingmen and their Jeffersonian allies for manhood suffrage for all white males won acceptance despite vigorous opposition from the representatives of property at the 1821 convention that drafted the new constitution. Other states with large cities quickly followed suit in the next decade.

All the old colonial cities had hastened to apply for new charters from the newly independent state legislatures in the 1780s. Confident of their capacity for self-government, they had sought and secured an abandonment of the close corporate form and a provision for local elections of councilmen and other officials. The governors retained the authority for a time to name the mayors and recorders in a few states, but soon abandoned it to the local councils—to the upper chambers where they existed. Granted in special acts by the variously constituted state legislatures, sometimes in accordance with carefully prepared local drafts, the charters of the old and new cities of America showed great diversity. They displayed an experimental vitality and a faith in popular government that contrasted sharply with the centrally controlled administrative governments of cities in Latin America and in many European countries. Even the British, who adopted a more liberal franchise in the Reform Act of 1832 and revived their earlier tradition of local self-government, retained a measure of central supervision. The Municipal Corporations Act of 1835 supplied a more uniform standard for urban civic development in Britain and her colonies, and assured great stability, as Toronto in Canada and Melbourne in Australia demonstrated; at the same time it restrained the local initiative so abundantly evident in the States.

A group of lively and articulate master craftsmen and professionals appeared in each town and vied with the merchants and landowners for leadership. In addition to the printer-editors, hotel keepers, attorneys, doctors, professors, and clergymen who served as unofficial spokesmen for the community, the towns produced successful builders, who sometimes served as street or market superintendents, and political activists who aspired for appointments as postmaster or nominations to the state or national legislatures.

Leading merchants, landowners, and bankers took turns in filling many local civic posts, though most of these men gave but one or two years to public service and made little impact. A few, however, such as Josiah Quincy of Boston and De Witt Clinton of New York, served several successive terms as mayor and helped transform their weak town governments into effective municipal administrations. Quincy, for example, after two undistinguished careers in the national and state legislatures, won election as mayor of Boston in 1823 and began work on the city's water and sewer systems, gave the streets their first thorough cleaning, removed a row of unsanitary hovels, opened several new streets, built a new market and additional public docks, reorganized the fire and police departments, and effected numerous other reforms that made Boston a model for conscientious municipal leaders throughout the country.

The number of dedicated civic leaders was limited, but frequently when a town discovered a need for a stronger charter or for the installation of sewers or lighting for its streets, its leaders would dispatch letters or emissaries to Boston, New York, or Philadelphia to gain the benefit of their experience. Philadelphia, because of the success of its water system and other achievements, became the model for the Ohio Valley towns, as Professor Wade has shown; Boston and New York for those to the Northwest. Many residents of the new towns eagerly accepted civic responsibilities, but few specialized in civic leadership. This was characteristic of the individualistic culture of the frontier. Occasionally, however, a leader such as William Carr Lane, who became mayor of St. Louis for five successive terms, brought to his job firsthand knowledge of several older and larger cities.

Other examples of the development of informal ties between the cities appeared in the character of their construction and the designs of their plans. Planned and constructed for the most part by private developers and builders, they lacked many of the substantial and formal qualities possessed by the more standardized urban structures of Europe and Latin America. They produced none of the estate-building projects that marked the expansion of London in these decades, yet many of their public buildings and the homes of wealthy merchants and planters displayed the influence of the Georgian and postcolonial styles of architecture. These and other patterns, distributed throughout America in manuals of architectural designs and building patterns, resulted in a profusion of local interpretations of the classical patterns, some by talented American architects such as Peter Harrison and Charles Bulfinch that won many expressions of astonishment and admiration from foreign travelers in the early years of the republic. The fearful rejection of urban ways and manners sometimes expressed by Jefferson and other champions of an agrarian, home-spun society were largely forgotten amidst the excitement of creating new towns in the wilderness and building communities that attracted the interest and praise of sophisticated visitors from abroad. Despite his romantic pre-dilection for the unspoiled wilderness, James Fenimore Cooper found life in New York marvelously congenial in the middle twenties.

Even Jefferson had become sufficiently excited by the prospect of the construction of a new capital on the Potomac to loan the patterns of European capitals he had previously collected to its architect, thus possibly assisting Pierre Charles L'Enfant in drafting his plan for Washington. Yet although it was hailed as the most elaborate and impressive urban design yet produced, few new towns in the West followed its lead. Most speculative promoters of new urban centers were more impressed by the simple and efficient layout provided by Philadelphia's gridiron plan, which was adopted in a master-plan extension of the New York City plan in 1813 and in many towns and subdivisions throughout the country. Some with foresight retained the occasional open squares of William Penn's original plan, while adjoining but independent town plots laid out by rival promoters at most strategic urban sites provided breaks in the gridiron pattern, as in New Orleans, that created opportunities for interesting and sometimes spectacular urban developments.

But if neither Jefferson's antiurban predilections nor the designs that he, L'Enfant, and the President chose for Washington had much effect on the character of American cities, the fact that Washington and Jefferson succeeded in locating the capital on the Potomac, rather than in New York or Phil-adelphia, did have considerable influence on the course of America's urbanization. It was the jealous rivalry of these two principal cities that enabled the two Virginians to capture the capital for the Potomac. The effects, however, were much more important, for the location of the government at a fresh site in a rural area removed it from influence by and involvement in the affairs of the major metropolises. For almost a century and a half Presidents, congressmen, and federal administrators would come and go virtually unaware of the increasingly urban character of the nation, and national historians would be equally oblivious of that development. Growing cities in America enjoyed a freedom from national direction unmatched in any other society.

Thus the heterogeneity that characterized the inhabitants of the cities of the young republic found similar expression in the variety of their structural and institutional forms and in the individual enterprise and vitality of their economic and civic life. The cities continued to play a generative role in the settlement and development of the nation and, because of their political and geographic diffusion, contributed to its democratic as well as its federal char-acter. In contrast with the early colonial days, when most towns had been isolated and seclusive, the cities of the new nation were open and receptive to newcomers and promoted economic and cultural bonds with distant cities in a rivalry for urban precedence that added, as we shall see in the next chapter, to the growth and productivity of the nation.

Table 2.   POPULATIONS OF PRINCIPAL U.S. CITIES, 1790 to 1830.*

Cities	1790	1800	1810	1820	1830
New York	33,131	60,515	96,373	123,706	202,589
Suburbs			(1) 4,402	(1) 7,175	(3) 39,689
totals			100,775	130,881	242,278
Philadelphia	28,522	41,220	53,722	63,802	80,462
Suburbs	(2) 15,574	(2) 20,339	(3) 33,581	(3) 45,007	(4) 80,809
totals	44,096	61,559	87,303	108,809	161,271
Boston	18,320	24,937	33,787	43,298	61,392
Suburbs			(1) 4,959	(2) 10,726	(3) 18,104
totals			38,746	54,024	85,568
Baltimore	13,503	26,514	46,555	62,738	80,620
New Orleans		9,000	17,242	27,176	46,082
Cincinnati		750	2,540	9,642	24,831
Charleston	16,359	18,924	24,711	24,780	30,289
Albany	3,498	5,349	9,356	12,630	24,209
Washington		3,210	8,208	13,247	18,826
Providence	6,380	7,614	10,071	11,767	16,833
Pittsburgh	376	1,565	4,768	7,248	15,369
Richmond	3,761	5,737	9,735	12,067	16,060
Salem	7,917	9,457	12,613	12,731	13,895
Portland	2,239	3,704	7,169	8,581	12,598
Troy		4,926	3,895	5,264	11,556
New Haven	4,487	4,049	5,772	7,147	10,180
Louisville	200	359	1,357	4,012	10,341
Newark			5,008	6,507	10,953
Total of Urban Residents	202,000	322,000	525,000	693,000	1,127,000
Number of Towns over 2500	24	33	46	61	90
Percent Urban	5.1	6.1	7.3	7.2	8.8
Total U.S. Population	3,929,000	5,308,000	7,240,000	9,638,000	12,866,000

*U.S. Census Office, *Seventh Census: 1850* (Washington, D.C.: U.S. Government Printing Office, 1851), p. liii; U.S. Bureau of the Census, *Thirteenth Census: 1910* (Washington, D.C.: U.S. Government Printing Office, 1911), *Population,* I, p. 80; U.S. Bureau of the Census, *Seventeenth Census: 1950* (Washington, D.C.: U.S. Government Printing Office, 1951), I, U.S. Summary, Table 15.

BIBLIOGRAPHY

Albion, Robert G. *The Rise of New York Port, 1815–1860.* New York: Charles Scribner's Sons, 1939.

Bender, Thomas. "James Fenimore Cooper and the City." *New York History,* 51 (April 1970), 287–305.

Deane, Phyllis, and W. A. Cole. *British Economic Growth: 1688–1959.* Cambridge: Cambridge University Press, 1962.

Gilchrist, David T., ed. *The Growth of the Seaport Cities: 1790–1825.* Charlottesville, Va.: University Press of Virginia, 1967. See especially the papers by Professors Julius Rubin and George R. Taylor.

Glaab, Charles N., and T. A. Brown. *A History of Urban America.* New York: The Macmillan Co., 1967.

Humphreys, R. A. *Tradition and Revolt in Latin America and Other Essays.* New York: Oxford University Press, 1969.

Livingood, James W. *The Philadelphia-Baltimore Trade Rivalry: 1780–1860.* Harrisburg, Pa.: Pennsylvania History and Museum Commission, 1947.

Mohl, Raymond A. "Education and Social Control in New York City: 1784–1825." *New York History,* 51 (April 1970), 219–37.

Niehaus, Earl F. *The Irish of New Orleans: 1800–1860.* Baton Rouge: Louisiana State University Press, 1965.

Rossiter, W. S. *A Century of Population Growth.* Washington, D.C.: U.S. Bureau of the Census, 1909.

Smith, Page. *As a City upon a Hill: The Town in American History.* New York: Alfred A. Knopf, Inc., 1966.

Spear, Dorothea N. *Bibliography of American Directories Through 1860.* Worcester, Mass.: Barre Publishers, 1961.

Wade, Richard C. *The Urban Frontier: The Rise of Western Cities: 1790–1830.* Cambridge, Mass.: Harvard University Press, 1959.

Wade, Richard C. *Slavery in the Cities: The South, 1820–1860.* New York: Oxford University Press, 1964.

3

Urbanization and the Commercial Revolution

The urbanizing process in America began to acquire a faster beat in the 1830s. As the national population increased and migration into the West accelerated, the need for new and larger cities grew still more rapidly. Part of the urban increase resulted from a new influx of immigrants who found homes particularly in the northeastern and new western cities. Urbanization was quickening in Great Britain and western Europe, too, as the industrial revolution gained momentum there in those decades. Industrial and technological developments also had an impact on urban growth in America, though most of its cities were more concerned with and more powerfully influenced by commercial rather than industrial innovations.

Again, as in the period of settlement, the cities of America assumed the initiative. They developed new trade arteries to safeguard their local interests and to expand their hinterlands. They also supplied leadership in the establishment of new economic, social, and cultural institutions. The rate and extent of their growth created new internal problems which revived serious doubts about the merits of urban expansion and, as we will see in the next chapter, stirred reveries of the good old agrarian days. Yet neither these doubts, held chiefly by small groups of social and intellectual critics, nor the disturbing occurrence of periodic economic slumps could halt the increasing tempo of the urbanizing process.

The urbanization of America first assumed the classic demographic format in the 1830s. Thus, while the nation's population increased 150 percent in the next three decades, that of its cities mounted three times as rapidly. Only the growth of the Old and the New West was more dramatic, but their sixfold increase included and was overshadowed by a thirtyfold upsurge of the western cities. The total number of the nation's urban places (over 2,500 in population) mounted from 90 to 392, and the urban percentage from 8.8 to 19.8. Moreover, the number of cities over 100,000 increased precipitously, from one to nine, and their percentage of the total rose from 1.6 to 8.4.

No other period in the nation's history could rival the urbanizing ratios of these decades, and the transformations that caused and resulted from this movement were far reaching. The cities again supplied the generative leadership for the building of the new arteries of trade that opened the West for wider settlement and enabled it to produce the surplus that attracted new-comers to the cities, where they found new job opportunities that made some cities processing and fabricating centers, and transformed their social and economic structures.

The pattern of urban growth in America differed strikingly from that in Great Britain. The resurgence of the English cities, especially those of the Midlands, was clearly related to the first occurrence there of the industrial revolution. Among the ten British cities of the second rank (those that ex-ceeded 100,000) in 1861, all but two old and somewhat isolated ports had experienced at least a fourfold increase in the preceding six decades. In the Midlands, where the chief industrial innovators—Manchester, Birmingham, and Sheffield—were located, even the port of Liverpool experienced a fivefold increase as it became the entrepôt for shipments of cotton and grain from America, and for migrating refugees from Ireland, as well as the principal exporter of the region's mounting factory output. These growth ratios and that of Glasgow, the industrial port of Scotland, overshadowed the nation's total population growth, which had barely doubled in this period. The total urban increment more than doubled that of the rural districts and contributed in large measure to a renewed national vitality, which contrasted sharply with conditions in nearby Ireland.

But even the urban growth in the Midlands could not match that of the nine American cities that reached the 100,000 bracket by 1860. Each of the nine exceeded and several doubled or tripled the growth rates of their closest British counterparts. The reasons for their superior growth rates are revealing. American cities performed a function not available abroad, that of promoting frontier districts or partially settled regions. They had, in addition, an un-matched source of newcomers whose labor and skill brought new supplies of power. By contrast, urban population increases in Great Britain depended on slow accretion from excess births over deaths, plus the addition of migrants from rural districts and from Ireland. The enclosure movement, which had for several decades been driving peasant farmers from the land, helped supply the cheap labor force that provided an incentive for technological innovations in industrial Manchester, Birmingham, and elsewhere. Rates of urbanization in these cities were striking partly because their rural districts were stagnant or declining—in sharp contrast with the situation in America, where almost all populations were booming.

The urbanization of the British cities was, as a result, more specialized. Their industrial start conformed fairly closely to the first stage of "export specialization" identified by Wilbur Thompson in his typology of urban growth. They progressed rapidly through the next stage of "more diversified exports," into the third stage of "economic maturation," where for a time they rested. No new trading centers or ports were required, and some of the older ones became resorts. Even in the thriving industrial and commercial cities, the newcomers—except for the Irish refugees and Scottish migrants—were, like the old residents, brother Englishmen, and these cities escaped some of the crises and the creative social tensions that marked urban developments in America. With the possible exception of Glasgow and Edinburgh, none of these British cities attempted to assume the metropolitan functions traditionally centered in London, which retained a supremacy that New York, despite its astounding growth, could not aspire to. The British industrial cities, supplying new economic opportunities for thousands of their fellow countrymen, attracted a heavy influx, particularly in the forties and fifties. But they could not hold all of Britain's dislodged inhabitants, some 500,000 of whom migrated in the second quarter of the century to the States, and another 1,050,000 to the British colonies. The English cities retained an even smaller proportion of the Irish migrants, over 950,000 of whom left for America before 1860.

The American cities, particularly those of the Northeast, the Mississippi Valley, and the Far West, acquired a more heterogeneous population than any in Europe. Despite a healthy excess of births over deaths, even the well-established eastern cities relied heavily on newcomers from neighboring and distant towns, and increasingly on immigrants from abroad. Locally born residents were constantly being lured away as the sons and daughters of the pioneers joined the ranks of those migrating westward, some to plant new cities beyond the Mississippi. All the eastern states were contributing heavily to the westward movement, to the towns as well as to the farms, but so great was the human surplus that, with two exceptions, both the old and the new states increased their agrarian totals and contributed generously to the population growth of regional cities and towns. Each of the thirty-five cities over 25,000 in population also attracted residents from other states but, except in the South, not in numbers comparable to the newcomers from abroad.

The mounting influx of immigrants supplied one of the unique features of the urbanizing process in America. Some Latin American cities would later experience a similar invasion from Europe, but only after their character had been firmly fixed. Many of the new colonial ports established in Southeast Asia harbored large colonies of foreign Asians in these decades, as T. G. McGee tells us, but the situation was not in other respects comparable. Other scattered cities, such as Paris, Constantinople, and London, attracted a heterogeneous influx of foreigners, but generally only of the merchant and student classes or as transient workers. None shared the experience of a dozen American cities which in 1850 discovered that over half their adult males were of foreign birth. In Milwaukee, St. Louis, and Chicago over half the residents, including the children, were born abroad, chiefly in Germany in the first two cities. The number of German parents in Cincinnati and of Irish parents in Boston, Albany, and New Orleans gave their populations, in the eyes of some old natives, now called Yankees, a foreign cast. In New York and Philadelphia, as well as lesser Rochester, Buffalo, and Chicago, the foreign contingents were more diversified and therefore less challenging to the Yankees.

The influx of immigrants would have a dramatic effect on urban economic and cultural developments, but curiously enough it tended to strengthen one demographic characteristic. In the older cities of the Northeast, where the native women tended to outnumber the native men, the same ratio held among the foreign-born, even in New York City, which was the only major center there that attracted more native men than women. West of the Alleghenies, however, where the frontier cities consistently attracted more native men than women, the frontier ratio held among the foreign-born as well, with the exception in this case of Chicago, where a surplus of Irish maidens tipped the balance. The immigrants of these decades, particularly those from Ireland, came in family groups, with females in the majority. Many migrants from

England and the Continent came in family groups, too, but the number of single men among them gave the males a definite majority, and on their arrival it was the men who pushed west to help build the new cities on the frontier.

European travelers, who continued to follow the migrants westward, had become accustomed to the dramatic growth of new towns on the frontier, but they were now repeatedly startled by the quality of the new urban development. After describing in detail the mechanical ingenuity of one of Rochester's flour mills and noting the exhibit by its leading seed firm of a newly invented "sowing cart," don Ramon de la Sagra, director of the botanical garden of Havana, could not help contrasting the industry that characterized the cities of America with the "indolence and laziness" so prevalent in Spanish cities. But while he marveled in 1835 "at the picture of activity which I behold," at the same time he was "surprised at the assiduity and steadiness of some men, who seem to look with indifference at the refinement of the social graces which riches can provide." Eighteen years later, however Fredrika Bremer was delighted to find Cincinnati "the Queen City" and "a cosmopolitan city" which "embraces in her bosom peoples of all nations and all religious sects. Germans constitute a considerable portion of the population of the city, which now amounts to 120,000 souls. The Germans live here as in their old Germany. They are *gemütlich*, drink beer, practice music, and still ponder here *über die Weltgeschichte.*"[1] Although deploring a neglect of the fine arts except for music, Miss Bremer became ecstatic over a marble figure by the Cincinnati-born sculptor Hiram Powers which she saw at the home of his patron, the city's leading real estate entrepreneur and horticulturalist, Nicholas Longworth.

COMMERCIAL EXPANSION IN THE NORTH

A major aspect of the rapid urbanization of America in these decades was the building up of its cities and the opening of new trade arteries. Most of the men involved in this construction were master craftsmen who received their training on the job in the older cities of the East or in Europe. Some engineers and contractors, however, had received advance training as a result of their participation in the construction of the Erie Canal. That great project, financed by the State of New York and completed in the mid-1820s, not only spurred the urbanization of the Great Lakes' region, reshaping the settlement pattern of the nation, but also intensified the drive of other Atlantic ports for western trade contacts and supplied the skills and confidence necessary to provide them.

The successful construction and operation of the Erie Canal, by opening a great water-level route to the interior, broadened the scope of America's urbanization and prolonged the era of commercial expansion. New York's great breakthrough diverted the attention of Baltimore, Philadelphia, and Boston from industrial developments and focused their efforts on the construction of

1. *The Homes of the New World* (New York: Harper and Brothers, 1853), Chapter 2, p. 166.

competing commercial arteries into the West. Boston delayed action until the success of several short rail lines to its industrial satellites encouraged it to build west to Albany on the Hudson, where in 1842 it tapped not only the canal trade but also that of the succession of pioneer rail lines that already linked New York's upstate cities. Philadelphia, which might have rivaled Birmingham or Manchester in industrial innovation, pressured the State of Pennsylvania to build a joint rail and canal system to link it with Pittsburgh on the Ohio, and within a decade of its completion in 1834 faced the task of replacing it with a more efficient trade artery. Baltimore made a more deliberate start on the construction of the Baltimore & Ohio Railroad. Projected to reach Wheeling on the Ohio 380 miles distant, it was the most ambitious railroad yet conceived, but financing and construction proved time consuming and Philadelphia was able to launch and complete its second great venture, the privately owned Pennsylvania Railroad, which entered Pittsburgh in 1852, several months before Baltimore reached the Ohio.

But Baltimore's rail connections with the West, like those opened by Philadelphia and Boston, proved more useful to merchants and other travelers journeying to and from the interior than to shippers of bulky goods or produce, who continued to follow the canal and other water routes to and from New York and New Orleans.

The success of the Erie Canal created a mania for internal improvements that quickened the development of several interior cities. Promotional groups appeared in Pittsburgh and Cincinnati, in Oswego, Syracuse, and Rochester, pressing for the construction of river improvements and new canals and for the chartering of railroads. The urban booms produced by the construction and operation of these improvements—in Rochester in the 1820s and in Cincinnati in the 1840s—represented the local responses to what later economists would call the external economies of the major improvements. But however they were described, the cities of America, which had from the beginning exercised a generative influence over their hinterlands, acquired, particularly in the West, the more positive characteristics of a "booster," as Charles Glaab has put it. A clear expression of this attitude was the frequent decision by many towns to take a new local census in order to demonstrate their rapid growth. The next step, as earlier in the Northeast, was to issue a local directory, and the population "threshold" for its appearance tended to decline as the frontier advanced.

Yet in the widespread scramble for urban status, a booster psychology was perhaps an advantage. With three hundred urban places competing for such facilities, few cities had railroads thrust upon them. When the Erie Canal bypassed Canandaigua, Geneva, and Batavia in western New York, these towns were eager to join with Rochester in building two feeder lines that later became links in the cross-state New York Central. Not only did local business leaders buy railroad stock, but they pressed their city councils to make sizable public investments in these enterprises. Only after local support was clearly demonstrated were the promoters of many rail projects able to secure the additional funds needed from investment bankers in New York, Philadelphia, and Boston.

Thus the pioneer railroads in a very real sense were built by the cities, represented an extension of their commercial enterprise, and spread their urban influences throughout their hinterlands. The rail lines, which increased from 8,500 to 30,000 miles during the 1850s, sharpened the competitive rivalries between various cities, but they also drew them closer together into an evolving system of cities.

The wider commercial concerns of the leading American cities contrasted with the industrial specialization in the British Midlands. Yet Philadelphia, the prime example in the States of diversified economic activity, pushed ahead of its British rivals, and even surpassed Glasgow, which was the most diversified there. Of course the port of Philadelphia could not rival that of Liverpool, nor did its textile and other factories equal those of Manchester, or its metallurgists match those of Birmingham, but the rail lines it built to the coal fields north of Reading and to the iron mines around Pittsburgh supplied its foundries and machine shops with fuel and raw materials for an abundant output. The Norris Locomotive Works, for example, was supplying engines to Prague and Moscow by the late thirties, as well as to the new roads of the Middle West. Two decades later, after Philadelphia had annexed its major suburbs, encompassing their factories and swelling its population to half that of New York, its highly diversified products surpassed in value the output of all rivals except New York (which it almost matched) and London.

British investors, reassured by the success of the Erie Canal, were ready in these decades to buy state bonds for internal improvements and to purchase shares in several private railroads. But evidence of large British investments in American industry is lacking, for few industrial ventures had yet attained the corporate structure that would have attracted foreign interest. Generally an enterprising craftsman with a new idea or a merchant craftsman eager to enlarge his trade found a venturesome friend to back him at the start, but further industrial expansion, even in England, still relied on the reinvestment of plant surpluses, and the emerging industrialists resorted to local banks only for operating expenses.

Boston, however, followed a somewhat different course. Shut off from direct trade with the West and faced with increasing competition from the more favorably located shippers of New York, some of Boston's merchants turned to the promotion of new industries. Constricted by the limited space within the city's natural boundaries, the merchants who formed the Boston Manufacturing Company located its first factories at nearby Waltham in the early 1800s. When the cotton factories erected there, and equipped with power looms designed by Francis Cabot Lowell after an observant visit to Manchester, prospered, the company, headed by Lowell, established a second and totally new industrial settlement at the falls of the Merrimack. The quick success of Lowell, as the new town was named, prompted an expanded group of businessmen called the Boston Associates to launch other new industrial satellites at Lawrence, Chicopee, and other power sites that were linked in the late thirties to the port of Boston by a series of rail lines spoking out from that hub, which acquired by the midcentury the largest rail network in the country, to serve its third largest concentration of industrial workers.

Lowell became more widely known for its labor-management innovations than for any technological advances. The cotton mills were the largest in

America, but they had many precedents in Manchester in both size and layout. There were a few English precedents, too, for the new industrial-town concept, though they were not as well-known and failed to capture the imagination of visitors as Lowell's quaint paternalism repeatedly did. Carefully planned as an industrial city, with ample space reserved for factories along the river and room for industrial expansion along a preexisting canal and its projected extension, Lowell broke new ground in urban planning, and the clusters of dormitories located nearby were equally innovative. Built almost entirely by the various milling companies organized by the Boston Associates to develop the property, Lowell outpaced all previous new towns in rate of growth and became a city of twenty thousand by 1840. Eight major companies had by that date opened factories that employed a total of eight thousand operatives, greatly outnumbering the artisans and tradesmen who usually comprised the majority in such towns. More surprising was the predominance of females in the work force, for the companies had recruited young women from the rural towns of New England, offering them a chance to earn a modest dowry by working for a few seasons in Lowell's model factories and living in its supervised dormitories. Impressed by its orderly plan and substantial construction, as well as by its unusual social customs, many visitors hailed Lowell as the model industrial city of the 1840s, yet by the close of that decade the glamour was wearing thin. The restrictive controls exercised by absentee landlords and mill owners cast a blight over its commercial and civic affairs. By the late fifties the mills of Lowell, like those of Lawrence and the other Boston satellites, were looking to the new immigrants for their labor force, and despite an increase in the number of its industrial corporations the city was fast becoming a company town, an important but minor pattern of urban development in the States.

New Haven, Hartford, and Worcester on the western fringe of Boston's sphere of influence experienced a strikingly different industrial growth. Again it started with an enterprising innovator, in this case Eli Whitney, whose invention of the cotton gin, which he produced in great numbers in a factory in New Haven, had transformed the economy of the South. His later role in the application of the principle of interchangeable parts to the production of machines and other articles provided the key for many new specialized factories that spread to neighboring towns in the Connecticut Valley and provided employment for the savings of former merchants and the skills of local workmen. Soon this district was almost as reminiscent of Birmingham in the early 1800s as Lowell and its neighbors were of early Manchester. Boston performed some of the functions of early Liverpool, including the distribution of a mounting influx of Irish refugees. Yet in size of population and economic output the greater Boston district of the 1850s was more comparable to the Midlands of the 1820s, while Philadelphia, with Pittsburgh and other Pennsylvania industrial towns in its trading zone, offered a more contemporary comparison.

New York, of course, enjoyed a uniquely advantageous situation which gave it a special pattern of commercial and industrial growth. Its ice-free harbor and central location had made it by the 1820s the chief entrepôt for foreign trade and migrants, and the successful opening of the Erie Canal together with the establishment of weekly packet service to Liverpool in that decade had clinched the port's control of the export trade as well. But it was the enterprise of its merchants that developed a similar dominance over the coastal trade, particularly with the booming cotton ports of the South. To maintain this commerce, New York's craftsmen developed a great variety of service trades and specialty shops. A similar pattern of small shops was dominant in its housekeeping industries, as well as among the dressmakers, tailors, shoemakers, and many other tradesmen who outfitted the incessant flood of travelers and immigrants thronging the bustling metropolis.

New York's economic functions were thus more comparable to those of London than to those of the Midland cities. Its growth in these decades was, however, more rapid than that of either of the two great urbanizing districts of Britain. Though only half as populous as the three Midland cities together in 1830, it exceeded their total by 1860. But London, which barely doubled its population in these decades, nevertheless grew by more than New York's metropolitan total and retained its unchallenged lead in international trade and finance, as well as in population and industrial output.

New York, however, in addition to its widening international contacts, its national leadership in imports and (except for cotton) exports, and its increasing dominance in banking, was developing an interior urban team which would help assure its continued growth. Five of the cities on the Erie Canal were among the first thirty in the nation throughout these decades, and four on the upper Great Lakes joined that group by the early 1850s. Most of these were important regional marketing centers, but four, whose products required industrial processing to prepare them for shipment, quickly became industrial fabricating centers as well. One of these was Chicago, the youngest of all, which mushroomed from zero to 109,000 between 1830 and 1860. All were linked to New York, and to each other, by an incomparable water-level route. And in the mid-fifties, when the last of the team members had completed their separately built feeder railroads, a consolidation of several of these lines into the New York Central & Hudson River Railroad was effected, with board control judiciously scattered along the route from Buffalo to New York. With the aid of its metropolitan backers, the New York Central soon secured a choice of alternate routes north and south of Lake Erie to connect with the Michigan Central or the Michigan Southern for an entry into Chicago by 1859, thus matching the westward extension of the Pennsylvania Railroad over the Pittsburgh, Fort Wayne & Chicago two years before.

Although bound to the New York port and to each other by water and rail lines, the members of this extended team were fiercely competitive and assertive of their independence from the metropolis. Troy and Albany were too close for comfort and vied for precedence in cultural efforts, as well as in trade and industry. Utica, Syracuse, and Rochester, at junction points with feeder canals, also built feeder railroads. Rochester investors backed the extension of telegraph lines throughout the West and promoted their consolidation into Western Union, which brought the city's chief industry, flour milling, a stability it had never known before and hastened its migration to the larger wheatfields of the Middle West. Buffalo, Cleveland, Detroit, and Chicago all established rail links with Pittsburgh and Philadelphia to assert their independence of New York, but of course that metropolis remained their chief outlet and trade center—services it increasingly performed for Philadelphia and Baltimore as well.

EXPANSION IN THE SOUTH AND WEST

The urbanization of the South was complicated by that section's "peculiar institution"—slavery. One simple technological advance, the invention of the cotton gin, had rejuvenated the plantation system and created an active demand for slave labor on the land. The mounting products of the cotton fields called for the development of market centers, and a half-dozen ports from Charleston south and west to New Orleans offered their services. But the pervasive fears of slave insurrections produced many restraints on the freedom of movement and activities of the blacks who comprised the major work force in most of these cities, and prevented the South from developing the cotton factories and other accessory trades its situation made possible. Although Savannah doubled and Mobile increased sevenfold in these decades, their black population declined as able-bodied male slaves were sold to plantation owners and Irish immigrants came to man their docks. Old Charleston, which grew more slowly, saw a rapid drop in the number of its slaves in the fifties, but attracted relatively few immigrants.

New Orleans, on the other hand, prospered from the more diversified flow of trade on the Mississippi. As its population increased fivefold in these decades, this old French port added several thousand Irish and German migrants to its residents and became the fifth city in total size, as well as the sixth in the number of foreign-born inhabitants. Its 116,000 residents in 1860 included 9,400 born in the North, yet New Orleans, like the other southern cities, neglected its industrial opportunities and ranked twelfth in the value added to its manufactured products. It stood second, and even first for a time, in exports, but as we have seen, permitted New York merchants and shipowners to handle that trade and to divert an increasing portion of the shipments and profits to New York. This unexpected languor in a booming port could not be attributed solely to the blacks, whose numbers, both free and slave, dropped sharply in the forties and fifties, particularly among the males. Yet here, as in the other southern cities, the system of bondage, by absorbing much surplus capital in a socially prestigious but unproductive investment in household slaves, sapped the community's vitality. Whatever the outcome of the long debate over the profitability of slavery in the plantation economy, its influence on the cities was negative. Despite the remarkable expansion of New Orleans, the astonishing growth of its trade, and the cosmopolitan splendors it attained, the Mississippi port failed to realize the great potentials its chief advocate, J. D. B. DeBow, publisher of *DeBow's Review,* claimed for it.

A number of borderland cities escaped the malaise of the Deep South and reaped benefits from the increasing trade between the sections. Scattered from Richmond and Baltimore west to St. Louis were six cities that displayed exceptional urban vigor in these decades. Richmond barely doubled while St. Louis increased tenfold, with most of the others approaching the latter rate; and although this fact was by no means the principal cause of their growth, slavery was important only in the Virginia capital. Blacks, predominantly slaves, comprised a third of its population, but unlike the cities of the Deep South, Richmond gave them productive employment in its iron furnaces and other industries as it processed the rich resources of its region. Its limited growth was more directly related to its failure to attract many immigrants, a group that comprised barely 13 percent of its population in 1860, the lowest ratio of any city over 20,000 in the country. Washington, with fewer blacks, most of them free, had a slightly higher percentage of foreign-born, while St. Louis, with barely 3,300 blacks, had 96,000 immigrants, over 59 percent of its total.

Each of the border cities experienced a distinctive growth pattern. Baltimore, the largest, displayed great vitality and increased 160 percent, despite a drop in the number of its slaves and free blacks and despite a smaller influx of immigrants than any other major city attracted. Its leaders pinned their hopes on the Baltimore & Ohio Railroad, which progressively established connections with the other borderland cities by linking with lines extending west to St. Louis in the middle fifties. Yet this hard-fought commercial achievement failed to sustain its statistical position as the city fell from a technical second (Philadelphia was larger but did not annex its suburbs as rapidly) to fourth place in population during the 1850s. In industrial output it was a poor eighth, surpassed even by St. Louis and overshadowed by Cincinnati, which was also attracting many immigrants and employing them to advantage in the processing of area products and the fabrication of consumer goods for valley markets. Cincinnati's output, in fact, exceeded that of Boston proper and challenged that of the Boston area for third place in manufacturing activity. It exceeded in population such old rivals as Pittsburgh and Louisville and was gaining on both Baltimore and New Orleans, though not as rapidly as was the rising new challenger for leadership in the Middle West, St. Louis, which needed only three hundred newcomers to oust Cincinnati from seventh place.

Except for New York, no American city had a firm grip on its population rank in these turbulent decades. In the promotional excitement of the period, all cities were acutely aware of these fluctuations and each had its boosters eager to promote its competitive status. An improvement of transport facilities was the prevailing objective, and most of the cities that specialized in industry did so as processors of area products—transforming the ore, lumber, grain, and livestock for easier shipment to distant markets. Moreover, Boston and its satellites, the apparent exceptions, were employing earlier shipping profits and regional labor skills to process imported cotton in order to retain commercial vitality. Even in the six northeastern states where urban occupations surpassed agricultural, commercial employment exceeded industrial.

This commercial emphasis was characteristic of all the major cities and of many lesser ones as well. Most of the successful towns had been strategically located at breaks in trade—Pittsburgh and St. Louis at the junctions of great rivers, Louisville at the falls of the Ohio, Buffalo at the eastern end of the upper lakes, Detroit at a junction of two lakes. Each hastened to exploit its advantages by developing accessory transport facilities, docks, roads, canals, or rail lines, to increase the volume of trade pausing at its door.

Through traffic, however, was of little value, as many towns that became way stations discovered. To avoid that fate, the town of Erie, Pennsylvania's port on Lake Erie, fought to retain the interruption of rail traffic which had developed because of the sharp differential in the gauges of the railroads that met there. When Buffalo and the New York Central secured alternate connections north of the lake to Detroit and Chicago, Cleveland and other Ohio interests helped break the roadblock at Erie, which did in fact become a way station. Other cities, such as Philadelphia and Cincinnati, delayed the laying of track across their central wards to connect their eastern and western railroads, and thus postponed until the sixties the development of through traffic.

The merchants of Cincinnati, advantageously located at a northern bend of the Ohio, were concerned by the rapid rise of St. Louis, but they hastened to improve connections with that Mississippi port. Cincinnati capital helped build the ill-starred Ohio & Mississippi Railroad through undeveloped southern Indiana and Illinois counties to St. Louis, and backed the construction of other lines north to Cleveland and Toledo on Lake Erie, as well as through Indianapolis to Chicago. These efforts assured its leadership in the rapid development of the Old Northwest in the late forties and fifties, but a major feature of that development was the emergence of a host of new cities in this area. In addition to the booming lake ports to the north, two interior state capitals, Columbus and Indianapolis, and several other aspiring towns made their appearance.

Of all the new cities, the most strategically located was Chicago. Situated at the southern tip of Lake Michigan, the most interior point to which water-level traffic with New York could reach, Chicago merchants quickly promoted the construction of roads, canals, and railroads into the nation's heartland. At its urging the State constructed the Illinois and Michigan Canal from Chicago to Peru, where it linked the two great water routes in the late forties. But Chicago promoters were more interested in building railroads to the south and west to head off the trade that might drain into St. Louis and turn it to their own lake port. As a result the tenfold growth of that upper Mississippi port in the forties and fifties was completely overshadowed by the mushrooming expansion of Chicago, which increased twenty-five times in those decades. New Orleans, Cincinnati, and St. Louis were still far ahead, but Chicago was rapidly gaining on them.

The most comparable range of cities was in European Russia, but the contrasts were more important than the similarities. Most of Russia's twenty largest cities in 1811 had been old cities located in the densely settled western portion of the country, with its forty million inhabitants. Some of these regional capitals and river- or seaports stagnated as nine other cities took their places among the top twenty during the next half-century. Several of the newcomers prospered, as Chauncy D. Harris explains, because of Russia's increased international trade, while others reflected the thriving internal commerce, but the urban population barely doubled in this period, and the total for the nation increased only 80 percent, in contrast with the 300 percent growth in the States and a fourteenfold increase of the cities. Russia would free its serfs in 1861, two years before Lincoln's emancipation of the slaves, but its urban ratio would fall to half that of the States, which, according to Weber, rose more rapidly than that of any other nation. Russia at this time had scarcely begun to develop its vast Siberian frontier.

In the United States, a host of new towns had already appeared west of the Mississippi River. At least twenty-two towns, mostly oases in a vast prairie, had reached five thousand in population by 1860, and nine already exceeded ten thousand. All but one were located at strategic river sites, but only three had railroad connections, although several of their lesser rivals had already acquired such service. The urbanization of the eight states and seven territories west of the Mississippi River had scarcely commenced, though the marketing needs of their almost four million residents were served by two major river ports, New Orleans and St. Louis, and on the west coast by San Francisco, which had mushroomed in a dozen years to become a city of 56,882 inhabitants. Centrally located on a promontory jutting into a spacious and beautiful bay and overlooking the Pacific Ocean, its spectacular site won the admiration of innumerable visitors drawn there in its early years by the fame

Table 3. POPULATIONS OF PRINCIPAL U.S. CITIES, 1830 to 1860.*

Cities	1830	1840	1850	1860
New York	202,589	312,700	515,500	813,600
Philadelphia	161,271	220,400	340,000	565,529
Brooklyn	15,396	36,230	96,838	266,660
Baltimore	80,620	102,300	169,600	212,418
Boston	61,392	93,380	136,880	177,840
New Orleans	46,082	102,190	116,375	168,675
Cincinnati	24,831	46,338	115,435	161,044
St. Louis	5,852	14,470	77,860	160,773
Chicago		4,470	29,963	109,260
Buffalo	8,653	18,213	42,260	81,130
Newark	10,953	17,290	38,890	71,940
Louisville	10,340	21,210	43,194	68,033
Albany	24,209	33,721	50,763	62,367
Washington	18,826	23,364	40,001	61,122
San Francisco			34,776	56,802
Providence	16,833	23,171	41,573	50,666
Pittsburgh	15,369	21,115	46,601	49,221
Rochester	9,207	20,191	36,403	48,204
Detroit	2,222	9,012	21,019	45,619
Milwaukee		1,712	20,061	45,246
Cleveland	1,076	6,071	17,034	43,417
Total of Urban Residents	1,127,000	1,845,000	3,543,700	6,216,500
Number of Towns over 2500	90	131	236	392
Percent Urban	8.8	10.8	15.3	19.8
Total U.S. Population	12,866,000	17,069,000	23,191,800	31,433,300

*Derived from U.S. Censuses in 1850, 1860, and 1910 (Washington, D.C.: U.S. Government Printing Office).

of nearby gold mines. No other city in America had enjoyed such a meteoric rise; and none were as predominantly male or rivaled the cosmopolitan urbanity San Francisco acquired. No other great port had achieved worldwide distinction so rapidly. It was the last great triumph of the era of commercial urbanization on the frontier.

BIBLIOGRAPHY

Berthoff, R. T. *British Immigrants in Industrial America: 1790–1950.* New York: Russell & Russell, 1953.

Briggs, Asa. *Victorian Cities.* New York: Harper & Row, Publishers, 1963.

Engerman, Stanley L. "The Effects of Slavery upon the Southern Economy: A Review of the Recent Debate." *Explorations in Entrepreneurial History,* Second Series, 4, no. 2 (1967), 71–97.

Ernst, Robert. *Immigrant Life in New York City: 1825–1863.* Port Washington, N.Y.: Ira J. Friedman, Inc., 1949.

Fishlow, Albert. *American Railroads and the Transformation of the Antebellum Economy.* Cambridge, Mass.: Harvard University Press, 1965.

Handlin, Oscar. *Boston's Immigrants, 1790–1865.* New York: Atheneum House, Inc., 1941.

Harris, Chauncey D. *Cities in the Soviet Union.* Chicago: Rand McNally & Co., 1970.

Jenks, Leland H. *The Migration of British Capital to 1875.* New York: Alfred A. Knopf, Inc., 1938.

McGee, T. G. *The Southeast Asian City: A Social Geography of the Primate Cities of Southeast Asia.* New York: Praeger Publishers, 1967.

McKelvey, Blake. *Rochester, the Water-Power City: 1812–1854.* Cambridge, Mass.: Harvard University Press, 1945.

Pred, Allan R. *The Spatial Dynamics of U.S. Urban Industrial Growth: 1800–1914.* Cambridge, Mass.: MIT Press, 1966.

Still, Bayrd. "Patterns of Mid-Nineteenth Century Urbanization in the Middle West." *Mississippi Valley Historical Review,* 28 (September 1941), 187–206.

Taylor, George. *The Transportation Revolution, 1815–1860.* New York: Harper & Row, Publishers, 1951.

Young, G. M., ed. *Early Victorian England: 1830–1867.* London: Oxford University Press, 1934.

4

Urbanization in Depth in the Merchant Cities

The pre-Civil War cities of the United States were commercially oriented centers of rapidly developing regions to which they supplied economic leadership and vitality. In their remarkable growth since the establishment of the British colonial ports two centuries before, they had assumed many social, political, and cultural functions, and their economic activities had acquired great diversity, but the commercial and generative functions remained dominant. They represented an advanced stage of urbanism, one which had taken a different course from that of Latin American cities, and one which was equally distinct both from the older urban patterns in Europe and from the newer industrial specialization developing in England. There were, however, similarities as well as contrasts with urban developments in Canada and Australia. Demographic and geographic components had helped account for the distinguishing characteristics of the American cities and considerably influenced the internal features that gave substance and form to these differences. An analysis of the changing internal structures and a consideration of some of the forces producing these changes will increase our understanding of what may be described as the urbanization in depth of the merchant cities.

URBAN CHANGE AND MOBILITY

The pre-Civil War cities can best be characterized as merchant cities. They had special attributes that did not fit either of the preindustrial patterns applied by Gideon Sjoberg to medieval and transition cities or the models of the commercial centers and colonial ports as conceived by other sociologists. They served as commercial centers, but in a dynamic sense, for their merchants were promoters as well as traders, interested in the marketing of their products and in the development of new regional potentialities. They were in a preindustrial transition stage, not from a stagnant feudal society, but from an enterprising homespun village society in which farmers and craftsmen alike, as well as practitioners of all other occupations, were fellow citizens. Unskilled workers in the towns, large and small, were known as mechanics, not laborers, and, except for the slaves in most southern cities, could aspire to become craftsmen or perhaps merchants and to see their sons and daughters climb the social ladder. Not all achieved advancement, and in fact the lower ranks increased more rapidly than the upper strata, as Edward Pessen has demonstrated, but this resulted in part from the rapid growth of towns, which brought progressively more newcomers. Yet the great majority continued to hope for advancement. Moreover, the larger towns and cities provided new opportunities for mechanics, merchants, and professional men alike.

Indeed, the cities were in a stage of rapid urbanization in more than one sense. Not only did their rate of growth exceed that of the nation as a whole, but the degree of their heterogeneity was increasing rapidly, and both the number and variety of their functions were expanding. Indeed, the momentum of these developments added zest to the urbanizing process and quickened the sense of community on both local and national levels. Despite an undertone of antiurbanism and rural nostalgia, the spirit of boosterism, the sense of participation in building the city, and the new-felt pride in the growth of both city and nation enabled the North American communities to absorb an unprecedented variety of newcomers.

Both the number and the variety of newcomers were significant. Thus the cities, particularly in the northern states, attracted a mounting flood of immigrants, swelling the number of the foreign-born in the fifty largest cities to a million and a half by 1860, or approximately 40 percent of their total. These growing cities drew a similar influx of rural or small-town natives, many from distant states, and since out-of-state residents comprised almost a fourth of all natives tabulated by the census that year, their proportions must have been much higher among the more mobile inhabitants of the cities. In the seven leading metropolises for which data on state of birth were tabulated in 1860, the city's home state was the principal source for those in the East, but supplied a diminishing share as the tabulators moved west, where the in-migrants decidedly predominated.

The in-and-out mobility of the urban population is dramatically illustrated by a study of the Rochester experience. A check of its city directories revealed that approximately 53 percent of those listed in 1855 had died or moved on before the end of that decade, despite a 10 percent increase in the city's total in those five years. The migratory ratios of this city, which because of its location on the major east-west artery probably exceeded those of many other places, had declined somewhat from the 65 percent who departed during the city's first five years two decades before. In a more exacting statistical study of mobility ratios in Boston during these decades, Peter Knights has recently found a similar overall decline, though the trends varied for different ethnic samples.

The effects of this mobility were far-reaching. Newcomers (even more than natives, according to Knights) who failed to find satisfactory places readily pulled up stakes and moved on. When (and if) they finally found suitable opportunities, they hastened to join or establish churches and other institutions similar to those of their homelands. The increased heterogeneity of the urban population was thus matched by an increased diversity of social and cultural institutions. Moreover, the eagerness with which most newcomers, whether native or foreign, endeavored to establish their identity by joining and supporting familiar organizations helped explain the greater number and strength of churches and schools in American than in European cities.

The migratory mobility likewise contributed to the upward mobility of many urbanites, since those who found the cards stacked against them in one town could readily make a fresh start in another place. Meanwhile, those who remained fixed in one city, whatever their talents, gradually acquired an old-settler quality that had its advantages in a sea of newcomers. The pioneers' associations were as characteristic of American cities as the Hibernian, St. Andrews, and Turner societies of the immigrant groups. Yet though prestigious and at the start powerful, the old settlers lost status or at least predominance in most growing cities and had to recruit talented newcomers, as Michael Frisch discovered in Springfield, to maintain the vitality of their institutions. Despite the advantages old settlers enjoyed, men of ability could rise more rapidly in new settings, with the result that the upwardly mobile made frequent migrations, and generally to larger or newer cities. Many Yankees from New England found attractive opportunities in New York City, for example. Not Yankees but numerous craftsmen from old England seized the opportunities for advancement in nearby Paterson, according to Herbert Gutman, while in Philadelphia, as Stuart Blumin tells us, it was the merchants who reaped the largest rewards. Whatever the direction, rapid change and development were endemic to American cities.

The dynamic character of America's urbanization was noted by many observers. Every travel journal focused on the cities and many commented on the ceaseless din of hammers and saws that greeted them on all sides. The invention and widespread use of the balloon frame, permitting unskilled workers to erect frame buildings from the generally abundant supplies of lumber, facilitated the rapid expansion of residential districts for homeowners and imposed on most growing cities the village pattern of single free-standing houses. The speculative subdivision of town plots and adjoining tracts by enterprising landowners further promoted urban expansion and gave it a private and in many places an unplanned character that generally followed more closely the prospect of profits than the contours of the natural site, the dictates of reason, or ancient tradition. Since the gridiron street pattern provided the most efficient scheme for the subdivision and sale of lots, most town promoters favored it, though the haste with which it was applied by plot holders along the roads branching out from many cities helped preserve a number of radiating natural thoroughfares that promoted continued expansion and made American cities open ended.

Some Canadian and Australian cities displayed several but not all of these tendencies. Both Toronto and Melbourne also started with gridiron street patterns to facilitate quick land sales, but in keeping with the British practice of centralized controls, as interpreted in the colonial capitals, they extended them with greater regularity than in most American cities. These and other British colonial cities in newly developing provinces in the 1840s relied more exclusively on newcomers from the British Isles and had less diversified populations than comparable American cities. Relative geographical isolation and slower rates of settlement limited their spatial mobility, depriving them of some of the vertical mobility characteristic of the States. Further research is needed to determine the extent to which British traditions also retarded social mobility, but greater homogeneity reduced the need for separate ethnic institutions and enabled Melbourne, as Asa Briggs has shown, to develop its formal structure and achieve elite standards with quite deliberate speed. As in the case of San Francisco, the discovery of gold within its province in 1851 quickened its growth as a merchant city, but while the California port acquired a cosmopolitan character, Melbourne remained Victorian.

Unlike the walled cities of Europe and elsewhere, American cities had no hard and fast boundaries. Incorporated in most cases by state charters, many repeatedly extended their corporate limits by making annexations with legislative approval. But there was no standardized distinction between rural and urban territory as in England, where the Borough and Corporate Towns Commission of 1837 drew enduring boundaries around 178 boroughs and prescribed both mandatory and optional functions. As the product in many cases of rival promoters of nearby or adjoining sites, many American cities had a dual or hybrid core, surrounded by numerous independently designed subdivisions. Their early tendency to expand was abetted by the desire of neighboring residents to share the services only the city could provide, but throughout these decades the lack of convenient and economical transit facilities held most cities within the limits prescribed by pedestrian convenience. Public omnibuses made their appearance in New York in the late twenties and in other metropolises in later decades, and seven cities acquired horse-car service on a few major arteries during the 1850s. But their total mileage, according to the 1860 census, was only 402.57, and the majority of urban residents, like their predecessors for centuries past, walked to work, to shop, and on most other occasions.

As the years progressed and the cities grew, travelers from abroad, particularly those who rated a tour by carriage, felt increasingly obliged to "visit the Lions," as Fredrika Bremer put it, for each town quickly acquired and took pride in a number of local showplaces. Among the more unusual "Lions" were Rembrandt Peale's museum of wax figures in Baltimore, as well as that of his father in Philadelphia, and Ormsby Mitchel's observatory in Cincinnati. Miss Bremer, who visited each of these, demonstrated her skill at hitting the high spots by describing the novel experience in 1853 of dispatching a telegraphic message at Rochester, where she also witnessed a performance by the Fox sisters, whom she described as "the little Barnums of the spirit world," and made a point of visiting Frederick Douglass, the fugitive slave whose autobiography she had found "deeply affecting."

There were many genuine accomplishments, but the pretentions, too, were widespread. Most towns acquired female academies before they erected water towers or other waterworks, though the compulsion to provide a system for combating fires was ever present, as the recruiting of volunteer fire companies and the digging of numerous storage cisterns indicated. Orphan asylums were almost as essential, particularly in cities on major traffic arteries, for a pathetic result of the flood of migrants into the cities and to the West was the appearance of homeless waifs on the downtown streets, lost or abandoned by their parents in transit. Fortunately, community consciousness was strong enough, particularly in its religious infrastructure, to produce a Protestant and a Catholic orphanage in most cities to shelter these children.

NEW CIVIC RESPONSIBILITIES

A major portion of the urban response to city needs in America was voluntary. Public-spirited individuals in every city, following Benjamin Franklin's example, took the lead in organizing athenaeums and young men's associations to maintain a library, reading room, and meeting hall. Others backed enterprising teachers in establishing academies and seminaries before the public school systems were securely launched, and in many places continued to maintain them as a means of social distinction. The active participation of many residents in public programs was, of course, generally related to some private interest. As the volunteer fire companies played politics in order to get better equipment and ultimately to secure positions of power for their favorite leaders, so the temperance societies, which started as friendly associations of reformed drinkers, became political factions with antiforeign overtones and prohibition as their objective.

The private and associational efforts that sufficed in the village and small town became inadequate, however, as the cities grew in size and heterogeneity. Not only did a half-dozen large cities replace their volunteer fire companies in the fifties with paid fire departments equipped with steam engines drawn by horses rather than boys, but several, particularly in the South, also replaced their night watchmen with uniformed policemen. In response to the city's growth and increasing complexity, the Boston police, as described by Roger Lane, passed their early responsibilities over sanitation and welfare on to newly created agencies and assumed the specialized functions of maintaining order and suppressing crime. Finally in 1859, following the lead of London and New York, Boston provided each policeman with a uniform. Meanwhile, the early practice of relying on stray hogs to remove the garbage thrown into the street gave way in most towns to the licensing of scavangers by the newly formed health boards. Numerous cities followed the example of Philadelphia in developing a public waterworks equipped with pipes to distribute water from impounded reservoirs, but the great majority of their residents still relied on private wells and water carriers.

In the field of municipal services the response of American cities contrasted dramatically with that of most cities abroad. Some of the capital cities in South America and in many countries in Europe, supported by their central governments, enjoyed excellent facilities in highly visible town halls, market buildings, and parade grounds, and with other foreign cities enjoyed a more effective police supervision than did American cities. Alerted by repeated contagions and other crises, the central authorities in France, Germany, and especially England developed sanitary regulations and provided agencies to implement them that supplied an example to cities in the States when their local leaders finally became aroused by the ravages of cholera in 1832 and after. A survey conducted by Dr. John Griscom for the New York Board of Health in 1845, following similar surveys in London and Bristol in earlier emergencies, first brought the wretched housing conditions in that city to light. The reports of health authorities in other cities, following the frightening epidemics of 1849 and 1852, were equally revealing and, as recently reviewed by Charles Rosenberg, generally resulted in the opening of a pest hospital and the permanent establishment of a local health board.

In civic matters the new western cities frequently followed the example of older cities in the East. Those in the Ohio Valley reflected Philadelphia influences, as we have previously noted, and those on the Great Lakes followed the New York model. Charters were granted by the state legislatures, which proved reluctant to authorize unusual functions or to extend taxing powers, and frequently a city had to submit repeated requests and prove that its needs equaled those of an older city before additional authority was granted. The New York State legislature endeavored for a time to maintain a degree of state control over the city governments by retaining the right to name the recorder who was to have a place on the city council. Rochester successfully broke that pattern by rejecting its first proposed charter in 1832, and the practice was abandoned after 1834. The legislatures by this date were ready to extend the vote to a wider class of citizens and, as Professor Still has shown, the chief advance made in the new western charters was the elimination of the property qualification for voters.

The crucial civic debates in most cities arose over the inadequacy of the taxing authority, not over the recognition of proper functions. None of the American cities received grants-in-aid from state or national authorities such as those supplied by Parliament after 1846 for local poor relief, sanitation, and police efforts. Left to its own resources, even New York, with a long-established power to build sewers, was able to provide them only in a fourth of its streets by 1857. And most of the 138 miles thus covered were served by drainage, not sanitary, sewers, since suitable pipes for the latter had only become readily available in the fifties. Their use, moreover, depended upon the prior installation of water pipes, and despite the progress made in a score of cities, none had yet achieved a wide distribution of either public or private water services. All, as a result, relied extensively on the traditional outhouses and on licensed night soil collectors whose performance fluctuated with the market for their product. The city's outlays for sewer construction, like those for street paving and the installation of water mains, were generally charged against the adjoining property, but this policy delayed improvements in the congested poverty-stricken neighborhoods that most urgently needed them.

Because of their limited powers and inadequate sources of revenue, the cities generally welcomed offers by private groups to provide needed services. Private companies had built wharves and bridges, as well as academies, public houses, and markets, since colonial times. Numerous towns had granted charters to private water companies in recent decades, but the most characteristic representative of the new group of public utilities was the gas company that now made its appearance in an increasing number of cities. Baltimore chartered the first such company in 1816, and by 1850 all the leading cities were served by at least one gas company, and the number of companies exceeded two hundred a decade later. They had by midcentury taken over a major portion of the street-lighting task and supplied lights to many public buildings and residences as well. Towns, many of whose inhabitants, like their rural cousins, had gone quietly to bed at nightfall, now experienced a new burst of activity. Struggling theaters acquired stability and increased in number in many cities shortly after the arrival of a gas company brought better illumination on stage and in the streets. Athenaeum lecture programs prospered as never before and reaped a surplus to expand their libraries, which now announced evening hours. Music halls and dancing pavilions extended their programs and added to the gaiety of many cities.

Not all the inhabitants of growing towns welcomed the new urban ways. Many objected to the make-believe and dissimulation of the theater and the promiscuity of the dance hall, as well as the dissipation produced by the newly specialized beer parks and saloons. Some former villagers of dominant sects even opposed the efforts of rival denominations to establish churches until they discovered, as in Rochester in 1824, that the town was not only becoming large enough to support more than one thriving church, but was also heterogeneous enough to need a variety of churches to counter less desirable aberrations. Citywide Sunday school unions and interdenominational temperance and other reform societies marked the growing sophistication of some communities.

In most places the transition from village to city was an evolutionary rather than a revolutionary experience. As the production of homespun in rural households faltered because of the dearth of house girls and other help, the increased reliance on specialized seamstresses, carpenters, and other artisans in the towns marked the progress of urbanization. In similar fashion, after former villagers from New England and the South had learned to live together in harmony in Cincinnati and other frontier towns, they were better able to accept and even welcome newcomers from abroad. Thus booming new cities such as St. Louis and Chicago received and assimilated proportionately larger influxes of immigrants with less internal friction than occurred in old Boston, much less than marked the outburst of nativism in several lesser and more single-minded towns. A diversity of ethnic origins, as Claude Griffen has noted of Poughkeepsie, was a key factor in maintaining a semblance of harmony.

The urbanizing process brought not only a greater heterogeneity of population and an increased diversity of institutional activity, but also new functions. Each of these trends supported the others. Thus, as the inrush of newcomers expanded the towns and diversified their social and cultural affairs, the cities became centers of assimilation, or Americanization, as one aspect of that process would later be called. The other aspect, the urbanization of rural newcomers, was more immediately pressing, for all failures added to the welfare and crime problems. Cities in England and on the Continent, with old established hinterlands that were producing a greater population surplus than they could normally absorb, faced less disquieting prospects. Some successfully developed industrial activities to absorb the new labor supply; others became emigration depots, dispatching the surplus migrants to the States or to other developing frontiers; but none, even of those that remained predominantly merchant cities, attained as diversified a character as their counterparts in America, and none faced comparable police problems or the need to assimilate dissident newcomers.

URBAN CORES AND RURAL HINTERLANDS

American cities, however, benefited from the continued growth of their hinterlands. The promotional efforts they expended on the development of regional potentialities sped the settlement and exploitation of their areas, increasing the flow of produce to the city markets and of orders for household furnishings and farm implements. Market towns and colonial ports established in the midst of native populations in South America and elsewhere could, by resorting to taxation and other devices, create a flow of produce to market, but their merchants faced a wall of indifference when pressing the sale of their merchandise. In the United States, by contrast (and in Canada and Australia as well), the cities grew up with and thus enjoyed a cooperative relationship with their hinterlands from the start. City residents took the lead in organizing agricultural and horticultural societies, in publishing farmers' papers, in manufacturing new plows and harvesters, in building plank roads to facilitate the inflow of produce and the distribution of merchandise, and in promoting agricultural fairs.

This close cooperation between rural and urban settlements hastened the development of processing industries in many market towns. Grain had to be transformed into flour or whiskey for easier shipment; logs into lumber and other milling products; wool, cotton, and hemp into thread, rope, and cloth. Market centers that possessed water power, or attracted sufficient raw materials to justify the installation of steam engines, became processing centers as well. The availability of natural power, as at Lowell, Louisville, Rochester, and many other towns at dependable waterfalls, or the accessibility of abundant coal supplies for steam power, as at Pittsburgh and Cincinnati, speeded the concentration at these sites of many fabricating handicrafts that had previously been scattered throughout rural villages. Thus, whereas a fourth of Monroe County's manufactured products came from the rural towns in 1840, by 1860 Rochester had absorbed nine tenths of all such production. Pittsburgh, which saw many of its industries spill out into industrial suburbs, experienced a decentralizing trend, but Cincinnati and Philadelphia, which successfully annexed their expanding suburbs, absorbed a still higher portion of the output of their counties. The rural districts adjoining these urban counties barely held their own in handicraft production during these decades.

Technological improvements also accelerated these trends. Thus the invention of the sewing machine and its successful application to the manufacture of both shoes and clothing drew rural and itinerant shoemakers, as well as tailors and seamstresses, into the cities. Carpenters and other woodworkers found jobs in urban lumber mills and chair and carriage factories, where new machinery increased their production, as well as in building homes for the expanding cities. Blacksmiths and other metalworkers converged on those cities where new techniques and other opportunities beckoned, including jobs producing new agricultural machinery. Printers likewise flocked to the towns where, on improved power-driven presses, they printed farmers' almanacs and agricultural weeklies, as well as the urban dailies that now made their appearance in every city of ten thousand residents. In addition, they produced so many books that American cities, which in 1820 had imported 70 percent of their book supplies from England, publishing only 30 percent themselves, completely reversed that situation during the course of the next four decades and imported only 30 percent to supplement the 70 percent they produced themselves.

That dramatic shift was not, of course, due exclusively to technological advances, though they helped there as in other industries. Numerous inventions contributed to urban growth. Mechanical planters and harvesters for the farms released workers from the fields and sent them to the cities looking for new jobs. Precut and assembled door and window frames and castiron fronts provided new and in the last case, supposedly fireproof building materials. The invention of machines to make lead, iron, and ceramic pipes permitted the wider expansion of cities by facilitating the distribution of water and gas and the collection of sewage. The invention of the telegraph made possible the speedy transmission of information from city to city and gave new stability to many urban ventures, including the newspapers. No improvement contributed more than the railroads, which brought an increased flow and diversity of both raw materials and merchandise at economical rates and assured a wider distribution of products. Economic historians are still uncertain whether the railroads produced or resulted from the economic "takeoff," but urban economists such as Wilbur Thompson recognize them as one of the most vital factors promoting urban development in America, for no one can question the large role they played in the growth of the cities, where they received as well as supplied great stimulus. Their chief contribution was to link many more or less isolated cities into a larger urban network, thus freeing each town from the limitations of its local region.

Of course the railroads did not prove equally beneficial to all cities. They sidetracked some, such as Troy, made way stations of others, such as Utica, and brought great economic advantage to many others. Most of the towns that prospered from the railroads did so by virtue of the energies they expended in building additional lines to tap the resources of a wider hinterland. In the excitement over the acquisition and construction of new rail arteries, the cities paid little heed to the effects of the competing lines on their local street patterns or on other aspects of their internal structure. At old terminal ports, the railroads generally entered along existing waterways or other channels to establish depots at points that soon became focal centers of commerce and travel and helped define the limits and shape of the evolving central business district. In many cities where the railroads plummeted through the town, linking it with distant places in each direction, the tracks created one or more barriers, breaking the city into segments of unequal size and salubrity. Even the newer cities, and the new subdivisions developed after the routes of the principal lines had been fixed, suffered dislocations from time to time as these powerful corporations, often controlled by out-of-town directors, shifted freight or passenger stations and opened or discontinued sidings as profits dictated, with little regard for local community interest. Invariably, as one of the segmented downtown districts evolved into a prosperous business center, its former neighbors now beyond the tracks degenerated into inner-city slums. Other nearby and outlying districts not blighted by that hazard, and therefore safe for the movement of carriages as well as pedestrians, became choice residential neighborhoods.

Yet the railroads were not alone in their influence on the development of urban cores in American cities. Except for the location of wharves, bridges, and raceways at appropriate natural sites, and the occasional designation of an open square or common, few of the original city plans had made any differentiation between business and residential property. The central four corners where the principal highways of the early village days intersected had frequently attracted stagecoach inns, general stores, banks, and other commercial enterprises, but the location of these facilities often depended on the lot holdings of the entrepreneurs involved. Public buildings erected on or overlooking a central square also helped determine the location of the central business district, as other merchants and tradesmen clustered within easy reach of the stage depot, banks, post office, and taverns. New and larger hotels arose nearby or on the cleared sites of pioneer taverns, theaters and concert halls made their appearance, and new and more ambitious builders provided office space for rent above their banks and stores.

Most American cities developed a central business district before they reached a population of twenty thousand. Boston, New York, and Philadelphia had seen the emergence of such districts in colonial days and, following the pattern set by London over two centuries earlier, each of these metropolitan centers developed specialized wholesale, retail, and banking districts in the early years of the republic. Other burgeoning metropolises—Cincinnati, New Orleans, and St. Louis—displayed similar tendencies in the 1850s, but most growing cities were content with undifferentiated business districts acquired as they approached the twenty thousand "threshold" point.

Despite the rapid increase in lot values in the emerging central districts of many American cities, the continued residence of many tradesmen in quarters over their shops and the increasing number of transients and more or less permanent residents who occupied suites in the hotels maintained a bustling downtown life that continued into the evening after the street lights were turned on. Although the throngs that tramped through the central districts of American cities were generally most dense and compulsive from midmorning until late afternoon, no American city saw the depopulation that central London experienced in these decades as trade and government took over, driving the inhabitants to the suburbs and creating a silent inner city after business hours.

The downtown life of American cities in the forties and fifties presented a sharp contrast to that of many quiet villages. Numerous transients, recent arrivals by train, steamboat, or stage, mingled with the busy residents who crowded the sidewalks in front of unbroken rows of shopfronts. An assortment of horse-drawn vehicles clattering along the roughly paved streets created a low rumble broken frequently by the shouts of impatient drivers and frustrated pedestrians. Travelers from abroad still marveled at the absence of beggars, but Americans were more surprised by the appearance in the fifties of an occasional Italian with a fiddle or hand organ or of a sandwich man shouting his wares. On warm Sundays the streams of worshipers filing in and out of downtown churches filled the streets before and after services. A widespread cessation of business and trade closed most shops, though despite the efforts of many church folk to maintain the traditional blue laws tavern doors often swung wide, particularly in the German districts in cities such as Cincinnati, St. Louis, and of course New York, where the constant movement between crowded Catholic churches and equally crowded saloons displayed a spirit of good cheer that contrasted with the sobriety in many Yankee sections.

All cities supplied new social opportunities on weekdays. In addition to the formal indoor entertainments, which now included an occasional opera performance in some of the larger cities, many provided amusements on scattered downtown squares or open fields where traveling circuses pitched their tents and other entertainers made their appearance. Militia companies, including the newly formed Irish and German units, practiced their marches on these open spaces, and in the fifties occasional matches between rival cricket teams drew curious spectators. Balloon ascensions invariably brought out vast crowds, as did the torchlight parades of rival political factions. Open-air beer gardens in the German section of town attracted patrons from other districts as well, while museums packed with curiosities from distant lands received an intermittent stream of visitors. A variety of athenaeum and temperance lectures drew interested audiences, and some of the more learned joined one or another of the gentlemen's literary clubs that made their appearance in several cities, following a pattern set in London a few decades before. Old and new secret societies attracted large numbers to fraternal ceremonies that provided symbolic ties with distant times and places.

NEW BUSINESS PATTERNS

Despite the new social and cultural facilities, the preoccupation of most American urbanites, according to many travelers, was with the city's economic opportunities. Their enterprising zeal was not new or markedly increased over that of earlier days in smaller towns, but new patterns of business activity were emerging. The boards of trade established in the 1790s in a few leading metropolises made their appearance in a score of enterprising cities and assumed informational and promotional functions of special interest to local merchants and speculators. Banks and insurance companies multiplied and, after the adoption in several states of general incorporation laws, the number of incorporated enterprises increased rapidly. Their power to issue stock of limited liability attracted support from many small investors for railroads and other public utilities, as well as for private commercial and industrial enterprises that had previously been owned individually or in partnership. As the cities assumed their place in a widening regional and world economy, the familiar bonds that had characterized earlier business relationships began to give way to more impersonal corporate dealings.

Yet, except for some of the railroads, there were few large corporations. Even the iron foundries and rolling mills springing up around Pittsburgh operated on limited capital resources that averaged around $150,000 in 1860, and except for several textile companies in New England few factories employed as many as five hundred operatives. Most of the ventures were headed by former merchants who had undertaken to process regional products for easier shipment and more profitable sale. Many had joined forces with talented artisans or secured the assistance of skilled craftsmen from abroad in manufacturing carpets and hosiery in Philadelphia, glass and iron products in Pittsburgh, pottery in Baltimore, and tools, textiles, and shoes in many New England cities. Despite the specialization already developing in a few places, based on a regional product or a large migration from a specialized district abroad, most cities had a diversified production keyed to the needs and opportunities of their still dominant commercial functions.

The boards of trade, headed by commercial leaders, practiced a more restrained form of promotional activity than that previously exercised by the speculative boosters of the pioneer period. East of the Mississippi River much of the rawness of frontier towns was disappearing, together with the patriarchical traditionalism of some of the older colonial cities. Only in the South, most notably in Charleston and Savannah, did the old ways and old leaders persist. In their place other cities were developing a bustling class of variously informed executives, managers, clerks, and salesmen who contributed to and depended on a mass of business information such as that published in the monthly issues of *Hunt's Merchants' Magazine,* produced in New York, and *De Bow's Review,* printed in New Orleans.

In addition to the boards of trade and chambers of commerce formed in a number of cities, merchants' exchanges developed in a few of the largest metropolises to provide a further means of coordination. These bodies had no official status, but served, in the absence of regulatory agencies, to keep the complex commercial activity on an even keel. As one observer, J. A. Scoville, recalled in his diary, the New York merchant's day had acquired a new routine:

"To rise early in the morning, to get breakfast, to go down town to the counting house of the firm, to pen and read letters—to go out and do some business, either at the Custom house, bank or elsewhere until twelve, then to take lunch and a glass of wine at Delmonico's; or a few raw oysters at Downing's; to sign checks and attend to the finances until half past one; to go on Change; to return to the counting house, and remain until time to go to dinner, and in the old time, when such things as 'packet nights' existed, to stay down until ten or eleven at night, and then go home and go to bed."[1]

The freedom of action enjoyed by the commercial and business leaders of the metropolis, and to a lesser extent of most growing cities, was seldom abridged by municipal, state, or federal authorities. In contrast with the situation in many metropolises abroad, where the national leaders were closely interested in and often associated with the major commercial, banking, and industrial enterprises, in America both the federal and the state governments were far distant and little concerned with the affairs of the leading commercial and industrial cities. Repeated efforts to revise the tariff and remodel the national and state banking systems to fit the needs of the cities became so entangled in politics that action was indecisive and the results questionable. British cities both at home and in the colonies were more effectively served in these respects by their national or provincial administrations.

Business groups in some of the larger American cities faced a potential challenge from the unions formed by their workers. Early craft and journey-

---

1. Quoted in Robert G. Albion, *The Rise of the New York Post, 1815–1860* (New York: Charles Scribner's Sons, 1939), p. 264.

men's associations had appeared in Philadelphia, New York, and a few other places in the late teens, but most had succumbed after staging ineffectual strikes. The movement did not receive wide support until the early thirties, when unions appeared in thirteen cities. The depression that blighted the end of that decade swamped most of these efforts, but unions again revived in the midforties and enrolled many newly arrived immigrant workers, some, particularly from Britain, with craft-union experience. Unions emerged in all but two of the cities with 10 percent or more of their workers employed in manufacturing. The two exceptions were Lowell and Lynn, the most completely controlled company towns. But even in the centers of their greatest strength, Philadelphia and Pittsburgh, the unions were unable to regain the advantages former craftsmen had enjoyed and saw the merchant-industrialists transform their members into shopworkers or machine tenders. Yet union members in American cities had access to the polls as natives or could easily acquire it through naturalization, as the workingmen's parties in several cities demonstrated, and the radical movements erupting in numerous cities abroad where the vote was denied received little support in the States.

Most of the manufacturing plants were so small, except in the textile towns, that their owners played minor roles in the local business groups. Nevertheless, increasing numbers of urban leaders were awaking in the forties and fifties to the desirability of local industry. Jesse W. Scott, a frequent contributor to Hunt's and De Bow's magazines, tabulated the industrial production of several western cities and analyzed their potentialities. But while the industrial prospects of Toledo and Detroit, Scott's favorite promotions, and of Kansas City, William Gilpin's "Centropolis," were still in the future, the industrial activity of a score of cities in the Northeast had already acquired major importance. In Philadelphia, Cincinnati, Newark, and several lesser cities industrial employment exceeded commercial, while combined urban occupations exceeded all rural employment in the seven northeastern states stretching from Massachusetts to Maryland.

Whether industry had become a major source of urban growth was still in doubt in most sections. Two economists at the University of Wisconsin, Jeffrey Williamson and J. H. Swanson, have recently concluded, after probing this question in depth, that at least in the 1840s the contributions of industry to urban growth were considerable, though industrial employment displayed less weight in the other pre-Civil War decades. In the three states in southern New England, however, it had become the mainstay of the economy. There, as Percy Bidwell has shown, the output of textiles, shoes, and machinery was the product of local power, enterprise, and capital, and there as in the British Midlands the factory owners imported their raw materials and much of their labor. Elsewhere most industrialists were still processors of regional products, yet they had by 1860 become so numerous and productive that the nation's manufactured products had reached a value of $1,885,860,000, which was five times the total of its imports from abroad. That ratio represented a dramatic shift from the country's dependence on foreign manufacturers for half of its merchandise five decades earlier.

Yet despite these and other accomplishments of the cities, the improvements they had effected in their internal structures and services, and the contributions they were making to the nation's development, an undertone of antiurban criticism persisted. The pastoral dreams of Thomas Jefferson retained a nostalgic hold on many citizens, strengthened by the evidence of increasing wretchedness among the swelling ranks of the newcomers, native and foreign, who crowded into the cities faster than accommodations or jobs could be created. Depressed and horrified by the misery they witnessed, men like Emerson and Thoreau, among other trancendentalists, deplored the materialism and artificiality of cities and idealized the advantages of country life and the peace and beauty of nature. But this antiurbanism, which had its counterpart in England, where Carlyle and Ruskin posed their varied criticisms of city life, was a minority view and had little effect on the course of urbanization in the states. Even the British travelers, many of whom came to America inspired by Rousseau and Wordsworth with a romantic interest in nature, displayed more excitement in their journals over the cities that had "sprung up over night in the midst of the forest" than over the grandeurs of nature that presented such tedious obstacles to their travels. And while a few novelists, including Herman Melville, and other intellectuals saw the cities as defilers of nature and corrupters of man, many more valued the superior cultural facilities the cities afforded. A half-century would slip by before some American sociologists would begin to view the city as a human phenomenon possessed of natural qualities. Meanwhile, whether knowingly or intuitively, most urbanites followed Alexander von Humboldt, the great German naturalist and explorer (who had visited the Americas between 1799 and 1804 and whose tomes on the cosmos were at last appearing in the late fifties), in viewing cities as the natural fulfillment of man's progress.

Table 4.   PERCENT OF TOTAL POPULATION IN CITIES OF 10,000+.*

	1800	1850
United States	3.8	12.0
England and Wales	21.3	39.4
Scotland	17.0	32.2
Belgium	13.5	20.8
France	9.5	14.4
Prussia	7.2	10.6
Russia	3.7	5.3
Ireland	7.8	10.1
Austria	4.3	5.8
Spain	14.1	16.2
Portugal	12.7	12.9
Netherlands	29.5	29.0
Denmark	10.9	9.6

*From Adna F. Weber, *The Growth of Cities in the Nineteenth Century: A Study in Statistics.* Originally published in 1899 for Columbia University by The Macmillan Company. First published for Cornell Reprints in Urban Studies in 1963 by Cornell University Press. Derived from Table 112, pp. 145–46, and arranged according to ratio of increased urbanization.

BIBLIOGRAPHY

Beckinsale, R. P., and J. M. Houston, eds. *Urbanization and Its Problems.* New York: Barnes & Noble, Inc., 1968.

Bidwell, Percy W. "Population Growth in Southern New England." *American Statistical Association Publication,* 15, no. 120 (December 1917), 813–39.

Glaab, Charles N. *The American City: A Documentary History.* Homewood, Ill.: Dorsey Press, 1963.

Handlin, Oscar, and John Burchard, eds. *The Historian and the City.* Cambridge, Mass.: MIT Press, 1963. See especially the essays by Handlin, Schorske, and White.

Lampard, Eric E. "Historical Contours of Contemporary Urban History: A Comparative View." *Journal of Contemporary History,* 4, no. 3 (1969), 3–25.

Lane, Roger. *Policing the City: Boston, 1822–1885.* Cambridge, Mass.: Harvard University Press, 1967.

Max, Leo. *The Machine in the Garden.* New York: Oxford University Press, 1964.

Mohl, Raymond A. *Poverty in New York: 1783–1825.* New York: Oxford University Press, 1971.

Pessen, Edward. "The Egalitarian Myth and the American Social Reality: Wealth, Mobility, and Equality in the Era of the Comman Man." *American Historical Review,* 76 (October 1971), 989–1034.

Rosenberg, Charles E. *The Cholera Years: The United States in 1832, 1849, and 1866.* Chicago: University of Chicago Press, 1962.

Still, Bayrd. *Mirror for Gotham: New York as Seen by Contemporaries.* New York: New York University Press, 1956.

Strauss, Anselm L., ed. *The American City: A Sourcebook of Urban Imagery.* Chicago: Aldine Publishing Co., 1968.

Thernstrom, Stephan, and Richard Sennett, eds. *Nineteenth-Century Cities: Essays in the New Urban History.* New Haven, Conn.: Yale University Press, 1969. See especially the essays by Griffen, Frisch, Gutman, Blumin, and Knights.

Tucker, Louis L. "Cincinnati: Athens of the West." *Ohio History,* 75 (Winter 1966), 11–45, 67–68.

Williamson, Jeffrey G., and J. A. Swanson. "The Growth of Cities in the American Northeast, 1820–1870." *Explorations in Entrepreneurial History,* Second Series, 4, no. 1 (1966), supplement, pp. 1–101.

PART TWO

Urbanization in an Age of Industrialism, 1860 to 1910

The scattered cities in the Northeast that had become manufacturing centers by the midcentury were making an early response to the industrial revolution, which had its origins in the British Midlands a half-century before. Manchester, its principal birthplace, had grown from a modest provincial market center into the world's leading industrial city by 1860, second in England only to London in value of production. A half-dozen other British cities had early felt the stimulus of the new industrial technology; together they had achieved an output of merchandise that had vastly expanded Britain's and much of the world's trade and greatly accelerated the urbanization process.

Defined as the concentration of an increasing number of people and mounting proportions of the population in more or less dense nonagricultural settlements, the urbanization process acquired a new dimension in America with the rise of industrial cities. The earlier merchant cities that had provided marketing and trade facilities for local craftsmen, as well as for agricultural and mining activities in their area, had been dependent on the resources of their regions and on the scope of the trade under their command. They had enjoyed a steady influx of newcomers from abroad, and they had improved their positions by promoting the development of their regions. Several had prospered with the opening of new and far-distant routes of trade or as a result of the discovery of new mineral resources. Most had developed handicraft industries to supply their increasing local needs and those of their trading area, but with the successful introduction of machine production and the use of new and more efficient and abundant forms of power, these cities and new ones located at convenient power sites experienced a burst of energy comparable to that which had brought vitality to the Midlands a few decades before. They too achieved new rates of growth and developed newly competitive capacities that had a wider and more aggressive impact on cities elsewhere.

The first effect of the British innovations on American cities had been to check the growth of handicraft production, as in Pittsburgh in the 1820s, and to speed the development of interior transport facilities. But the latter action had increased the number of urban centers whose business leaders soon faced the task of processing a mounting flood of regional products. Their bright prospects attracted an inrush of settlers and immigrants, many with new technical skills that enabled the American cities to duplicate on a broader scale the industrial fabrication taking place in Britain, and sometimes to improve on Britain's technological accomplishments. This industrial transformation commenced, as we have seen, in New England before the Civil War and spread rapidly after that conflict. No one would have guessed in the midseventies, when the American economy, with powerful factions working at cross-purposes, had ground almost to a stop, that another quarter-century would see the emergence of a system of cities capable of unprecedented production. The beginnings of industrialism sparked an urban economic "take off" throughout the States, which, because of the constantly widening base of supplies and the multiplication of participating cities, would overshadow the British and European industrial output before the close of the century.

America's mounting production also reflected the efficiency of increased specialization. Its industrial cities, like those of Britain, developed a greater degree of specialization than their merchant-city predecessors. The textile, shoe, and heavy-industry cities were all distinctly different, and although some also produced related machine tools, other cities specialized in that line, and still others in men's or women's wearing apparel, or in woodworking or food-processing industries. This specialization depended in part on regional resources of raw materials or power, or on available transport facilities or labor skills. Managerial talents and sources of capital also played a part, and as the decades advanced the economic decisions in industrial cities became less responsive than in their merchant predecessors to the free swings of the market and more closely tied to the emerging corporate structure. In contrast with most European cities, where public enterprise supplied most of the municipal utilities, corporate enterprise in America generally built the utilities, as well as the factories, and only after the turn of the century did the Progressive movement provide public regulatory safeguards.

We will examine these contrasts in greater detail in Chapter 6 as we develop the relationships between ethnic diversity and moral reforms, free enterprise and public control, volunteer benevolences and social welfare. And we will consider some of the democratic implications of these contrasting urban styles in Chapters 6 and 7, noting particularly the relative degrees of mobility, the different social and cultural priorities, and the increasing interchange of techniques and insights as the urbanizing process became worldwide.

5

Industrial Urbanization

When the full force of the industrial revolution finally reached America in the 1860s it was no longer a new phenomenon. England had been the first to feel its impact over a half-century before, and some who had participated in it there had since migrated to the States, bringing elements of its technology with them. Like many other innovations in history, the industrial revolution had originated on the periphery, not at the center, of the dominant urban society. Thus Richard Arkwright had located his factory in Manchester in 1781, and James Watt's steam engine had found its first industrial application in that same modest town a few years later. But these events, occurring far from England's great metropolis, acquired significance because of the world-wide trade London had already developed. Britain's early awareness of the new situation made it eager to end the War of 1812 in order to open the American and European markets to its mounting store of goods. The industrial revolution had already given a powerful stimulus to a half-dozen cities in the Midlands, and with the return of peace their products flooded world markets. It would only require a few decades for the cities of Europe and America to duplicate the British achievement.

Artisans and tradesmen alike felt the new challenge, and in several American cities, as well as in some on the Continent, they hastened to copy and sometimes to improve on the English innovations. Americans, in fact, had been the first to develop a practical steamboat in 1807, and they were quick, as we have seen, to take the lead in building steam railroads. Their success in the improvement of transport lines contributed to the nation's expansion and to the planting of new towns in the interior, but it also made America the bread and cotton producer for Britain's factory workers and diverted attention for a time from local industrial developments. The American cities, however, already possessed the essential ingredients for industrial growth, as the early beginnings in New England and Pennsylvania in the 1840s demonstrated; after a series of reversals in the fifties, these forces would achieve wider application in each succeeding decade.

AMERICAN INDUSTRY AND INNOVATIONS

We can get a better understanding of these forces by observing their first appearance in England in the late eighteenth century. A combination of circumstances had made the small city of Manchester the center of industrial innovation. Agricultural developments and the enclosure movement had driven many workers from neighboring farms and created a surplus of cheap labor in town, thus prompting Arkwright, who had developed and patented his spinning jenny in nearby Nottingham only to encounter hostility from rival craftsmen there, to open a new and enlarged workshop at a water-power site in Manchester. The increased output he achieved spurred the establishment of other spinning factories nearby, and when one introduced a Bolton-Watt steam engine in 1790 the basic components of the factory system were joined.

The full story of these developments belongs, of course, to economic history, but it impinges here because only a preexistent urban environment could have brought these and later events into such a fruitful combination. The steam engine, for example, had not sprung magically onto the scene, for James Watt had spent years of study and experimentation in Glasgow and Birmingham, with side trips to London and Paris, exhausting the resources of his first partner and trying the patience of a second before he achieved a workable machine. Its potentialities for industrial production were more clearly demonstrated in 1820 when several mill owners introduced power-driven looms into their spinning factories. By 1846 Manchester had one hundred such establishments, a few of them employing one thousand workers each, and, with those in other manufacturing towns, produced goods that comprised half the value of Britain's exports.

Manchester was also the first city to realize the full effects of the industrial revolution. Its cotton factories created a demand for steam engines and prompted the establishment of foundries to build them. These and other shops also manufactured the machines needed to operate the cotton, woolen, and silk mills, as well as the chemical dyeing plants, the printing firms, and other industries drawn to the thriving town. To facilitate the import and export of its raw and finished products, Manchester's business leaders hastened to build a railroad to the docks at Liverpool. Soon four additional lines provided links to other cities and brought, among other useful items, an abundant supply of coal to the expanding city. To supplement a branch of the Bank of England acquired in the 1820s, four other financial institutions established their headquarters or branches there, and local merchants organized an exchange to help direct the city's commercial and industrial growth.

The increased output and reduced costs of production with power-driven machinery had a multiplier effect on the city's growth rate and produced other important results. Mill owners profited from the internal economies of increased size and output, and their growing number created external economies that benefited the manufacturers of accessory products. But many skilled craftsmen who failed to secure key positions in the new factories found themselves reduced to operatives and their prospects for advancement curtailed. Some migrated to other industrial towns in Britain or America, thus assisting in the wider dissemination of the new technology. Meanwhile, many unskilled workers from the fields, who welcomed the factory jobs, soon found them monotonously simple and, to derive some pleasure from their new urban environment, resorted to the pubs and playing fields for relaxation. Some of both groups, however, refused to be appeased, and the rising industrial capital also became the capital of the discontented, as Asa Briggs has aptly put it. Thus Manchester increasingly supplied leadership to the struggle for the Reform Bill, to the Chartist movement, and to the Anti-Corn Law League. As the gap between the rich and the poor widened, some merchants joined the reformers and made their city the base for the development of the new free-trade doctrine that captured the imagination of men in the street as well as in the House of Commons before the midcentury.

Long before the full ramifications of the industrial revolution had become evident, most of its basic ingredients had crossed the Atlantic and become established in several of the new cities of America. The increasing number of American towns demonstrated an abundance of entrepreneurial talent. Although the presence of vast open lands ready for settlement drew off many potential workers, a mounting flood of newcomers from abroad constantly replenished the work force and brought in many with new technical skills. Lowell in Massachusetts was not the only beneficiary of British technology, for Philadelphia and Pittsburgh, as well as Providence, Paterson, and several other cities, shared in the influx of skilled craftsmen who participated, as R. T. Berthoff has ably demonstrated, in the establishment of shops and factories modeled on the latest British innovations. Moreover, the railroads built in the forties and fifties supplied facilities for the interchange within the American borders of raw and finished products and of skilled and unskilled workers that far surpassed those of more compact Great Britain.

The industrial transformation of the urbanization process was delayed somewhat in America by a recession in the midfifties and by the distractions of the Civil War in the early sixties. Economic historians are divided as to whether the war promoted or retarded industrialization, but if the withdrawal of hundreds of thousands of men for army service seriously checked construction and other aspects of growth in many cities, it created new demands in others. Everywhere the need for new facilities spurred rapid developments in the late sixties, and the nation's urban growth ratio for this decade, as calculated by Adna F. Weber, reached 261, well above that for the fifties and second only to the halcyon forties. The only cities over fifty thousand that doubled in population were Chicago and San Francisco, and these, with several other western cities that experienced a dramatic growth in this decade, such as Kansas City and Omaha, were predominately regional market centers at the time. A few small eastern and midwestern cities that had already acquired thriving industries—Scranton, Jersey City, Cleveland, and Indianapolis— likewise more than doubled in population and, with Pittsburgh, Newark, and most other industrial cities, increased their output severalfold. According to Colin Clark, the nation's net income from manufacturing increased 77 percent during the sixties—a gain exceeding that of Britain and Germany combined— and finally achieved first place among all industrial nations.

The accomplishment was more remarkable in view of the nation's absorption with other matters. In spite of the distractions of civil war and the demolition of several southern cities, the total urban increase in the sixties slightly exceeded the rural gains for the first time, and yet popular attention again centered after the return of peace on the rural areas, where three fourths of all inhabitants still resided. Despite their moderate growth in numbers, the farmers increased the value of their products by slightly more than a billion dollars, well above the monetary gains in manufacturing. They were able to achieve this result, however, partly because of the increased mechanization of agriculture, and numerous cities prospered from the manufacture of farm implements. The farmers were able to market their increased output because of the new rail lines the cities built across the prairies and mountains, linking the East, the Middle West, and finally the Far West and the South in one vast network before the close of the decade.

New cities mushroomed on the expanding frontier in America, as they also did in Russia, which pushed into Siberia in these years. Again those located at strategic breaks-in-trade experienced sudden booms, notably St. Paul at the last steamboat stop on the upper Mississippi River, and Portland, Oregon, and Oakland, California, at the western ends of the first transcontinental trails and rail lines. A waterfall, such as that which fixed the site of Minneapolis, or the discovery of a new source of fuel, such as natural gas at Toledo, proved equally stimulating and transformed these and other regional market centers into industrial processors of area crops and fabricators which supplied regional needs for bulky implements and furniture. Their economies displayed the mixture of commercial, industrial, and service occupations that had characterized earlier processing centers.

Because of the growth of the rail network, which tripled in mileage during the seventies and eighties, some urban processors lost control of their earlier specialties but acquired new opportunities. Thus Rochester, once the leading flour miller, and Cincinnati, the prewar porkopolis, were both superseded by new western giants, and both developed more diverse industrial characters producing for national as well as regional markets. Rochester, for example, with new shoe and clothing factories and many other shops established by immigrant artisans, including some that produced machine tools and optical instruments, kept a host of traveling salesmen on the road and grew in size and productivity in the seventies and eighties. With other former processors and trade centers, such as Milwaukee and Buffalo, it advanced from the second to the third of Thompson's growth stages and became an industrial city with more than 55 percent of its workers engaged in manufacturing. Of the frontier cities of the sixties, only Minneapolis, the new flour-milling city, acquired industrial status, with at least 30 percent employed in manufacturing by 1890.

Although few of the major American cities rivaled the industrial concentration of Manchester and several other industrial specialists in Britain, or that of a half-dozen on the Continent, Pittsburgh was an exception and frequently attracted interested visitors. Willard Glazier, a British traveler in 1884, found it especially spectacular at night when its gleaming furnaces lit up the sprawling city and its surrounding hills. "This is the domain of Vulcan, not of Pluto," he declared as he praised the industrial accomplishments of its ironworks and glassworks, its coal and oil producers, and the lesser firms that combined to make "thirty-five miles of factories." Although America's urban population barely equaled that of Great Britain and trailed that of Bismark's Germany, the nation's manufacturing output now exceeded the combined total of its two leading competitors. Moreover, the value added by manufacturing in the 1880s for the first time exceeded the total output of the nation's farms, though its cities scarcely numbered half the rural population by the close of that decade.

The productive energies of the American cities were evident on every hand, and their innovations generally promoted further urbanization. Even new towns on the last frontier that had scarcely outgrown their regional trading-center status, such as Los Angeles and Seattle and slightly older Denver, experienced such rapid growth that their building trades became major industries. Indeed, in most cities the construction industry had entered a highly specialized stage and attained major importance. And in a few great metropolises, notably Chicago, St. Louis, and New York, where cast-iron front buildings had appeared in the sixties and seventies, some rising to eight and ten stories, a few architects were experimenting with iron and steel frame construction. The successful development of a safe passenger elevator encouraged the effort to build more lofty structures, and by the close of the decade Chicago and New York had their first skyscrapers, thus introducing a new and challenging architectural form.

Numerous other inventions, both technological and organizational, contributed to the changing patterns of the urban economy. The telephone, invented by Alexander G. Bell in the midseventies, was displayed at the Philadelphia Exposition and won such favor that numerous cities soon had pioneer lines in operation. The great benefits it provided by speeding communications were partially matched in the eighties by the new application of electricity to street lighting and finally for indoor use with the development of Edison's incandescent bulbs. These improvements hastened the formation of electric companies in most cities and presented new franchise and public safety problems, as well as new opportunities for commercial and industrial development. Thus the telephone and the electric light found an immediate use in the expanding department stores that appeared in downtown New York, Philadelphia, and Chicago, as well as in many lesser cities, eventually transforming the merchandizing customs of most urbanites. And these facilities, joined by the typewriter, speeded the development of great office forces, which created an urgent demand for the skyscrapers that would add a new dimension to the downtown scene.

British travelers were beginning to recognize with some surprise the advanced achievements of some American cities. "The effect of the [electric] light in the squares of the Empire City can scarcely be described, so wierd and so beautiful is it," exclaimed a visitor from Britain in 1882, as quoted by Bayrd Still.[1] Another Englishman described a ride on the Sixth Avenue "El" as more pleasant than one on a London underground, but others viewing it from the street level found the aerial railroad offensive. Yet one visitor from London, the mercantile capital of the world, did not hesitate on viewing A. T. Stewart's dry-goods store to declare, as Still records, that its equal was "not to be found in any other shop of its kind in the world."[2]

The expanding size of the department stores and the rising height of the

---

1. *Mirror for Gotham* (New York: New York University Press, 1956), p. 209.
2. *Ibid.,* p. 219.

office buildings matched the increasing dimensions of many new factories and the growth of the railroad and other utility networks. These developments suggested the emergence of a larger and coarser grain in the American urban economy, but the suggestion was as yet only a hint, for outside the utility field all the big companies were exceptions, surrounded by a host of small independent stores and workshops whose owners and employees often shared the same tasks and aspirations, separated as in the past chiefly by age and skills. Even in industrial employment, the average number of workers per establishment in a hundred leading cities tabulated by the censuses declined in the eighties from 18.3 to 15.3, as the number of new establishments mounted more rapidly than the work force. But except for the handicraft and other service shops, the age-old family system had virtually disappeared.

Despite the existence of a number of large industrial firms, only a dozen placed their shares on the New York Stock Market, where the railroads and other utilities shared the attention of investors until the nineties with the dealers in wheat, corn, and livestock on other markets. The banks, too, presented widely diffused financial structures operating under varied state and national charters, with the central reserve functions of New York under the National Banking System declining in importance as the domestic trade increasingly overshadowed foreign imports and exports. Private investment brokers such as Morgan and his associates, with large foreign resources to draw on, were increasing in power, however, as were some of the railroad kings and other utility magnates. Demands for state regulation of these and other monopoly ventures produced a number of laws and supporting court decisions, but the proportion of industrial firms incorporated was still low, and the traditional reliance on the free market persisted as most urbanites still relied on the voluntary restraints of private enterprise. A prime example was supplied by the clearinghouses organized by local bankers in many cities to facilitate the exchange of notes and checks. Their courageous practice of issuing loan certificates during periods of tight money, pioneered in New York in the late 1860s and applied in six other metropolises in the depression of the midseventies, seemed an added proof of the resourcefulness of the system.

PROBLEMS OF THE GROWING CITIES

America's urban growth, like its industrialization, was not achieved single-handedly. Most of the more than ten million immigrants who came to America in these three decades, over half of them in the eighties, settled in the cities, particularly in the rapidly growing western and industrial cities. Some were skilled artisans dislodged from British or Continental towns as machine production superseded the handicrafts, but many more were unskilled peasants driven from the farms by enclosure movements, pogroms, and political disturbances, or by a surplus of births over deaths. Both the skilled and the unskilled found their best opportunities in the cities, where they comprised a major portion of the industrial workers by 1890. Immigrant contributions of technological and entrepreneurial leadership and professional talent were considerable, but in these fields they faced stiffer competition from descendants of earlier immigrants.

The urban population was becoming increasingly heterogeneous. Americans of longer standing were widely scattered across the land, but their representation in some of the more rapidly growing cities was thin. Second-generation Irish and German residents of Cincinnati, St. Louis, and Chicago, as of many new western cities, shared important roles with the descendants of the Yankee founders and with the more recent migrants from rural America. The federal census failed to distinguish those born in each city from those who had moved there from other parts of the state, though migrants from other states were reported separately. These groups varied from city to city and decade to decade, and the proportion of the native-born increased as the children of the foreign-born multiplied and as the city grew in size. Thus the high immigrant ratios of St. Louis and Chicago in 1860 fell in three decades from 50 percent to 25 and 40 percent respectively as the ratios of the children of foreign-born parents mounted to 42.3 and 37.5 percent. Even New York and San Francisco, the leading ports of entry, saw their ratios drop from 47 and 50 percent respectively to 42.2 percent, which in 1890 gave them the largest as well as the most diversified representation of the foreign-born of all major cities. Only a few rapidly growing industrial towns, such as Paterson, Fall River, and Manchester, New Hampshire, attracted larger proportions of immigrants in these decades.

Boston, now a less active port of entry, had achieved a measure of stability. Although the Irish influx had tapered off, newcomers from French and British Canada maintained its foreign-born ratio at better than 35 percent throughout these decades. A state census for 1885 reveals that 38.5 percent of its inhabitants were born in Boston, and 11 and better than 16 percent in other parts of Massachusetts and in other states respectively. Adna F. Weber, who in 1899 made the first probing study of *The Growth of Cities in the Nineteenth Century,* noted that Boston drew proportionately about as many of its residents from the rest of America as London, or Glasgow, or Amsterdam attracted from their national hinterlands. The big difference was the much larger foreign influx, which chiefly accounted for Boston's more rapid growth than these European cities experienced. New York City, with its still larger foreign influx, and some western cities more centrally located with respect to the American hinterland, notably Chicago, enjoyed even higher rates of growth.

The mobility of the urban population, though difficult to measure, remained a striking characteristic. In Rochester the stability ratio, or percentage of a sample of those listed in its city directories who reappeared there five years later, fluctuated upwards from 43.2 to 61.8 percent between 1860 and 1880, a trend that may have reflected the greater stability attained by its immigrant groups. Stephan Thernstrom, in his study of Newburryport, discovered that less than a fifth of the families resident there in 1850 were still represented in 1880. In relating this geographic mobility to upward mobility he found that the migrants included a large number who were "permanent migrants," misfits everywhere, while among those who remained put, many tended to rise in social status. But this question merits fuller discussion for the entire half-century in Chapter 7.

The remarkable population growth and industrial output of American cities astonished many foreign visitors. Some, as in earlier days, expressed admiration, but an increasing number took note of the less favorable social and cultural contrasts with cities abroad. Charles Dickens felt impelled in 1867 to praise the New York police as the best he had seen "at home or abroad," and touring artists and entertainers, such as E. Catherine Bates, generally spoke highly of the courteous reception they had received. Other visitors, like James F. Hogan from Australia, were more critical of the pretentious display they saw on every hand. Hogan attributed this tendency and other deficiencies of the American cities to their devotion to the "Almighty Dollar." Some Americans were equally criticial. Mark Twain, for example, found New York a lonely, unsatisfying city, lacking in the warmth and stimulation a true community should supply. Walt Whitman, on the other hand, was one of many who had an opposite experience, while, as Bayrd Still has shown, George T. Strong, New York's most faithful diarist, was ambivalent in his reactions. Contemporary magazines such as *Galaxy, Scotts Monthly,* and *The North American* carried numerous articles by American writers on the city, some laudatory and some critical. No foreign observer in this period was more widely respected or more devastating in his indictment of the American city than James A. Bryce, who declared in 1888 that "the government of cities is the one conspicuous failure of the United States."

Numerous mayors, including Seth Low, reform mayor of Brooklyn who wrote one of Bryce's chapters, would have agreed. They would, however, have stressed that the failure was not due solely to the cities, but was shared by all, especially by the states that refused to grant adequate powers. City administrations had in fact been in turmoil for many years in most of the leading towns. In Philadelphia, a Citizen's Municipal Reform Association of 1871, later reconstituted as a Committee of One Hundred, set a pattern for reform activity copied in numerous cities. But generally when the reformers ousted a corrupt administration, as Samuel J. Tilden did in 1871 when he routed the Tweed ring in New York, the victors found themselves unable to cope with the complex municipal problems and soon gave way to more untiring vested interests. Gas company executives in Philadelphia, beer and liquor dealers in Cincinnati, and leaders of a strong ethnic group in Boston represented more enduring factions and could frequently appease a sufficient number of voters to retain control of the council and safeguard their interests. The wide suffrage increasingly assured to all adult male citizens after the Civil War spurred vigorous efforts by rival party leaders to speed the naturalization of recent immigrants in order to secure their votes. Boss Cox in Cincinnati and Boss Aldridge in Rochester became especially active in this respect in the late eighties. Ethnic political and marching clubs appeared in most cities, and many of their leaders secured nomination and election as councilmen, justices, and even mayors as the years progressed.

This democratization of city governments exceeded that achieved in any cities abroad. It also assured a sense of participation, as the leading ethnic groups supplied policemen and firemen as well as ditchdiggers, schoolteachers as well as pupils, and commissioners as well as voters. Critics protested that the major objective of the leaders, even the honest ones, was to increase their share of the appointments, not to secure improved public services, but the tax-conscious reform groups that occasionally seized control had nothing more than economy to offer and were quickly swept out again by "bosses" ready to supply services at a price. Thus William M. Tweed, in his last months of control in New York, made a generous grant of city funds for the construction of the privately incorporated Metropolitan Art Museum on a public site in Central Park.

Despite their democratic base, most American cities lacked the civic consciousness that was welling up in these decades in a number of cities abroad. Thus, whereas Leeds, an aspiring industrial city in the Midlands, invited Queen Victoria to help dedicate their new town hall in a memorable ceremony in September 1858, and the Queen occasionally participated in other municipal ceremonies, the only comparable event in America was the opening of Brooklyn Bridge in May 1883 with President Arthur, his cabinet, and the governors of three states in attendance. It was more a commercial than a civic triumph, and as such appeared more worthy of state and national recognition.

The most widely representative community body in the American city was usually the chamber of commerce, and its leaders were generally more interested in low taxes and freedom from municipal control than in public services. If they looked for precedents abroad they looked to Manchester, with its free-trade doctrine, rather than to Glasgow, Birmingham, or Dusseldorf, where the emphasis was already focusing on improved civic services. No American mayor of the period rivaled Mayor Joseph Chamberlain, who made Birmingham "the world's best governed city" in the midseventies. Yet, as Asa Briggs has reconstructed it, this was not a single-handed accomplishment, but required the earnest collaboration of many groups and the persistent agitation of numerous religious and social reformers before the complacent junta in charge of the city was ousted and an administration emerged that was prepared to tackle the sewer and other sanitary problems and was ready to pay the price to acquire the water system, gasworks, and other needed improvements.

This "municipal trading," as the British described it, or "state socialism," as it was termed in Germany, introduced an aspect of urban development that few cities in the States experienced. Baltimore and numerous other American cities had helped finance the construction of regional railroads before the Civil War and some continued to back strategic extensions, though New York and other state legislatures increasingly restricted such investments after the losses suffered in the depression of the seventies became known. The more modest sums required for city waterworks and gas companies, and the quicker profits they promised, attracted enterprising private investors in American cities, while in Britain and on the Continent municipal leaders, backed by national loans and subsidies, assumed the task of building needed utilities or pressed for their early purchase by the city. The task of constructing and managing these major services attracted able men into the municipal councils, as E. P. Hennock has demonstrated in his study of the borough councils of Birmingham and other British cities in the 1870s. Most American cities, content to rely on private franchise companies, would wait two decades or more before the evils of franchise grabs aroused a sufficient number of citizens to launch reform.

The problems, of course, were already present and several were attracting attention. When the Metropolitan Board of Health, established in 1866 by the state legislature in response to earnest requests from a citizens association, successfully warded off a threatened cholera epidemic in New York, several less fortunate cities moved to strengthen their boards of health and to staff them with doctors instead of politicians. Such boards surveyed local sanitary conditions, made regular inspections of wells and cisterns, milk and meat dealers, and undertook to record all births and deaths. The city schools, though severely handicapped in most places by a shortage of funds, were recognizing new subjects. A graded elementary system topped by a high school open to more gifted pupils had become standard in most cities, but the enrollment of increasing numbers of children of immigrants who could not speak English presented challenging new problems to teachers and administrators alike. The innovations of Dr. Edward A. Sheldon at Oswego, who undertook to equip teachers to meet this task, and those of William R. Harris at St. Louis, who devised an elementary program that included instruction in science and also experimented with kindergarten techniques imported from Europe, marked further advances on the cultural side of America's urbanization. Milwaukee, with 19.7 percent of its residents over ten unable to speak English—the highest in the land—was one of several cities that offered evening courses in English and other elementary subjects to adults in the 1880s.

Except in the field of education, the American cities were reluctant to assume public responsibility for community problems. They continued to rely on private and institutional efforts, particularly in the welfare field, where the public almshouses of earlier decades now proved totally insufficient. In addition to the denominational orphan asylums and friendly homes of pre-Civil War days, many cities acquired industrial schools for the widows and orphans of that conflict, rescue missions to sober up and redeem the many homeless males who for the first time tramped from city to city, and humane societies to safeguard the rights of children and the welfare of the dumb animals that still hauled and carried man's major burdens through the city streets. These and other social problems became increasingly acute at each successive slump in the economy, and the depression of the midseventies brought them dramatically into the foreground.

RESPONSES TO POVERTY

Responsible leaders in many cities faced a major dilemma in the midseventies. The hardships of the poor, as unemployment mounted in city after city during the depression, called for generous outlays for relief, both public and private. But nagging fears lest the free distribution of food and other supplies encourage the growth of pauperism, as in some cities abroad, were strengthened when the number of immigrants among the needy became known. Federal census data in 1870 disclosed the startling fact that 30 percent of the country's paupers in June that year were foreign-born, as well as 26 percent of the inmates of prisons. Few observers considered the fact that 22 percent of all adults, rural and urban, were foreign-born and, as newcomers resident for the most part in cities, were generally the first to lose their jobs during a layoff. The possibility that some might refuse jobs to qualify for relief prompted the opening of a stoneyard in many cities, where unemployed men were required to break stone for use on the highways as a test of their worthiness as relief recipients.

The problem was not peculiar to the American city, but it was there that the discovery of poverty in the United States occurred, as Robert Bremner has vividly demonstrated, and it was there rather than in the state legislatures or the halls of Congress that the great debate over its causes and cures commenced in the seventies. In Britain, Parliament had accepted responsibility in the 1830s for directing and partially funding relief in all parts of the realm. Similar responsibilities for the amelioration of the hardships of the poor had early been assigned to the counties and towns by most of the states. But charitable folk in the cities of both countries had supplied additional provisions for widows, orphans, and other unfortunates. The new challenge of unemployment in an urban setting required a fresh response. To make sure that the Christian obligation to one's neighbor would not endanger the ethic of individual self-reliance, a group of humanitarians in London, headed by Octavia Hill, had formed the London Charity Organization Society in 1869 to supervise the distribution of relief. Similar efforts in American cities dated from the organization of the New York Society for the Prevention of Pauperism in 1817, but since this and most other early societies were either Protestant or Catholic in affiliation, their aid was unwelcome in some homes. A fresh effort was needed and, after several false starts elsewhere, Buffalo successfully established a charity organization society in 1877 that supplied a model for many to follow. Its moving spirit was the Reverend S. H. Gurteen, who had formerly been a volunteer in the London society. Under his direction "friendly visitors" were recruited who visited all applicants for relief within certain districts. The volunteers did not have the final say on the grant of relief, but their contacts with the recipients gave increased assurance that the aid would be properly used.

As the charity organization movement spread from city to city in the late seventies, it sometimes became entangled with a temperance crusade which was likewise sweeping the cities in these years. Temperance, its advocates believed, was the true remedy for poverty, and since its appeal was strongest among the Protestants, who chiefly supported the charity organization movement, the temperance crusade superseded its rival in several cities, such as Rochester, where the YMCA and the rescue mission also displayed renewed vitality. These and other institutions battling for a middle-class ethic were strong in those industrial cities where the more evangelical church groups outnumbered and outweighed the Catholics, Episcopalians, Congregationalists, Unitarians, and Jews, who seldom backed these moral reform efforts. Except for the Catholics, who maintained separate charities, the latter denominations often cooperated in promoting organized charity efforts, and after the temperance crusade had subsided somewhat in the early eighties these groups, with the Presbyterians, revived the charity organization societies in numerous cities.

The *Monthly Register,* published by the Philadelphia society, reported the existence of twenty-five similar organization societies in 1883 in a dozen other cities. A major objective was to reduce the miscellaneous giving of alms and to channel charitable funds through institutions that would administer relief only to the worthy poor, with rehabilitation as the goal. A serious defect was the lack of authority over member societies. The Denver body formed in 1887 as a federation of fifteen local societies endeavored to remedy this lack by conducting a unified drive for funds, but the effort collapsed in the third year when the response proved inadequate. Several organization societies established new special-function bodies to meet urgent city needs, such as the Crèche for children in Buffalo, which also maintained a provident woodyard in winter months, the remedial loan societies of St. Paul, Boston, and elsewhere, and the shelters for homeless men in New York and a dozen other cities.

But the organization societies, which began to restructure themselves as associated charities in the late eighties, had no monopoly over new welfare techniques, several of which appeared independently in these years. The Legal Aid Society, formed in New York City in 1876, was such a body and later spread to other cities. Perhaps the most significant response to the baffling problems of the cities was that of the settlement houses introduced in New York, Chicago, and Boston in the late eighties. Modeled on Toynbee Hall in London, they marked the effort of humanitarian middle-class leaders to bridge the widening gap between the Yankees and the immigrant inhabitants of the big cities by establishing resident homes in the slum districts where the two groups could live together and learn to understand each other as neighbors.

Several of the older charitable societies made new moves to meet the problems of the cities. Thus the YMCAs, at the start primarily evangelical, developed a gymnastic program in the late sixties and established a number of special railroad branches with dormitory facilities to supply a home away from home for railroad workers who were forced to spend frequent nights on the road. The West Coast Ys also formed clubs and conducted classes and special programs for Asians who could not speak English. And the YWCAs and Women's Educational and Industrial Unions, first launched in Boston in 1877, endeavored to provide downtown restrooms and lunchrooms, as well as dormitories and parlors, where single women forced to work in the city could find shelter and opportunities for wholesome associations. In addition to these interdenominational efforts, several of the Protestant and Catholic churches developed clubs and societies to provide church-related activities for their young people as well as for older men and women. These organizations, often promoted to keep members in the fold and check the urge to affiliate with out-of-church fraternal clubs or to participate in more worldly activities, served a real need in the urbanization of recent migrants from rural or small-town America and from similar backgrounds abroad. Some neighborhood churches delayed the transition of their ethnic members from a rural old-country heritage to the more impersonal urban industrial society.

Fraternal societies, secret and otherwise, multiplied in the postwar decades, and so did the trade unions. The unions, of course, had a more activist objective, to safeguard and improve the economic position of their members in the rapidly developing economy. They also supplied a sense of belonging and, particularly in the Knights of Labor at the height of its popularity, a sense of power to many humble workingmen, most of them newcomers from abroad. From their parades and public rallies during innumerable strikes (the census of 1880 placed the number for that year tentatively at 762) the unionists experienced an increased participation in the affairs of the local community. Most of these confrontations occurred in the cities and mining towns of Pennsylvania, New York, and Ohio, for the textile and shoe towns of New England were not effectively organized. But even in these centers of strength their influence on industrial policy, except in the mining towns and other small industrial cities, was limited. Unions were most numerous in the building trades, but the wide diffusion of this activity dissipated their strength. The railway unions posed a real challenge for a time to the expanding networks, yet these conflicts had only an indirect impact on the cities. The typographical unions played a more direct role in the urbanization process as they brought increased standardization and professionalization to the publishing industry, with its newspaper and book firms scattered in every city in the land. As a result of the limited victories of these two groups and of several branches of the metalworkers, the unions acquired a respectability that won their marchers a place in Fourth of July parades and brought the recognition of Labor Day as a community holiday in most cities after 1887.

The unions played a role in the urbanization not only of their members, but of other groups of citizens as well. Their generally peaceful tactics and the publicity they secured for their grievances often won the support of leading clergymen and other popular spokesmen who in the process acquired and promoted a broader concept of community well-being. The appeal for a ten-hour and later an eight-hour day, for a living wage, even for union recognition, often seemed justified and gradually awakened many citizens to some of the transformations that had taken place in the urban economy. Mayors and police chiefs as well as leading educators and clergymen addressed labor gatherings in the 1880s with increased respect. And when trade associations in some industrial towns endeavored, by the employment of Pinkerton detectives, to weed out potential organizers, popular protests, supported at times by the local police, sometimes forced even a chamber of commerce to frown on such tactics and to assist, as in Rochester in 1889, in the reorganization of the offending company. The reaction could and often did go the other way, most dramatically in the bloody Haymarket riot in Chicago three years before, when the explosion of a bomb turned the police and the public against the Knights.

CITY SERVICES AND PLANNING

Many cities of modest size acquired a democratic image as communities of average citizens. The widespread provision of paid uniformed police placed many humble citizens, including some of immigrant origins, in positions of authority, but generally made them defenders of the public and, except in the southern cities where the police units relied more heavily on large numbers, prompted them to seek popular support for their sometimes dangerous duties. The disciplined reviews and parades sometimes conducted by the uniformed police forces that numbered from one hundred to twenty-five hundred in the largest cities in 1880 often helped build community as well as police morale, but they lacked the dramatic excitement provided by the brother force of firemen. The firemen, in the larger cities now organized in paid companies, were equipped with horse-drawn steamers as well as ladder and hose trucks, and their clanging response racing through the streets to battle a fire provided some of the most animated civic scenes of the period.

The quelling of fires and the suppression of crimes were essential aspects of the urbanization process. It was easier to tabulate the 567,731 arrests made by the 13,500 policemen in all cities over five thousand in population in 1889 than to measure the work of the fire departments, most of them still volunteer in the smaller cities. But nobody could question the glamor or the vital importance of the firefighter's job as he frequently battled conflagrations that threatened the entire city. The Chicago fire of 1871, which swept over an area of 1,688 acres in the heart of the city, consuming buildings valued at over two-hundred million dollars, was only the most destructive of a number of great city fires, such as that in Boston a year later which spurred a reconstruction as dramatic as that achieved in Chicago.

Two closely related new developments in these decades were the organization of the National Board of Fire Underwriters and the widespread drive for the requirement of fire resistant construction in congested urban districts. The New York City Board of Fire Underwriters, including representatives of local insurance companies, took the lead in the organization of the national body after a serious fire in Portland, Maine, in 1866. Its policy of examining local ordinances and inspecting local fire fighting equipment and fire hazards before establishing local insurance rates created a powerful drive for local improvements and helped upgrade building codes in many cities.

Health authorities, as we have seen, exerted a similar pressure in New York in the sixties for housing improvements. The charity organization movement in the seventies renewed that pressure and extended it elsewhere, prompting the appointment of the first city building inspectors in Chicago and a few other metropolises. Unfortunately the rapid influx of poor newcomers overcrowded many of the older districts in the larger port and industrial cities and encouraged the construction of many flimsy tenements on vacant lots. Many modest frame houses, some with the currently popular machinecut Gothic trimmings, sprang up on the outskirts of cities in the North, while brick and stucco houses appeared in profusion elsewhere. Some of the steam railroads serving the larger metropolises scheduled commuter trains to nearby suburbs, and the four largest each numbered passengers in excess of a million per month by 1890. San Francisco built its first cablecar lines in the 1870s, and Chicago and a few other cities followed a decade later. New York completed its first elevated line in 1876 and soon had two others. But the limited area served by the horse-drawn lines on which most cities still relied, and the necessity for the great majority to walk to work, kept most cities within limited confines. This increased the pressure on the inadequate housing of the older districts, which now in several cities became wretched slums. In New York the housing reformers, seeking sanitary improvements, compromised with building developers and secured the enactment in 1879 of a Tenement House Law that permitted the construction of dumbbell apartments that spread their blight over much of Manhattan during the next decade.

Reports and descriptions of new housing ventures in several British and Continental cities prompted several ambitious attempts to meet these problems in America. Alfred T. White's model tenements in New York and Brooklyn in the late seventies and scattered ventures in other cities failed, however, to provide an economic model for low-rent inner-city dwellings, and they were soon lost in an avalanche of speculative building. In similar fashion the few enlightened industrialists who laid out and developed new communities in the vicinity of new plants on the outskirts of the great metropolises, such as Mariemont near Cincinnati and Kingsport in Tennessee, were quickly lost in the unplanned spread of suburbia. Thus George Pullman, despite the model designs copied in part from a similar town development in Essen, found it difficult to impose the German residential patterns even on his immigrant workers in America.

Architecture and city planning had little influence on American cities in these decades. The surging forces of commercial and industrial growth had swept away many choice details of the early town plans, engulfing some of the colonial squares and blocking off river and lake vistas. Architects continued to win commissions to design the principal public buildings, and Henry H. Richardson of Boston achieved a reputation for the Romanesque arches and style incorporated in the stone churches and railroad passenger stations he built there and in other cities. Many architects followed his lead or reproduced details from the great styles of Europe, including the French mansard roof, which had achieved such popularity at the Centennial Exposition at Philadelphia in 1876 that it was in demand not only for mansions and public buildings, but also on modest frame houses where machine-cut veneer made it possible to achieve a bit of elegance. The chief contribution of the planners in these years was in the design of an occasional park or cemetery, and here the leadership achieved by Frederick Law Olmsted in the fifties in the development of New York's Central Park won him commissions and spread his influence to many cities across the land. The full impact of these developments would not appear until the nineties and after, as we will see in the next chapters.

Table 5.   CONSTITUENTS OF THE POPULATION OF THE GREAT CITIES, 1890.*

Native of Native Parents /////   Foreign ·······

Native of Foreign Parents |||||||||| Nonwhite ▦▦▦▦▦

PERCENT	0	10	20	30	40	50	60	70	80	90	100

Milwaukee

New York

Chicago

Detroit

San Francisco

Buffalo

St. Paul

Cleveland

Jersey City

St. Louis

Cincinnati

Brooklyn

Pittsburgh

Boston

Rochester

New Orleans

Newark

Minneapolis

Allegheny

Providence

Louisville

Philadelphia

Baltimore

Washington

Omaha

Denver

Indianapolis

Kansas City

*U.S. Bureau of the Census, *Eleventh Census: 1890* (Washington, D.C.: U.S. Government Printing Office, 1895), I, pt. 1: plate B, p. xcii.

Table 6.   POPULATION OF CITIES THAT REACHED 100,000 by 1910.*

Cities	1860	1870	1880	1890	1900	1910
Albany, N.Y.	62,367	69,422	90,758	94,923	94,151	100,253
Atlanta, Ga.	9,554	21,789	37,409	65,533	89,872	154,839
Baltimore, Md.	212,418	267,354	332,313	434,439	508,957	558,485
Birmingham, Ala.			3,086	26,178	38,415	132,685
Boston, Mass.	177,840	250,526	362,839	448,477	560,892	670,585
Bridgeport, Conn.	13,299[1]	18,969	27,643	48,866	70,996	102,054
Buffalo, N.Y.	81,129	117,714	155,134	255,664	352,387	423,715
Cambridge, Mass.	26,060	39,634	52,669	70,028	91,886	104,839
Chicago, Ill.	109,260	298,977	503,185	1,099,850	1,698,575	2,185,283
Cincinnati, Ohio	161,044	216,239	255,139	296,908	325,902	363,591
Cleveland, Ohio	43,417	92,829	160,146	261,353	381,768	560,663
Columbus, Ohio	18,554	31,274	51,647	88,150	125,560	181,511
Dayton, Ohio	20,081	30,473	38,678	61,220	85,333	116,577
Denver, Colo.		4,759	35,629	106,713	133,859	213,381
Detroit, Mich.	45,619	79,577	116,340	205,876	285,704	465,766
Fall River, Mass.	14,026	26,766	48,961	74,398	104,863	119,295
Grand Rapids, Mich.	8,085	16,507	32,016	60,278	87,565	112,571
Indianapolis, Ind.	18,611	48,244	75,056	105,436	169,164	233,650
Jersey City, N.J.	29,226	82,546	120,722	163,003	206,433	267,779
Kansas City, Mo.	4,418	32,260	55,785	132,716	163,752	248,381
Los Angeles, Cal.	4,385	5,728	11,183	50,395	102,479	319,198
Louisville, Ky.	68,033	100,753	123,758	161,129	204,731	223,928
Lowell, Mass.	36,827	40,928	59,475	77,696	94,969	106,294
Memphis, Tenn.	22,623	40,226	33,592	64,495	102,320	131,105
Milwaukee, Wis.	45,246	71,440	115,587	204,468	285,315	373,857
Minneapolis, Minn.	2,564	13,066	46,887	164,738	202,718	301,408
Nashville, Tenn.	16,988	25,865	43,350	76,168	80,865	110,364
New Haven, Conn.	39,267[1]	50,840[1]	62,882[1]	81,298	108,027	113,605
New Orleans, La.	168,675	191,418	216,090	242,039	287,104	339,075
New York, N.Y.[2]	1,174,779	1,478,103	1,911,698	2,507,414	3,437,202	4,766,883
Manhattan Borough	813,669	942,292	1,164,673	1,441,216	1,850,093	2,331,542
Bronx Borough	23,593	37,393	51,980	88,908	200,507	430,980
Brooklyn Borough	279,122	419,921	599,495	838,547	1,166,582	1,634,351
Queens Borough	32,903	45,468	56,559	87,050	152,999	284,041
Richmond Borough	25,492	33,029	38,991	51,693	67,021	85,969
Newark, N.J.	71,941	105,059	136,508	181,830	246,070	347,469
Oakland, Cal.	1,543	10,500	34,555	48,682	66,960	150,174
Omaha, Nebr.	1,883	16,083	30,518	140,452	102,555	124,096
Paterson, N.J.	19,586	33,579	51,031	78,347	105,171	125,600
Philadelphia, Pa.	565,529	674,022	847,170	1,046,964	1,293,697	1,549,008
Pittsburgh, Pa.[3]	77,923	139,256	235,071	343,904	451,512	533,905
Portland, Oreg.	2,874	8,293	17,577	46,385	90,426	207,214
Providence, R.I.	50,666	68,904	104,857	132,146	175,597	224,326
Richmond, Va.	37,910	51,038	63,600	81,388	85,050	127,628
Rochester, N.Y.	48,204	62,386	89,366	133,896	162,608	218,149
St. Louis, Mo.	160,773	310,864	350,518	451,770	575,238	687,029
St. Paul, Minn.	10,401	20,030	41,473	133,156	163,065	214,744
San Francisco, Cal.	56,802	149,473	233,959	298,997	342,782	416,912
Scranton, Pa.	9,223	35,092	45,850	75,215	102,026	129,867
Seattle, Wash.		1,107	3,533	42,837	80,671	237,194
Spokane, Wash.				19,922	36,848	104,402
Syracuse, N.Y.	28,119	43,051	51,792	88,143	108,374	137,249
Toledo, Ohio	13,768	31,584	50,137	81,434	131,822	168,497
Washington, D.C.[4]	61,122	109,199	177,624	230,392	278,718	331,069
Worcester, Mass.	24,960	41,105	58,291	84,655	118,421	145,986

1. Population of town; town and city not returned separately.
2. Population of New York and its boroughs as now constituted.
3. Includes population of Allegheny as follows: 1900, 129,896; 1890, 105,287; 1880, 78,682; 1870, 53,180; 1860, 28,702; 1850, 21,262; 1840, 10,089; and 1830, 2,801.
4. Population as returned from 1880 to 1910 is for the District of Columbia, with which the city is now coextensive.
*U.S. Bureau of the Census, *Thirteenth Census: 1910* (Washington, D.C.: U.S. Government Printing Office, 1913) I, p. 80.

BIBLIOGRAPHY

See previously cited books by R. T. Berthoff, Asa Briggs, Allan R. Pred, and Bayrd Still.

Belcher, Wyatt W. *The Economic Rivalry Between St. Louis and Chicago: 1850–1880.* New York: AMS Press, Inc., 1947.

Bremner, Robert H. *From the Depths: The Discovery of Poverty in the United States.* New York: New York University Press, 1956.

Clark, Colin. *The Conditions of Economic Progress.* 3rd ed. New York: The Macmillan Co., 1957.

Cochrane, Thomas C. "Did the Civil War Retard Industrialization?" *Mississippi Valley Historical Review,* 48 (September 1961), 197–210.

Glaab, Charles N. *Kansas City and the Railroads.* Madison: State Historical Society of Wisconsin, 1962.

Gutman, Herbert G. "The Workers' Search for Power." In *The Gilded Age: A Reappraisal,* ed. H. Wayne Morgan. Syracuse: Syracuse University Press, 1963.

Hennock, E. P. "The Social Composition of Borough Councils in Two Large Cities, 1835–1914." In *The Study of Urban History,* ed. H. J. Dyos. New York: St. Martin's Press, 1968.

Hoselitz, Bert F. "The City, the Factory, and Economic Growth." *American Economic Review,* May 1955, supplement, pp. 166–96.

Lampard, Eric E. "The History of Cities in the Economically Advanced Areas." *Economic Development and Cultural Change,* 3, no. 2 (January 1955), 81–136.

Mandelbaum, Seymour J. *Boss Tweed's New York.* New York: John Wiley & Sons, Inc., 1965.

Marshall, Leon S. "The Emergence of the First Industrial City: Manchester, 1780–1850." In *The Cultural Approach to History,* ed. Caroline F. Ware. New York: Columbia University Press, 1940.

McKelvey, Blake. *Rochester: The Flower City: 1855–1890.* Cambridge, Mass.: Harvard University Press, 1949.

Mohl, Raymond A., and Neil Betten, eds. *Urban America in Historical Perspective.* New York: Weybright & Talley, Inc., 1970.

Pierce, Bessie L. *The History of Chicago.* Vols. I and II. New York: Alfred A. Knopf, Inc., 1934, 1940.

Still, Bayrd. *Milwaukee: The History of a City.* Madison: Society Press, 1948.

Turner, Ralph E. "The Industrial City: Center of Cultural Change." In *The Cultural Approach to History,* ed. Caroline F. Ware.

Vartanian, Pershing. "The Cochrane Thesis: A Critique in Statistical Analysis." *The Journal of American History,* 51 (June 1964), 77–89.

6

Urbanization
and the Progressive
Movement

The widespread urban growth and numerous technological advances achieved
in the eighties had more than economic repercussions. Improvements in transit
and communications encouraged the growth of larger cities that required the
development of improved municipal and social services. Increased industrial
output not only sustained the larger growth, but brought a higher standard of
living, including more leisure and new demands for popular forms of en-
tertainment. As the more animated cities drew increasing numbers from rural
areas in America and abroad, stimulating in the nineties new migrations from
southern and eastern Europe, the greater heterogeneity presented new challenges to the manners and customs of American cities. Most of the newcomers
were forced by poverty to join the working class, which gave the mounting
conflict between labor and management an ethnic dimension that increased the
social, political, and economic tensions.

    Industrial cities in Europe had experienced economic and political turmoil
and civic rebirth in earlier decades. Their urbanizing response to industrialism had, however, escaped some of the complexities faced by American cities.
Not only was the heterogeneity of the urban population much greater in America, but it was also acquiring a new diversity in an era of continued growth of
cities in both population and geographical area. Despite the pulsating growth,
the fortunes of individual cities and of their inhabitants, rich and poor, were
in constant flux, but they attracted little of the state and national concern so
evident in European countries. Urban civic problems, competing groups of
entrepreneurs, the contending forces of capital and labor, and the conflicting
aspirations of dissimilar ethnic groups and individuals gave increased intensity to local political contests. In their struggle to control and determine the
changing urban patterns, various groups couched their arguments in moralistic
terms, for indeed many ethical as well as ethnic standards were facing revision. The most vocal and persistent group of reformers called themselves "progressives" and branded the opposition as the "bosses," the "old political ring,"
the "spoilsmen." But although the Progressive movement had important moral

aspects and achieved wide national implications, in its relation to the city it was a product of the urbanization process in an era of rapid industrialization, continued technological advance, and increased demographic heterogeneity.

NEW SOCIAL AND CULTURAL PROBLEMS

American industries in the 1880s had achieved a 113 percent increase in the value added to their products. This remarkable advance spurred continued urban growth, almost doubling the population of the nation's cities as well as the number employed in manufacturing during the next two decades, and more than doubling the value of their products. Although the ratios of these increments were less dramatic than those of the eighties, they represented a vigorous and remarkably quick recovery from a serious depression and two subsequent recessions. They also reflected a sustained urban development which exceeded that of all major nations abroad and more than doubled the gains in population and in productivity of America's agricultural districts.

These statistical advances were accomplished as the cities drew increasing numbers from rural areas in America and abroad. Not only were the rural districts of New England experiencing a decline, despite their high birthrates, but the drain from the farms was also evident in Pennsylvania, New York, Ohio, Indiana, Iowa, and Missouri. Mushrooming regional cities absorbed many of these rural migrants, although others continued to press into the scattered pockets of undeveloped land—the last phase of the westward movement that added 1,800,000 farms, or a 35 percent increase in the total, in these two decades. This wider occupation of the land, despite the symbolic closing of the frontier in 1890, was made possible by a 60 percent extension of the railroad network. But to develop all out-of-the-way areas it was also necessary to establish many new market centers, mining towns, and trading cities. As a result, the total number of urban places increased 61 percent, reaching 2,262 by 1910.

The continued diffusion of the American system of cities was unmatched elsewhere and greatly exceeded those of Great Britain, Russia, and China, which had thirty-eight, thirty, and forty-two (est.) cities of 100,000 respectively by 1907, to forty-eight in the United States. This diffusion, however, was now overshadowed by the more substantial growth of existing cities. New York City, for example, aided by the annexation of Brooklyn and three other suburbs, trebled its population. Despite the sudden rise of Chicago to second place in 1890, New York retained its lead, exceeding the total of its three nearest rivals in the States and surpassing all but London in the Western world. Chicago, Cleveland, Pittsburgh, and Detroit, partly by annexing their overflow, more than doubled in population, while smaller Los Angeles and Seattle on the West Coast and Atlanta and Birmingham in the South increased severalfold. A few scattered cities elsewhere that rivaled these gains, notably São Paulo in Brazil and Tashkent in Siberia, developed as commercial and processing centers in widespread and newly productive agrarian societies that continued to maintain dominance. In contrast, the number of cities of 100,000 in the States almost doubled in two decades and their combined population exceeded twenty million in 1910, which was almost half the nation's urban total and almost as many as all the cities had reported two decades earlier.

It was the civic plight of these larger cities that chiefly commanded attention in the Progressive era. They achieved their growth by continuing to attract newcomers from abroad, but the percentages of the foreign-born in their midst were dropping sharply as the children of earlier immigrants swelled the ranks of the native-born to 70 percent and more in all but New York, Chicago, Boston, and ten smaller but heavily industrial cities, chiefly in New England. These and other industrial cities drew increasing numbers from southern and eastern Europe to fill their workbenches, sufficient to comprise 40 or more percent of their immigrant population. The proportion of the foreign-born engaged in manufacturing rose from 32.7 to 43.4 percent as the poverty-stricken Italians, Hungarians, and eastern Europeans competed for any jobs available. Cleveland absorbed over 100,000 of these newcomers, Chicago a third of a million, and New York over a million, while in Newark, Bridgeport, New Haven, and Pittsburgh they constituted over half of the foreign-born.

These newcomers supplied the manpower to stoke the furnaces and operate the mills of the rapidly growing industrial cities, but they also presented many new social and cultural problems. Unable on arrival to speak English, they encountered special problems of communication and imposed new difficulties on cities such as Cleveland, Detroit, and Milwaukee, where the number of adult males who were thus handicapped exceeded twenty thousand each by 1910. Even New York and Chicago, long accustomed to this problem, saw the numbers of such people double and triple in this decade. Many of these newcomers clustered in ethnic colonies speaking their native tongues, but the formation of new colonies of these proportions in old congested cities brought the displacement of earlier inhabitants, thus adding to the urban turmoil and calling for the development of new mediating services.

Yet the clustering of ethnic groups into distinctive though seldom exclusive neighborhoods, while often a source of friction at the start, had several benign effects. The communities of ethnically related migrants not only tended to assume responsibility for the order and welfare of their own newcomers, but also gave them a sense of belonging. Since these newcomers could acquire that sense of belonging only in large cities, the urbanization process itself contributed to their adjustment. And as the early arrivals acquired citizenship and mastered English they found themselves drawn into politics, generally on the side from which benefits had been received. As they became a majority in their districts, some of their members received minor posts and eventually won election as aldermen, supervisors, and state legislators. They posed serious threats only to previously dominant groups that had tried to block their advance. Yet a multiplicity of ethnic minorities also checked the dominance of any one group. Thus, by their participation in the affairs of the larger city, the ethnic leaders contributed to its democratic development and assured the gradual integration of their neighborhoods into the larger society.

The new ward leaders naturally sought improved services and additional favors for their constituents. As the Irish, according to Edward M. Levine, had overcome their earlier alienation by increasing their representation in the police, fire, and street departments of Boston, New York, and other heavily Irish cities, and the Germans in Cincinnati and Milwaukee, so many Italians, frustrated by the increasing notoriety of the Mafia and the Black Hand in the 1890s, formed patriotic societies in eastern cities or migrated to new settlements in the West, as Andrew Rolle has shown. They also pressed for admittance to the municipal services in Chicago and elsewhere, as the Poles and the eastern Jews did in Buffalo among other places. The new ethnic neighborhoods also sought extensions along their streets of water and sewer mains, gas and electric lines, and trolleys. Since a powerful boss could best assure the continued flow of jobs and services to poor districts unable to pay a proportionate share of the taxes, these ethnic neighborhoods became the strongholds of political machines in Cincinnati, St. Louis, New York, Philadelphia, Boston, and many lesser cities.

These and other developments brought to power in many of the more rapidly growing industrial metropolises leaders who were tolerant of strange customs and ready to accommodate new interest groups. Not only did they relax the enforcement of unwanted restraints against saloons, Sabbath amusements, and houses of ill repute, especially when suitable payments were offered, but they were often ready, for more substantial considerations, to grant valuable franchises to transit and light companies, as well as construction and paving contracts to other obliging interests. The lost utility revenues and the added costs for padded services had in the seventies prompted a short-lived effort in many cities to cut taxes, but unlike the more permanent reform regimes achieved in such British cities as Birmingham and Glasgow, most of the early reform efforts in American cities, preoccupied with economy, had succumbed to the pressure for more adequate services and other benefits in the crowded immigrant districts. All districts wanted improved services, and in the prosperous eighties few protested the mounting costs.

REFORM POLITICS

Before the depression of the midnineties revived the demand for economy, the tactics of the bosses in several cities had aroused new reform efforts. In Cincinnati the flagrant disregard in the German districts for Sunday closing laws and other regulations brought a reaction by old Yankee elements that effected an alliance with recent inner-city migrants and successfully launched a new city boss who was ready, as Zane Miller has shown, to supply new utility services. Boss Cox, by maintaining firm links with Cincinnati's boosters, survived the economy drive of the midnineties. Boss Rasin of Baltimore, on the other hand, lost to the good government forces there in 1894 when their indignation over the ring's corruption, joined with the complaints of inner-city job hunters, brought a temporary overturn. The reformers, though strong in university circles and among Baltimore's old families, as well as in its predominantly black wards, failed to attract support from the German element that generally backed the dominant southern Democratic machine, which soon resumed control.

Baltimore's reformers, relying on their prestige in a tradition-bound community, accepted a compromise that gave them a limited say over the boss's nominations. Their arrangement was somewhat comparable to that of some conservative industrialists in Leeds, England, who entered local politics to assure more efficient and adequate services. In turbulent Detroit, on the other hand, the business leaders who in 1889 chose shoe manufacturer Hazen S.

Pingree as their leader in a battle against a corrupt Irish ring, although they had the same objectives, had to make a broader appeal. In order to assure his election they balanced the ticket by naming candidates of German, Polish, and Irish, as well as Yankee, origin. Mayor Pingree, a newcomer to politics, soon discovered that the task of governing a rapidly growing industrial and cosmopolitan city required the strengthening of these ethnic ties, even at the cost of a lax enforcement of the liquor laws. Elite groups of old-family industrialists and professionals could not control even the city's bounding entrepreneurial energies. The mayor needed all the support he could rally from the public to check corruption in street and sewer contracts, on the school board, and in the operation of ferries and tollroads.

These first conflicts were soon overshadowed by Pingree's difficulties with the City Railway Company. A horse-drawn line whose service was sadly inadequate, its influential backers demanded an extension of their exclusive and lucrative contract as the price for conversion to electricity. A strike by the company's drivers won popular support and gave vent to much public resentment. But when, after three days of violence, the company agreed to arbitrate the strike issues, it received an unexpected extension of its franchise from the city council. Charging a sellout by the aldermen, Mayor Pingree vetoed that act and three subsequent franchises submitted by local and national transit groups during his first term. The powerful interests he opposed threatened to block his renomination by the Republicans, but he had attracted a sufficient following to defeat their efforts. He served his second and third terms as the people's mayor and forced the insertion of model provisions in the franchises finally granted to the transit and gas companies. He also established the first major publicly owned electric generating plant in the nation.

Mayor Pingree discovered in the early nineties, as Melvin G. Holli has ably shown, what many large-city mayors were to learn in succeeding years. Not only was it necessary for urban reformers in industrial cities to enlist the support of ethnic groups to win at the start, but it was also essential to collect adequate revenues in order to maintain the municipal services, including the distribution of welfare payments during the depression. With the needed revenues in mind, Mayor Pingree looked to the franchise returns and soon found himself battling some of the most prestigious groups in the city to secure both additional revenue and improved, economical services. Finally, to acquire the necessary power to regulate gas rates, Pingree ran for governor and carried his battle to the state capital.

The reformers in Philadelphia, despite repeated efforts, could not muster sufficient support to break the alliance between Boss James B. McManes and the local gas trust and transit combine. Dismayed as these power groups extended their holdings into other communities, the reformers moved in 1893 to invite municipal reformers from other cities to a conference in Philadelphia. Delegates from twenty-nine organizations in twenty-one cities responded, and the National Municipal League, organized at that first gathering, soon increased the number of its affiliated societies to 180 scattered in cities across the country. Although the league had no official status, its annual meetings, the work of its numerous committees, and the exchange of information it promoted created a vital new relationship between the more conscientious leaders of the nation's cities. The "Model Program," adopted in 1900 after much debate at the conference in Columbus, supplied helpful direction to reform groups active in a hundred cities by that date.

The reformers who gathered at the annual good government congresses were a diverse lot. Some were reacting to the waste and extravagance of political spoilsmen, as in Cincinnati; some were indignant over the pervasive moral corruption, as in Minneapolis; some were seeking educational reforms, as in Rochester; some were battling utility rings, as in Philadelphia. They included many public-spirited business and professional men, some of whom had served a term or two in elective office, and a number of public administrators who were devoting their lives to urban service. They constituted what was later described as a democratic elite, for they seldom attracted the more rough-and-tumble politicians or the representatives of labor or ethnic minorities. Predominantly Protestant, they included some Catholics and Jews as well, generally of the upper strata, and they were battling for more than the preservation of a threatened prestige or a traditional order, for the programs they formulated generally pointed toward a more effective administration of the increasingly complex urban functions and higher standards of service for all residents.

But while the reformers debated their model programs, practical politicians battled for control of the cities. In some of the most rapidly growing cities new leaders arose who challenged both the spoilsmen and the reformers and explored new aspects of the urbanization process. Toledo, which experienced a 60 percent growth in the nineties, produced Samuel M. Jones, the "Golden Rule" Mayor, who won reelection as a people's candidate when his refusal to bludgeon some poor criminals cost him the support of the regular parties. Mushrooming Cleveland produced Tom Johnson, a wealthy businessman whose chance reading of Henry George converted him into a champion of the unemployed during the depression and made him a battler for improved transit and other utility services at such reduced rates that his struggles won nationwide attention. Yet despite his successful launching of a publicly owned transit company, its failure to force improvements in the service of the older company reemphasized the need for regulatory power, which turned Johnson to state politics.

These dramatic regimes provided substantive contrasts to the corruption which a group of journalists began to expose in the early years of the new century. Lincoln Steffens, whose articles on "The Shame of the Cities" were published in *McClure's Magazine* in 1902 and 1903, alerted thousands of readers to the complexities as well as the corruptions of a half-dozen leading cities. With Ray Stannard Baker and other "muckrakers," he helped win a wide following for the urban progressives and other reformers whose programs generally lacked the sensational qualities that brought out the voters. Yet the sudden outburst of critical journalism, a reaction to the fin-de-siècle optimism of a year or two before, and promoted by the appearance of a group of competing urban journals seeking to capture a national audience, soon spent itself and left the sober reformers struggling to effect rational improvements in municipal services.

A new generation of progressives was emerging in many cities around the turn of the century. Dana White has called them urbanists, whose detached concern for city problems distinguished them from the earlier mugwumps animated generally by moral indignation. Many delegates to the National Municipal League congresses, enlisted originally in a righteous crusade, gradually acquired a more objective approach after serving on special study committees and hearing several sides to a question. The experience and practices of European cities proved especially enlightening on several issues, not only in the extent of national fiscal support many enjoyed, but also in the degree of professionalism some had attained, and the central direction and supervision they received. Socialistically inclined reformers noted that the wide adoption of public ownership of utilities had freed European cities from what was a major source of corruption in America. Although the situation in which American cities found themselves was strikingly different from that in Europe, progressive urbanists endeavored to devise new procedures to attain some of the advantages enjoyed abroad.

The National Municipal League provided a focus for much of this effort. Its model program of 1900, revised and updated a decade later, supplied a partial though strictly admonitory substitute for the legislative directives issued by Parliament in a series of acts prescribing the functions and powers of boroughs and cities in England. France, Germany, and some of the other European countries supplied similar municipal codes, which generally prescribed more specific and unified functions and responsibilities than the states granted to their cities. But the efficient administration attained by many European cities was more directly related to the bureaucratic character of their staffs. In most countries municipal suffrage was limited by or weighted in respect to real property holdings, and the power of the councilmen to appoint the administrators was narrowly prescribed. The efficiency and honesty sometimes attained, particularly when special events drew some of the abler citizens into public service for a term or two, attracted praise from many observers and engendered a spirit of pride among the residents, but few felt the thrill of citizen participation.

Urban progressives in America, on the other hand, were beginning to recognize the value of wide citizen participation as a unifying force in heterogeneous communities. They were trying in some cities to entice ethnic groups away from the bosses, but they also hoped to improve efficiency. Their civil service reforms, designed to remove appointments from political patronage, pointed in that direction. The establishment of bureaus of municipal research and legislative reference libraries in a dozen cities, following New York's lead in 1905, supplied sources of information that greatly assisted conscientious administrators. The formation in this decade of national associations of various municipal officials spurred the development of professional standards and promoted a wider diffusion of improved administrative techniques. Even new political appointees could be drawn more quickly into their bureaucratic units after attending one of these conventions.

In the provision and management of utilities the European cities generally followed a different course from that prevalent in America. The early reliance on public enterprise in Glasgow and Birmingham and in several cities on the Continent produced such exemplary services that many conservative as well as liberal municipal authorities in other cities assumed responsibility for supplying water, gas, electricity, and public trams, and at moderate rates. In the more rapidly growing American cities, enterprising men, seeing the prospect of large profits from future growth, competed eagerly for the opportunity to supply these facilities, and their rival bids for utility franchises helped at the start to assure early and reasonable services.

Once the franchises had been granted, however, and the facilities built, the situation changed drastically. Often constructed ahead of the market and in anticipation of future demands, the early gas and transit companies in America found their returns inadequate and as a result curtailed service or sought increased rates. Public officials who chartered competing companies to assure improved services quickly discovered the disadvantage of repeated disruptions in the streets. A city's best chance of securing adequate service at moderate rates depended on a tightening of its franchise provisions or the introduction of regulatory powers, but the pressure of rival franchise groups on the aldermen repeatedly frustrated such efforts. Few cities solved this problem locally, but while Governor Pingree's efforts to provide regulatory powers to the cities of Michigan were blocked in the legislature, other progressive governors, notably Charles Evans Hughes in New York and Robert M. La Follette in Wisconsin, secured the passage of measures establishing state regulatory commissions with jurisdiction over the rates and services of local as well as statewide utilities.

But if reform mayors such as Pingree and Johnson frequently found themselves battling prestigious groups engaged in exploiting lucrative franchises and advantageous contracts, some of the more soft-spoken urbanists discovered that many influential business leaders were ready to back the regulation of municipal utilities, as well as railroads and other out-of-town monopolies. The regulation of local utilities became more popular as out-of-town combines absorbed them. The intensely competitive character of the American economy created a climate as hostile to utility monopolies as to socialistic ventures in their public ownership. Urban progressives could thus rally support from respectable business groups and residents who wanted more and better transit service and gas and electricity at cheaper rates. The great mass of working men, who in England and on the Continent frequently supported public ownership of these utilities, were in America less responsive to such radical proposals, partly because of their greater hope for personal advancement under the enterprise system and partly because they had come to share the reformer's fear of the corruption of most political leaders. An investigation in 1907 of the labor-management relations in the municipally owned utilities of a half-dozen American cities revealed that drastic upheavals had occurred at each shift in party control. Partisanship was also rampant in private utilities, another investigation declared, but all agreed that city or state regulatory commissions promised the best safeguard for the interests of the many urban groups that had little hope of achieving a position of dominance.

SOCIAL WELFARE AND ECONOMIC CONTROL

In the field of social welfare, urban reformers were also turning from moral to pragmatic goals. The hardships of the depression of the midnineties had convinced many leaders of the Societies for Organized Charity and other bodies that the major evil was not pauperism but poverty. Local employment offices had attracted more applicants than they could handle, and remedial loan societies had quickly seen their funds exhausted. An increasing array of social settlement houses located in the depressed immigrant districts of many cities were enlisting adults as well as children in neighborhood guilds and other programs and endeavoring to develop more wholesome communities. The formation of a national federation of settlement houses in 1911, the same year that saw the start of a national association of Societies for Organized Charity, signaled the recognition by these workers of the need for professional status and for wider cooperation in their attack on urban welfare problems. Earlier attempts in several cities to publish welfare journals had resulted in the merging of the two strongest into *Charities and the Commons* in 1910, which was soon renamed *The Survey*. Four training schools for social workers made their appearance before the close of the decade.

Although the social workers, like the progressives in government, generally sprang from the more educated ranks of the middle class, they were able to develop relationships with poor immigrants in crowded slums that opened new channels of communication. Nurses and doctors who offered instruction in sanitation and public health at the settlement classes learned much in return about slum conditions and immigrant needs, while volunteers who undertook to supervise youth clubs and adult forums acquired the skills of group workers and a new appreciation for the talents and customs of the inner-city residents. The establishment of numerous branches of the Educational Alliance in scattered cities after 1893, the organization by one of these of a Breadwinner's College in New York, and the launching of a university extension program in a downtown settlement in Chicago and of a group of adult social centers in inner-city schools in Rochester all represented cooperative achievements in the most difficult and crucial aspect of America's urbanization. Baltimore's three-day City-Wide Conference, which assembled several hundred participants from 132 local organizations to discuss pressing urban problems, supplied another demonstration of the awakening civic consciousness.

The increased awareness of communitywide interdependence was reflected in and promoted by many improvements in intracity communication. Although telephones had made their appearance in the seventies and numbered over 200,000 by 1890, it was only as they multiplied tenfold in the next decade, reaching into private homes as well as offices, that their potential value to the cities was revealed. The efficiency and speed they brought to day-to-day business transactions strengthened the position of the administrative elites. At the same time, electric trolleys increased their passenger loads to a total of six billion by 1902, three times the number of a decade before. The outward extension of their tracks sped the expansion of many cities, while the construction of elevated lines in Boston, Chicago, and New York, and of subways after the turn of the century, greatly facilitated internal movement and communications in these great metropolises. In similar fashion, the construction of electric interurban lines, branching out in several directions from many thriving regional cities, drew the residents and activities of nearby and distant towns more closely into the urban orbit and transformed their regional centers into budding metropolises.

These technological developments had far-reaching effects on the social and economic life of the cities, as well as on their municipal affairs. The

increasing flow of commuters into the downtowns of the central cities promoted the development of thriving retail shopping districts with large department stores, hotels, and banks to serve their needs. Large office buildings
appeared there, as well as theaters and other commercial amusements. Some of
the old shops and mills near the center, spurred by the increased influx of
workers, expanded their existing plants and operations; others moved to more
spacious sites on the outskirts but near an active freight artery and a convenient transit line. The social and economic effects of these movements were
sometimes considerable, but only in the case of slaughterhouses and oil mills
were the cities beginning, as in New Orleans in 1873, to assert a power to
control their location.

The wider extension of the railroad network and its increased capacity to
deliver raw materials to any city and to distribute finished products throughout the country spurred the consolidation of companies and the building of
larger factories. Although the number of wage earners per establishment
doubled in these two decades, that gain was based on a 50 percent increase in
the number of factory workers and a 25 percent reduction in the number of
plants. The number of incorporated manufacturing companies, on the other
hand, increased from forty thousand in 1900 to seventy thousand a decade
later, absorbing three quarters of the wage earners and producing 79 percent
of all manufactured products. New York City, the unchallenged leader in
number of establishments, wage earners, value of products, and value added,
was first also in many specialty industries that did not lend themselves to
large factory production. Its millinery shops, clothing shops, and printing establishments contrasted with the slaughtering plants and foundries of Chicago,
the woolen factories and machine foundries of Philadelphia, and the growing
factories of most other industrial cities. Detroit, with the sudden growth of the
automobile industry, achieved a 196.8 percent gain in the value added to its
products. It doubled the national average of twenty-four workers per establishment, but it did not yet rival Lawrence, whose cotton and woolen factories had
an average work force of two hundred. Of course the big companies were
much larger, and five hundred forty, as reported in the census of 1909, employed in excess of one thousand workers each.

Nationwide statistics fail, however, to reveal the threatening surge toward
monopoly control during these two decades. The trust movement of the
eighties had been checked by the Sherman Anti-Trust Act of 1890, following
court decisions upholding a similar state law in 1889, but other devices were
found, and in the nineties a number of gigantic corporations emerged, con-
solidating groups of railroads, metal firms, and other key industries. Functional consolidation had at the same time drawn large clusters of similar firms
into strategically located cities where they could share common pools of labor
and marketing skills and reap the benefits of accessory industries. Providence
captured 25 percent of the jewelry business on this basis, Philadelphia 21
percent of the hosiery and hat trade and 31 percent of the carpet business, and
Detroit 24 percent of the automobile production. But this type of consolidation, which marked progress toward the technical virtuosity of Thompson's
fourth growth stage, was within the competitive tradition of the free enterprise system. In contrast, the formation of the mammoth Standard Oil Company based in Cleveland quickly presented a monopolistic threat to Toledo

interests, as the American Bicycle Company also did to a score of cities when it drew much of that expanding industry into Springfield, Massachusetts, in the late nineties. The free-swinging market on which merchant cities had relied was outmoded. A renewed drive for the enforcement of the antitrust provisions in 1903 checked the formation of vast holding companies, but the internal economies of large-scale production and the accompanying external economies which had boosted the number of firms employing over ten thousand workers to eighty-one by the turn of the century continued to operate.

These developments prompted the adoption of new measures to safeguard community interests and new strategies on the part of organized labor. New or revived boards of trade or chambers of commerce appeared in most cities and assumed new informational and promotional functions. In several industrial cities, following Milwaukee's lead, the chambers organized and conducted annual industrial expositions, and Philadelphia was the first of several to see the opening of a commercial museum, where its products were kept constantly on display. The commodious headquarters of some of these chambers rivaled those of the exchanges in British and Continental cities, providing a sense of community to local business leaders and sometimes to the charity and welfare workers they helped organize and support. In 1870 the chambers and boards of trade formed the National Board of Trade to assist in the coordination of their efforts. An aggressively conservative faction formed the National Association of Manufacturers in 1895 to support industrialists in their struggles with unions. Yet none of these organizational efforts rivaled the promotional effect of the new advertising techniques which created vast new markets in foreign and American cities.

THE UNION MOVEMENT

Of all urban residents it was the workers who faced the most drastic readjustment in industrial cities. Earlier apprentice practices were readily abandoned as young men and women from the rural districts and unskilled immigrants welcomed the opportunity to move more quickly into the status of a machine tender. But there they quickly discovered that further advancement had virtually ended. They were free to shift to a similar post in another factory, or to start fresh at another calling, but the great majority were trapped in the ranks of an army of workers whose only hope of improving their lot appeared increasingly to lie in unionization. Like the industrialists in the head offices, they had to organize or perish, or at least accept a subsistence wage. For many their chief hope for improvement and a slight degree of distinction was membership in a trade union that might secure them slightly higher wages than their neighbors.

As a result, the 1890s brought an era of business unionism. The bread-and-butter strategy of most unions in the American Federation of Labor, each negotiating with company managers for special contracts and cautiously posing the threat of an occasional strike, proved more attractive to many urban workers than the mass action of the Knights or the ideological stance of the Socialists. And as union leaders became less responsive to antimonopoly campaigns and the membership accepted its working-class status, some industrialists grew more willing to negotiate business contracts. They admitted that the workers' representatives, like any other suppliers, were entitled to binding agreements. This concept of labor as a commodity fit neatly into the new technology of the efficiency experts and prompted some plant managers to grant union recognition on that basis, and to institute a check-off system under which they deducted dues for the unions, thus bringing membership into the open. This was more acceptable when several small unions were involved, since it eliminated collections in the factory without posing a threat to management. Membership in the unions mounted rapidly after the depression and surged over the two-million mark in 1904.

Yet despite the increased numbers in the unions, a shift in the economy from one of slow currency deflation to one of slow but long-term inflation erased most of the advantages of increased production as far as the workers were concerned. Only the simultaneous decline in unemployment supplied assurance of increased income to many workers and strengthened the hand of the moderate union leaders who displayed caution in calling strikes. Some unions appointed local business agents to maintain discipline among their members and to develop regular contacts with plant managers. All sent delegates to regional and national conferences and to local trade councils, which now appeared in most cities and supplied a new communitywide forum on related matters. The central trades councils, as they were generally called, staged annual Labor Day parades and picnics, endorsed and sometimes gave material support to strikes by member unions, publicized the efforts of member unions to improve their wage rates and reduce their hours, promoted the adoption and use of union labels and the establishment of public employment offices, and occasionally endorsed labor reforms proposed by the progressives.

However, union leaders as well as the great majority of their members were becoming skeptical of, if not indifferent to, political action. Many of the national unions had sickness and benefit programs, and their members were slow to respond to occasional advocates of workmen's compensation laws such as the nations of Europe were enacting in these decades. They were equally lethargic in supporting the pleas of settlement house leaders and others for anti-child-labor laws and for laws regulating the hours and conditions of women workers. Disillusioned by the results of earlier campaigns against monopolies and for eight-hour laws, which the courts sustained only for those employed on public works, they focused their efforts on contract negotiations for their own benefits. Many were suspicious of the efficiency experts and opposed the piecerate offers and other schemes sometimes advanced by management, but the pressure of rising prices forced some to consider the merits of arbitration and mediation as alternatives to frequent and costly strikes.

It was a threatened steel strike that prompted a group of the old Chicago Civic Federation to reorganize and establish the National Civic Federation in 1900 to promote conciliation between labor and management. The federation enlisted the cooperation of many mayors, including Seth Low, who served as chairman for several years, and of Samuel Gompers and John Mitchell, the moderate heads of the American Federation of Labor and the reorganized United Mine Workers, as well as numerous industrialists, in promoting the negotiation of contracts in coal, steel, clothing, and transit in many cities. It helped persuade President Theodore Roosevelt to appoint a board of conciliation to supervise a coal settlement in 1903 and to mediate other controversies. In order to promote conciliation locally, the federation organized urban branches in Pittsburgh, Detroit, and Milwaukee, among other cities, and held national conferences to bring industrialists and labor leaders together.

The conciliatory efforts of the National Civic Federation revealed some of the deep divisions that had developed among industrialists in several cities. While some of the larger corporations, as Robert Wiebe has demonstrated, were eager to reach peaceful agreements with their workers, many businessmen, particularly in the smaller industrial cities, opposed this movement. An employers' association in Dayton originated the "open shop" campaign in 1901 to counter the drive of many unions for a "closed shop," and two years later, with the support of the National Association of Manufacturers, founded the Citizens' Industrial Association of America to wage open war on organized labor. The CIA soon had units or affiliates in a hundred cities and helped account for the slight decline in union membership in 1906 and the slower growth thereafter.

Labor organizers in many cities faced a critical division among rank-and-file workers. Most unions had supported the drive to ban the importation of contract labor in the 1870s and had helped secure a ban against Chinese labor in 1885. Union complaints assisted in the passage of revisions designed to strengthen these restrictions during the next two decades. But many foreign-born workers were eager to bring friends from their hometowns as well as members of their own families to America, and their efforts to assure them of jobs were threatened by the restrictive legislation. Unions pressing their organizational drives in immigrant districts faced this divisive issue, but their top leadership generally supported the campaigns of various antiforeign groups, such as the Immigration Restriction League organized by prestigious Bostonians in 1894, for more drastic limitations.

The division among the workers, who were chiefly affected by immigrant competition, was matched by the ambivalence of many urban and national leaders to immigration restriction. Some industrialists, wishing to retain the steady flow of labor, opposed it, and many cities eager for continued growth endorsed that stand. But others in both groups, concerned over the mounting number of new immigrants who presented more difficult language and other cultural adjustments, pressed for additional restraints. The progressives, too, were ambivalent, for there, as in so many other issues, they were not as responsive to ideological arguments as to the practical needs of their communities. Since the choices were not clear cut, the progressives continued to support institutions that promoted the integration and Americanization of all newcomers. The final decision on immigrant restriction was postponed until new developments brought action at a later date.

Thus the progressives transcended their original moral reaction to the evils of the city and assumed the lead in promoting cultural innovations. The increased specialization fostered by technological advances brought new spatial and functional concentration, but also heightened the interdependence of cities and promoted moderation and accommodation. The conservative reforms advanced by the American progressives contrasted with the more radical demands of dissident groups in European cities, where labor achieved few of the modest gains shared by immigrant workers in America. With those who had arrived earlier, even the recent newcomers had a part in developing new cities in a new country and enjoyed a degree of social as well as spatial mobility unknown abroad. The very size of the immigrant influx increased the momentum of urban change and permitted the reformers to assume moderate rather than radical positions. At the same time the diversity of origins created a Tower of Babel factor, as Stephan Thernstrom has aptly put it, that inhibited more concerted efforts.

Despite their remarkable growth and the numerous innovations introduced in the Progressive era, the American cities fell short, in the opinion of Arthur Shadwell, of their counterparts in Britain and Germany on many counts. Not only were they more prone to corruption and violence, but few metropolises had as yet discovered what several in Europe knew, that the chief function of a city was service, not growth, performance, not profit, and that increased output could only be judged by widespread evidence of improved well-being, public as well as private. Still the advantages, as Shadwell

Table 7.   COMPARATIVE URBANIZATION TRENDS.*

	1870	1890	
	Cities over 2,000	Cities over 10,000	Cities over 2,000
England and Wales		61.73	72.05
Scotland		49.9	65.4
Australia		41.4	
Belgium		34.8	
Netherlands		33.5	
Uruguay		30.4	
Germany	36.1		47.0
Argentina		27.8	
United States	25.7	27.6	37.7
France	31.1	25.9	37.4
Denmark	25.2	23.6	32.4
Spain		29.6	
Italy		20.6	43.4
Ireland	22.2	18.0	26.4
Canada	18.8	17.1	27.3
Chile		17.1	42.0
Norway		16.7	22.2
Sweden	12.9	13.7	18.0
Japan		13.1	
Mexico		13.0	
Brazil		10.2	
Russia	10.6	9.3	12.3

*From Adna F. Weber, *The Growth of Cities in the Nineteenth Century* (Ithaca, N.Y.: Cornell University Press, 1963). Derived from Table 112, pp. 145–46.

hastened to observe, were not all located abroad. The American cities had not only increased the mobility of most residents, but had also supplied more freedom to women and youths and more opportunities for voluntary expression. And, as repeatedly noted, they presented a greater diversity of ethnic contacts and influences. Moreover, acting independently and without the support and direction accorded cities in Europe, they had launched progressive reforms that marked "the emergence of a sense of civic consciousness," the "true miracle," as Professor Oscar Handlin has put it, of America's urban development. If their sense of order and the quality of their products left much to be desired, the vitality of their productive energies, the abundance of their output, the creativity of their innovations, and the confidence of their promoters were unsurpassed and helped produce significant internal transformations, as we shall see in the next chapter.

BIBLIOGRAPHY

Chalmers, David M. *The Social and Political Ideas of the Muckrakers.* Freeport, N.Y.: Books for Libraries, Inc., 1964.

Crooks, James B. *Politics and Progress: The Rise of Urban Progressivism in Baltimore, 1895–1911.* Baton Rouge: Louisiana State University, 1968.

Hennock, E. P. "The Social Compositions of Borough Councils in Two Large Cities, 1838–1914." In *The Study of Urban History,* ed. H. J. Dyos, New York: St. Martin's Press, Inc., 1968.

Holli, Melvin G. *Reform in Detroit: Hazen S. Pingree and Urban Politics.* New York: Oxford University Press, 1969.

Hooson, David J. M. "The Growth of Cities in Pre-Soviet Russia." In *Urbanization and Its Problems,* ed. R. P. Beckinsale and J. M. Houston. New York: Barnes & Noble, Inc., 1968.

Kolko, Gabriel. *The Triumph of Conservatism, 1900–1916.* Chicago: Quadrangle Books, Inc., 1963.

Levine, Edward M. *The Irish and Irish Politicians.* Notre Dame, Ind.: University of Notre Dame Press, 1966.

McKelvey, Blake. *Rochester: The Quest for Quality: 1890–1925.* Cambridge, Mass.: Harvard University Press, 1956.

Miller, Zane L. *Boss Cox's Cincinnati: Urban Politics in the Progressive Era.* New York: Oxford University Press, 1968.

Rolle, Andrew F. *The Immigrant Upraised: Italian Adventurers and Colonists in an Expanding America.* Norman, Okla.: University of Oklahoma Press, 1968.

Shadwell, Arthur. *Industrial Efficiency.* London: Longmans, Green and Co., 1909.

Warner, Sam B., Jr. *Streetcar Suburbs: The Process of Growth in Boston, 1870–1900.* Cambridge, Mass.: Harvard University Press, 1962.

White, Dana F. "The Self-Conscious City: A Survey and Bibliographical Summary of Periodical Literature on American Urban Themes: 1865–1900." Ph.D. Thesis at George Washington University, 1969.

Wiebe, Robert H. *Businessmen and Reform: A Study of the Progressive Movement.* Cambridge, Mass.: Harvard University Press, 1962.

7

The Internal Structure and Social Dynamics of Industrial Cities

Urbanization in an age of progressive industrialization led to rapid growth, increased productivity, and advances in economic and civic technology. It also brought extensive social and cultural transformations. These developments were characteristic of urbanizing trends everywhere, and their rates and priorities in each case reflected local circumstances. Thus in America the wide expanse of the land frontier and the successive waves of immigrants that sped the growth of old and new cities not only combined to achieve unprecedented commercial and industrial advances, but produced a richly varied assortment of institutional responses. The urbanization process effected different results in commercial and industrial cities, in the older northeastern and the newer prairie or far western cities, in southern and other predominantly native American cities and those that attracted and absorbed large numbers of newcomers from abroad. Moreover, an awakening consciousness of the process and of some of the problems involved transformed the experience from one of natural history into a deliberate part of the nation's history.

An early hint of this growing awareness of urbanization as a process came at the annual meeting of the American Social Science Association in 1895. Its president, Franklin J. Kingsbury, a banker and trustee of Yale, delivered a memorable address that year on "The Tendency of Men to Live in Cities." After taking note of contemporary indictments of cities as "the rotten spots in our body politic" and the "menace of our civilization," he observed that nevertheless "our cities . . . attract rather than repel residents." It was the city, not the country, that gratified man's needs for gregariousness, he declared, satisfied his desires for excitement, and fostered his creative impulses. Kingsbury's positive approach presented a scholarly challenge to his fellow social scientists, but, fearful as they were of a stand that might promote or condone the booster element, most of them continued to focus their attention on the problems and deficiencies of American cities.

THE GHETTO AND URBAN MOBILITY

A major source of America's urban problems, many contemporary observers felt, was the mounting flood of immigrants inundating its cities. The contributions these newcomers made to the nation's urban growth and industrial productivity were sometimes forgotten by nativists who resented the competition of immigrants in urban politics and feared the disruption they posed to old social and cultural traditions. The growth of antiforeign sentiment failed at the time to impose restrictions on immigrants, but considerably affected their opportunities for advancement. Circumstances differed sharply between cities, especially those of diverse regions, and the transformations they effected in internal social and cultural institutions were still more deviant and contrasted dramatically with contemporary developments in cities of other lands.

As the decades advanced and the post-Civil War immigrant migrations increased in volume and diversity, several of the largest metropolises developed a patchwork of ethnic neighborhoods that displayed their cosmopolitan character. Except perhaps in New York, few of these immigrant districts were exclusively occupied by any one nationality, though mounting hostility to strange newcomers, particularly in the depression of the 1890s, served to intensify the clustering process for some of the late arrivals. Earlier migrants, particularly the Irish and the British, who together had comprised the majority of adults in many northeastern cities in the 1860s and before, were so widely scattered in most places that local "Dublins" and "Caledonias" were at best vaguely bounded districts in which foreign-born residents clustered around a church or some other old-country institution. The Germans, who hastened to establish German Protestant or Catholic churches, had an additional incentive for clustering because of their language difficulty, but districts where German was spoken daily also attracted German Jews, whose temples in turn drew to these districts the early Jewish migrants from Poland and Russia. Because of their familiarity with the ghettos of eastern Europe, the Jews often referred to their American settlements as ghettos, too, and the term gradually acquired a wider application to all ethnic neighborhoods, though the voluntary and mixed character of their residents contrasted sharply with the exclusive and compulsory character of such districts abroad.

Despite their open boundaries and the mobility of their residents, the ethnic neighborhoods or ghettos played a significant role in American cities. They enabled newcomers to find lodgment among their ethnic fellows, where mutual concerns helped develop familiar institutions and thus provided community ties that gradually expanded to involve these newcomers in the affairs of the larger city and nation. Many of these adventurous folk quickly acquired the restlessness characteristic of most Americans and moved frequently in search of better accommodations in other parts of town or better opportunities elsewhere. Their removal and that of their children made room in the old districts for new arrivals from the home country, or newcomers from other lands, who thus inherited and sometimes remodeled the institutions of their predecessors to serve their own needs.

Thus the ghettos, as voluntary residential enclaves, served a succession of ethnic newcomers in the great ports and in some large and rapidly growing industrial cities. The transitory nature of their inhabitants contributed to the spatial mobility of American cities and to the social mobility of these newcomers. With the ravages of time and of repeated remodelings, the physical structure of these neighborhoods, whether consisting of the old mansions of the original founders or of tenements built to replace the shantytowns of the poor, deteriorated, and these districts, unless cleared by fire or appropriated by expanding commercial districts, became the base for the inner-city slums that increasingly blighted the older central cities of the Northeast. Yet even the late arrivals, such as the Italians and several groups of eastern Europeans, frequently managed to develop congenial if ephemeral communities by reconverting the churches, clubrooms, and stores to serve their own ethnic needs.

An increased public recognition of the ghetto's existence added in the 1890s to the awakening consciousness of the city and its problems. The vivid articles by Jacob Riis in the *New York Tribune* and *Scribners,* and later in his seminal book, *How the Other Half Lives,* not only alerted many readers to the problems of the cities, but popularized the concept of two societies as a challenge to the American dream. Settlement houses, institutional churches, and other reform efforts of native Americans, as well as varied housing programs, responded to this challenge, but many ethnic groups had from the beginning demonstrated their determination to maintain their own community activities. Their churches, schools, benefit societies, social and marching clubs—all except the churches unfamiliar in the home country—closely resembled institutions that had served the native Americans on their migration to the cities in earlier decades. Native Americans continued to make use of these institutions, and new arrivals from the farms hastened to join volunteer fire companies, athletic clubs, and building-lot associations, as well as congenial churches. Thus the ghettos performed an urbanizing function similar to that of the small cities, both contemporary and of an earlier day, or of the neighborhood in the metropolis.

But the American ghettos and the American industrial or port cities contrasted with similar districts and cities in other lands. Cities in South America that attracted large numbers of immigrants in these decades, notably several in Argentina and Brazil, housed the great majority of them in shantytowns on the outskirts and admitted only the well-to-do merchants and highly skilled craftsmen to the inner city, where the more successful natives of Spanish or Portuguese ancestry resided. That division between the substantial inner city of the well-to-do and the cruder habitations on the outskirts had persisted since the earliest colonial days, when the Indians had been encouraged to rebuild their villages beyond the walls. Except for the household slaves, most of the blacks had been settled in camps on the periphery, too, and when a new immigration from Europe, especially from Italy and Syria, commenced in the midnineteenth century, all but the most wealthy found lodgment on the outskirts. This pattern was not unique to South America, for European cities that attracted immigrant workers generally settled them in colonies on the periphery, reserving the inner city for the residences of affluent citizens in convenient proximity to the civic and cultural institutions, as well as the better shops and stores. In eastern Europe the real ghettos had for centuries been confined to the outskirts. In Southeast Asia, as we noted earlier, the expanding colonial port cities of the nineteenth century, Singapore and Batavia among others, had planned districts for the alien Chinese and Indian immigrants who sometimes outnumbered the native Malayans, and for the much smaller European colonies which in every case occupied the choice residential districts.

This structural contrast between the inner-city ethnic neighborhoods or ghettos in the northeastern cities in the States and the foreign settlements on the outskirts of leading cities abroad had more than a physical significance. Both the inner-city and the outlying ghettos exerted urbanizing influences on their formerly rural inhabitants, though the often congested inner-city district, with a full battery of urban institutions already at hand, offered a more intensified urbanizing training. But the important difference sprang from the ultimate objectives of that experience, as determined in each instance by the philosophy and the politics of the larger society. In theory, the American policy was unique in that it welcomed newcomers to full and equal citizenship, with integration as the objective, though the existence of distinctive and increasingly wretched ethnic neighborhoods raised serious questions about the application of the theory.

The questions were part of the broader one of the extent of social or democratic mobility in American cities. The physical mobility exercised by those who moved out of the ghettos, as most residents of European origin did in those decades, involved an element of social mobility since many now became homeowners, although such moves did not always result in social advancement. Some of the old neighborhoods had achieved distinction as important subcultural centers, such as the Lower East Side in New York, to which former Jewish residents returned periodically for social and cultural renewal and which sometimes, as Moses Rischin tells us, drew Jews from other parts of the metropolis and other cities as permanent residents. Moreover, as Warner and Burke have argued, most immigrants even in the major cities never resided for long in exclusive ethnic neighborhoods. The Irish and the British were in many cities too numerous for inner-city confinement and, with their close relatives the Canadians, lived singly or in pockets in all parts of the city. The Scandinavians were too few, except in Minneapolis, to establish neighborhoods, but the Germans and later the Italians, the Poles, and the eastern Jews, as well as the blacks and the Chinese, did form distinctive neighborhoods. New York and a few other northern metropolises developed patchworks of such neighborhoods, including in some cases three or four widely separated concentrations of the larger ethnic groups. But even in such cases, as H. S. Nelli has demonstrated for the Italians of Chicago, for a time their largest settlement, many were never resident in any of the distinctively Italian neighborhoods and yet they faced the problems of urbanization and the struggle for upward mobility, which for poor newcomers from rural areas were the basic questions.

Critics of the two-cultures concept early developed the rival concept of the melting pot as the means for realizing the American dream of equality. Yet persistent and mounting hostilities, especially against certain groups of newcomers, distorted the process of assimilation in some cities and raised serious doubts as to the efficiency of the melting-pot process. Later scholars replaced the two-cultures analysis with a four-layered stratification (upper, middle, working, and lower classes) and related it, as Warner and Burke have shown, to four major "socioreligious identifications—white Protestant, white Catholic, white Jewish, and Negro Protestant." This more complex stratification seemed to explain some of the difficulties encountered by certain ethnic groups in specific cities, and it also recognized the extreme handicaps faced by blacks in any situation. Probing studies of shifting patterns of intermarriage in New

Haven and of cross-cultural relations in Detroit supported this synthesis, but according to Warner and Burke failed to account for the experience of the great majority of immigrants who escaped contact with the ghettos. While they concluded that no single factor accounted for the progress many newcomers enjoyed in these decades, the diversity of the American cities provided many stairways. The bottom doors remained locked, however, to those lacking the proper keys.

Yet no one could deny the exceptional degree of mobility available in American cities, despite the increased stratification brought about by industrialization. Mobility, though practically nonexistent in long stagnant Lima, Peru, before the late nineties, was more evident in dynamic São Paulo, according to Richard M. Morse, and yet if it was harder for an Italian or a German to become a proper Bostonian than to win membership in the elite of São Paulo or Buenos Aires, as Warren Dean maintains, more of their destitute fellow countrymen were able to climb a rung or two on the urban ladder in North than in South America. Inner-city districts in some northeastern cities were progressively becoming wretched slums, but, as Thernstrom has observed, the same people did not live in them for long. Their inhabitants moved on, some to better locations in the same or larger cities, some into more wretched situations, but seldom did they return to the farms. The cities of Germany were likewise attracting migrants from small towns and rural areas in these decades of rapid industrialization, as Wolfgang Kollmann tells us, and this horizontal mobility gave many there an opportunity for social advancement, too, perhaps for the first time in history. But the 75 percent expansion of the working class overshadowed the increase of all other groups in the larger German cities and absorbed most of the in-migrants. Newcomers from the farms and from other towns took the poorer jobs, but the influx was not as great as in American cities and, except for seasonal workers in border cities, it was not a handicapped minority that sometimes served to push the earlier arrivals upward.

Yet the greater mobility enjoyed in the States was not evenly distributed in time or place, or among various ethnic groups. Thernstrom has discovered that young men reared in native families secured a higher start and enjoyed greater occupational mobility in Boston than those born and reared in rural Ireland or born in America but reared in recent immigrant families. He also finds that second-generation immigrants and even the first-generation youths who grew up in post-Civil War Boston had a greater mobility than their parents, especially if they were of British or west European origin. Apparently religion was a significant variable, as well as the state of the economy, in occupational mobility. Institutionalized religion also served as a ladder for some upwardly mobile sons of poor parishioners, enabling ambitious immigrants to surmount ethnic barriers. The hurdling of ethnic barriers was even more dramatic in the field of sports; by the turn of the century professional teams were eager to recruit talented youngsters of any background. Only with the formation of professional teams able to pay their players did the poor immigrants have a competitive chance against the more affluent natives, however.

The contributions of organized sports to upward mobility were only beginning to appear in the eighties and nineties and slumped drastically during the depression. The geographical mobility of American urbanites also fluctuated with the times. In Rochester, for example, the ratio of stability over five-year periods declined from 62.5 to 58.4 percent between the prosperous eighties and the unsettled early nineties and then rose to a new high of 66.2 percent with the return of prosperity. A comparable mobility occurred in greater Boston, where Thernstrom has demonstrated that it was generally the failures who moved on and often downward into a class of permanent migrants. With persistence some of the disadvantaged Irish mounted to positions of power in Lawrence, Boston, and elsewhere, and many of their fellows shared in the new dignity conferred on their churches and ethnic institutions. In cities that attracted large concentrations of specific ethnic groups, some of their members attained modest successes as storekeepers and other merchants serving their fellow countrymen, and many by investing their meager savings in real estate achieved the increased stability and added status of homeowners. Several industrial cities with high percentages of foreign-born and foreign-parentage residents, such as Buffalo, Cleveland, Detroit, Milwaukee, Minneapolis, Rochester, and St. Paul, reported 40 percent and more of their families as homeowners in the 1890 and 1910 censuses.

Of cities over 100,000 only a few in the Far West, principally settled by migrating midwesterners, rivaled these percentages of home ownership. Many smaller cities in the Midwest, also predominately of native origins, equalled or exceeded these standards, but none in the South or (except Nashville) in the border states, where the black population practically displaced the immigrants, reported home ownerships of more than 25 percent. Moreover, except for San Francisco's Chinatown and New Orleans' Storyville, neither the far western nor the southern cities had as yet developed ghettos, partly because the European-born were relatively few and widely scattered, while the blacks who migrated to the southern and border cities after the Civil War built new shantytowns on the outskirts. As in the case of the Indians, blacks, and poor immigrants of South American cities, Negroes in the United States were not expected to achieve integration, though the development of neighborhood tradesmen and professionals, as Constance Green has discovered in Washington, marked a response of these oppressed people to an urban environment that had significant implications for the future. The mobility potentialities of Negroes were even more evident in New York, where the multiplicity of ethnic groups forestalled the suppression (though not the oppression) of any one minority and enabled the blacks who crowded in great numbers into Harlem in the early 1900s to enjoy what was frequently described as a renaissance. With all their limitations the cities of America, particularly the industrial cities of the Northeast and Midwest, supplied opportunities and agencies for upward mobility to a larger and more diversified influx of newcomers and displayed a wider participation in home ownership and civic activity than most cities abroad could boast.

HOUSING AND CITY PLANNING

Yet the limitations in American cities were numerous, and in some respects, notably housing, they were becoming more troublesome. The sheer speed of urban growth partially accounted for the failure of many cities to meet their housing needs. The reliance on private enterprise and the almost total absence of civic direction presented additional contrasts to most cities abroad. Only in the great ports and industrial cities of the North, where crowded inner-city districts were producing slum conditions, were some distraught leaders awakening to the housing problem, and their responses contrasted sharply with those of similar authorities abroad. But throughout the country civic leaders were developing a new interest in city planning, and in this case the exchange of ideas was again, after a long period of isolation, on a worldwide basis.

Efforts to improve urban housing sprang from a recognition of the needs and opportunities presented by continued population growth and increased density. Private investors in estate developments in Britain and on the Continent and in the construction of individual houses and blocks there and in America had met most needs unaided before the 1850s. The display of two model houses for workingmen, sponsored by Prince Albert at the London Exposition in 1851, spurred philanthropic societies there and in Paris and Berlin to launch model housing projects as an antidote to revolution. The Association for Improving the Conditions of the Poor erected the first "workingmen's home" in New York in 1855, and, despite the disadvantages soon discovered by the inhabitants of its eighty-seven apartments, the Peabody Foundation and other agencies promoted several housing projects in New York and Boston in the late sixties. These efforts were soon overwhelmed by the mounting tide of poor newcomers who overcrowded the converted houses of earlier residents and prompted the boards of health that conducted sanitary surveys in New York in 1867 and in Chicago a year later to press for regulations that became operative in New York in the sixties and in Chicago and a few other cities in the next decade. These regulations, as strengthened in New York in 1879 after a second survey, tried to assure the maintenance of minimal standards of light and ventilation and the provision of sanitary facilities and fire escapes for all multiple dwellings. But the restricted accommodations of the four- and five-story dumbbell apartment tenements that spread in conformity with these laws over much of Manhattan created a density unrivaled elsewhere. The worsening conditions could not be overlooked and prompted repeated efforts to find a solution.

The housing aspect of the urbanization process followed a different course in most other cities. Most of the rapidly growing port and industrial cities of the Northeast conducted surveys and enacted regulations that followed New York's lead in some respects, but except for limited districts in Boston, St. Louis, Cincinnati, and Chicago the densities were so much less extreme that the major deficiency was the lack of inspectors to enforce the regulations. Mounting expressions of concern prompted Congress in 1892 to call for an investigation of the slum conditions in sixteen cities, but a last-minute cut in the appropriation limited the survey to the four largest metropolises and produced findings that were promptly outdated by the depression of the mid-nineties.

Philanthropic efforts to supply model housing made more effective gains in Europe, though not without some impetus from the States. Alfred T. White's model apartment projects in New York in the late seventies helped spur the more widespread development of cooperative housing projects in Britain and on the Continent in the next decade. Several German cities began in the nineties to acquire land for housing and open-space use, and the appearance in 1898 of Ebenezer Howard's famous treatise on *Garden Cities of Tomorrow* gave the movement new direction. Although the first dramatic embodiment of the new concepts occurred in England and on the Continent, at Letchworth in 1904 and at Bromma in Sweden in 1908, and would not cross the Atlantic for another two decades, the whole movement had an interesting relation to urban developments in America, as Walter L. Creese has demonstrated. Howard, as it happened, had spent four years in Chicago in the mid-seventies and visited Frederick Law Olmsted's ideal suburban development in Riverside, which was hailed as a revival of Chicago's "Garden City" traditions. On his return to Britain a few years later he had occasion to read Bellamy's *Looking Backward,* which his friend William Morris was asked to review. Impressed by the American's bleak picture of what Boston would become in the year 2000, the two men worked to promote the garden city concept of a new and more satisfactory environment for man.

If Olmsted had a distant influence on the development of the garden city concept, he had a more direct relation to the revival of city planning in America. The spreading fame of his work as the landscape architect of Central Park in New York had brought him commissions to plan parks, cemeteries, and other public grounds in a score of cities from Brooklyn to San Francisco during the next three decades. In addition to Riverside in Chicago, he designed attractive suburbs for Newark and Detroit, and when Chicago was preparing for its inauguration as a major world city at the Columbian Exposition it engaged Olmsted to landscape the fairgrounds. Each world's fair since the first in London over four decades before had served a special urbanizing function. But neither the new conception of enclosed space conveyed by the Crystal Palace at London in 1851, nor the new realization of the popularity of art and museum exhibits acquired at Paris four years later, nor the new potentialities of mechanical instruments displayed in Philadelphia in 1876 had as great an effect on American cities as the lagoons and sculpture courts surrounded by the impressive classical structures of the White City. To millions of visitors from small towns and large cities the memory of hours spent in that charming setting stirred new desires for urban rather than rural opportunities and persuaded many of the possibility of making their cities more attractive.

Daniel Burnham, who shared with Olmsted the chief credit for the White City's form, soon received invitations, along with Olmsted, Sr. and Jr., and others, to draft plans for Cleveland, St. Louis, San Francisco, Detroit, Chicago, Washington, D.C., and numerous other cities. Some of these cities, Detroit and Washington, for example, had originally had plans of great distinction, but everywhere rapid growth and frequent political turnovers had compromised the original design and obliterated many choice features. Thus in the national capital a railroad had cut its way across the Constitutional Mall designed by L'Enfant for Washington before such "improvements" were dreamed of. Fortunately Burnham and his colleagues on the new planning commission were able to secure the railroad's withdrawal into a well-located central station and to restore the basic lines of the L'Enfant design before the capital had reached its first 300,000 residents. With renewed growth Washington would double in size in the next three decades and achieve an urban style that was the envy of many capitals abroad, as well as of some of America's more dynamic industrial cities which failed to attain its balanced proportions. Most of the other American cities, plagued by the needs of their factories, the urgencies of immigrant workers, and the insistent projects of the great railroad magnates on whom they depended, modified or shelved major aspects of their new city plans. Content in some cases with the completion of a new civic center and a new railroad terminal and plaza, as in Cleveland, or with a well-designed park system, as in Kansas City and Minneapolis, many American cities deferred to another date the more difficult tasks of city planning.

Most of the new crop of city plans were, however, little more than two-dimensional drafts prepared by out-of-town experts who had made only superficial studies of the city's needs. Paid for by chambers of commerce and other volunteer groups, they lacked official or political backing and quickly fell apart when challenged by a major utility or other vested interest. They paid little or no attention to the arrival of the skyscrapers.

By the late nineties many American urbanites were looking to the new utilities—the electric trolleys, the telephone and light companies—for escape from the inner-city problems that concerned the more enlightened planners and housers. The exodus to the suburbs that had commenced in the largest metropolitan cities in earlier decades, when steam ferries and trains had made distant commuting possible, now spread to many more cities as the trolley companies extended their lines beyond the city limits to old villages and new subdivisions that rapidly acquired a semiurban status.

Some of the new suburbs were planned as model villages, some as industrial satellites, but the great majority developed as unplanned overspills of central-city inhabitants and represented a new shift in the urbanization process. Even the model tracts, such as Tuxedo Park near New York, by withdrawing able and wealthy residents from involvement in central-city affairs sapped the city's vitality. Model industrial satellites, such as Homestead near Pittsburgh and Pullman near Chicago, dependent on the whims of the joint owner-employers, became demoralized in time and some eventually erupted in violent strikes. The more normal suburbs provided a welcome escape for harried urbanites from the congestion of inner-city districts blighted by commercial or industrial activities and offered the more successful immigrants and their children an opportunity to break loose from ethnic neighborhoods and start afresh in new houses, sometimes as homeowners, in a more evenly mixed environment. The trolleys and, after the turn of the century, the increasingly plentiful automobiles made possible frequent trips back to the old neighborhood and its institutions, but as the suburbs filled up, schools, churches, and stores were required, and the new communities acquired a self-conscious identity that brought dramatic changes in the religious and cultural structures of the larger, now metropolitan, community.

THE ROLE OF THE CHURCHES

A secondary aspect of the urbanization process was the transformation wrought in many traditional institutions. The new responsibilities assumed by the civic and welfare authorities were in part a response, as we have seen, to mounting needs; they also marked the development of a new social consciousness, which was an outgrowth in turn of new religious responses to the problems of the cities. Few institutions experienced more extensive and diversified changes in the process of urbanization than the churches, which continued to play a larger role in American than in European cities.

The most numerous of the several types of churches that served the American city in these decades were the transplanted churches, as Professor Cross has characterized those established by each group of newcomers. Most urban churches had such an origin, and the increasing variety of newcomers of both native and foreign origin, together with the need most of them felt to reestablish familiar bonds in their new setting, assured a steady increase in the number and variety of such churches. Among the Protestant churches of the evangelical type, the pre-Civil War emphasis on recurrent revivals gave way to an increased reliance on Sabbath school and other group-work activities to strengthen their hold on their particular communities. The ethnic churches and synagogues transplanted from the mother countries displayed a similar readiness to organize societies and programs to strengthen the traditions and associations of the newcomers. Products, in a sense, of a transition stage in urban development, the zeal of the leaders of these transplanted churches was often enhanced by the struggle for survival in a changing society.

But the expanding cities presented serious challenges to many traditional churches. Some of the older churches, established by the founders near the center of town, saw their parishioners migrate to more salubrious districts as the city grew, and sold their valuable downtown sites at a profit to build more handsome edifices in new communities on the outskirts. A few of the older Protestant churches retained their original locations and built adjoining social halls, even gymnasiums in some cases, in an effort to serve both the young and the adult new inner-city residents who had replaced their original members, some of whom continued to support their programs. Most of these new institutional churches, as they were called, developed a broad social-gospel approach that emphasized the Christian's responsibility for the welfare of his neighbor of whatever creed. Their leaders helped promote the reform and welfare programs of the progressives and served to quicken the community consciousness of the emerging metropolises.

The downtown Catholic churches and Jewish synagogues were similarly challenged by urban growth, but with different results. Most of the original Catholic churches in American cities had or soon acquired Irish priests, and, although a number of strong German Catholic churches developed in many cities that attracted immigrants from that country, the Irish managed to acquire leadership among the bishops and other members of the hierarchy of the ninety dioceses formed around America's principal regional cities. As Catholic migrants from Italy and eastern Europe increased in number, the inner-city churches, replaced in many cases by cathedrals, endeavored to serve their parishioners drawn from diverse countries by organizing ethnic societies and by naming associate priests to represent the different nationalities. Despite the efforts of some bishops to maintain an integrated parish system throughout their dioceses, the reluctance of many immigrants to attend churches staffed by priests who could not speak their language prompted the establishment of Italian, Polish, and other Catholic churches in the neighborhoods of their concentration. Except for some of the Polish churches, which asserted their independence and organized as Polish national churches, most of these ethnic churches retained their affiliation with the regional Catholic diocese, and, because of the incessant migrations, some dropped their foreign tongue and became in time integrated parish churches.

The Jews had a more divisive experience in American cities. As their original temples, established by the German Jews in pre-Civil War days, responded to the liberalizing trends in Germany and followed the adjustment of many of their members to American ways, new Jewish migrants from eastern Europe in the eighties and after found their services unsatisfactory and established new Orthodox synagogues of their own. Some of the Reform temples, as the liberals were now designated, had been located in inner-city areas that by the nineties were largely occupied by eastern Europeans, and they attempted to supply integrated services and to perform socializing functions similar to those of the institutional churches. But these efforts often aroused the jealousy of the less affluent Orthodox leaders, just as the Protestant programs stirred the indignation of Catholics and Jews who feared their proselytizing effects. A removal to a new site on the outskirts of the city offered a more peaceful course and helped transfer congregational ties to a new and more typically American district. If the removal represented a flight from the inner city, it also helped develop the vitality of other urban neighborhoods within the wide expanse of the emerging metropolis.

Downtown churches of all faiths and denominational leaders whose responsibilities extended beyond their neighborhoods faced grave social problems in these decades. Several religious groups responded directly to specific urban needs. Thus the Salvation Army, introduced from London in 1880, established its barracks on the skid rows of many cities to serve lonely down-and-outers, much as the settlement houses served needy immigrant areas. Earlier YMCAs and YWCAs multiplied and, with Catholic and Jewish youth centers, met the special needs of single young men and women. A variety of Pentecostal tabernacles appeared in most of the cities that attracted migrants from the rural areas of the South and the borderland states, and the emotion-packed testimonials they featured gave opportunity for expression to many unsettled newcomers. The rapid spread of Christian Science churches from their first establishment at Boston in 1875 demonstrated the anxiety many urbanites felt over the health problems created by congested cities.

But no movement aroused the volume of support and opposition engendered by the Anti-Saloon League, the WCTU, and related opponents of the liquor interests. The very mention of the Women's Christian Temperance Union as an influential body marked the increased prominence of women in urban life, a development many European travelers, particularly British ladies, enviously commended. Although the local branches of these earnest champions of a puritanical ethic never matched the number of saloons that catered to the thirsty inhabitants of cities and towns across the land, their success in securing Sunday closing laws and other restraints created enforcement problems that resulted in a continuing struggle in many cities. Deeply involved in this conflict were several related issues. In opposition to the puritanical morality derived from a temperate, middle-class, rural background was the urban workingman's thirst for a glass of beer and desire for the conviviality of the friendly pubs he had known in the old country. Many native middle-class Protestant urbanites supported the prohibition cause, but few foreign-born Catholic workers did, and social prejudices were not far below the surface. Many charity workers were convinced, for example, that drunkenness was a prime source of poverty, and many law-abiding citizens believed it was also a major cause of crime. Every city provided graphic evidence in support of both arguments, which increased in intensity as the decades advanced.

INCREASING URBAN SERVICES

The battle for law and order had several other crucial aspects. As we have noted in earlier chapters, the urban police were undertaking to suppress crimes of violence, incendiarism, and other attacks on property, and to perform these duties more effectively they were enrolling members from local minority groups. This strategy became increasingly important and difficult as the cities attempted to add the force of law to the earlier moral restraints against gambling, vice, and intemperance. Such regulations challenged the mores of varied ethnic groups, and not only accentuated the political pressures on the police, but gave them tasks that many were reluctant to perform. Policemen enrolled from the neighborhoods resented orders from commissioners appointed by state authorities responsive to rural views, and even after New York City regained control of its police in 1870, officers in the ethnic districts, as James F. Richardson has discovered, resisted the efforts of commissioners from the outlying middle-class wards to enforce Sunday closing laws and the like. On the other hand, in Boston, according to Roger Lane, the taxpayers denied adequate support to the police until the state legislature took full control away from the city's Irish-dominated administration.

Few cities were ready in these decades to adopt prohibition laws, but campaigns against vice and organized gambling were widespread and produced stringent municipal ordinances in many places. Unfortunately, in the predominantly male atmosphere of most cities, these practices proved hard to suppress. Not only were the youthful immigrant men, some brought over in work gangs, eager for excitement and quick gains, but many single young men from the small towns and farms of America also longed for companionship. Institutional efforts to meet their needs were nowhere as plentiful in the inner cities as the corner saloons, commercial dance halls, gambling dens, and brothels. In 1880, when the federal census reported on the number of houses of prostitution, it found thirteen cities in which they exceeded one hundred each, most of them cities with an excess of adult men. Except in rapidly growing western cities, such as Minneapolis, Omaha, Seattle, Portland, and San Francisco, and in heavy-industry cities such as Pittsburgh and Chicago, the male predominance had disappeared by 1900, but the number of single men between twenty-five and twenty-nine years of age exceeded the number married in two thirds of all cities over 100,000. The census no longer tabulated brothels, but the problem had not disappeared.

Antivice crusades organized by indignant moralists and antigambling drives by harried police chiefs marked an increased awareness of these problems in midwestern metropolises. Few if any observers as yet saw such behavioral infractions as by-products of the urbanization of rural newcomers, native and foreign. Yet scattered advocates of the social gospel, more urban than their evangelical predecessors, were discovering a significant relationship between the city's social problems and its basic demographic and economic conditions. Thus Walter Rauschenbusch, who conducted a survey of Rochester's social needs for the YMCA in 1904, discovered that local wage rates had denied many young men incomes that would encourage early marriages and that the city's frugality had restrained it from providing playgrounds and gymnastic facilities to supply legitimate outlets for youthful energies. With similar leaders in other cities he called for the correction of these deficiencies and for public support of libraries, galleries, music halls, and other cultural facilities to extend intellectual and artistic opportunities to the many citizens who could not afford to patronize the commercial offerings in these fields.

Many local progressives were promoting similar expansions of urban services. Numerous cities established public libraries and playgrounds and expanded their earlier park systems around the turn of the century. But most American communities, unlike some abroad, relied on volunteer associations for the establishment of art galleries and science museums and for the maintenance of orchestras and choral societies. Yet these and other manifestations of high culture attracted sufficient support to prompt the opening of such institutions and numerous theaters and opera houses in cities large and small. Symphony orchestras staffed by professional musicians made their appearance in a dozen metropolises before 1910, while amateur orchestras by the score supplied opportunities for participants and audiences in numerous other cities. The civic pride engendered by these efforts was surpassed only by that manifested by the crowds that gathered daily during the summer months at the new baseball parks on the outskirts of every city. The successful organization of the National League in 1876 and, after a false start, of a rival American League in 1900 provided the structure for new intercity relationships that were unmatched abroad.

Partly because of their frontier heritage, American cities developed a back-to-nature movement which added new functions to their parks and hinterlands. Animated by an Arcadian myth, as Peter Schmitt describes it, the movement gave a special emphasis to the pastoral landscaping of the city parks and the rustic ornamentation of choice residential subdivisions. European city parks sprang from an older tradition, that of the palatial estates of the local aristocracy, and had favored the renaissance design of formal gardens. A Gothic revival brought new variety and vitality, but of a different kind from that of the frontier in America, where summer camping in rustic cabins in the mountains vied with the more traditional vacation at an ocean beach or lakeside hotel. European urbanites had their resort beaches and their mountain spas, but they did not develop the Boy Scout and Campfire Girl approach to nature and other aspects of the Arcadian myth.

There were many little-understood contrasts between the urbanization of America and that of Europe and other continents. The greater centralization of authority in Europe made possible the development of a sense of national responsibility and firmer controls in the fields of public health, welfare, and police, as well as in the provision of facilities for high and low cultural expression. Yet different countries assumed varying degrees of responsibility that reflected basic aspects of their societies. Thus, while the Catholic church assumed the task of supplying institutional and other provisions for some of the disadvantaged in Latin countries of Europe and South America, the greater diversity of sects and beliefs in England and in central and northern Europe encouraged the development of a variety of religious and other voluntary efforts there, as in the American cities. The awakening social consciousness alerted the national authorities in Europe more readily than in America and produced programs that fell more directly within national fields of action and administration. Britain's relief and public health measures have already been noted; Germany's health and employment insurance programs of the late seventies and after represented another significant response that was geared to national or state action and served to strengthen that authority. The greater central control of banks and of urban fiscal policy in European countries favored more liberal grants of aid and bonding privileges to their cities for local utility developments, parks and theaters, even housing, which facilitated the provision of civic services in cities such as Birmingham and Dusseldorf that no American city could match. More locally oriented and democratic in their approach, the American cities displayed an even more variegated outpouring of voluntary efforts, and as we have seen, generated a Progressive movement that was striving in many ways to tackle the urban problem from the municipal rather than the national level. Education and the schools seemed more important, viewed from that perspective, and temperance, an extension of the suffrage, and the attack on corruption in politics all acquired a relevancy they did not possess in the more centralized societies abroad.

Urban leaders in America were, however, becoming increasingly alert to urban trends abroad. Not only were American artists, architects, and city planners journeying in increasing numbers to European cities to study their techniques and accomplishments, but European opera and theatrical stars and companies were touring American cities and stirring new efforts in many places. Members of the National Municipal League and other officials were making comparative studies of the civic programs and objectives of European and American cities, and after years of graduate study abroad many American professors were returning to revitalize the universities and seminaries in the States, which now supplied opportunities for college training in practically all cities over 100,000 and in many more of lesser size.

Some American scholars were excited to discover that many Europeans were struggling to master urban problems similar to their own and that a few were achieving new insights into old dilemmas. For half a century, as Jean B. Quandt summarizes it, several European social scientists had been

"developing typologies to indicate the contrast between a rural, homogenous, and group-oriented society and an urban, differentiated, and individualistic one. . . . Maine's status versus contract, Spencer's militant versus industrial society, Tönnies' community (Gemeinschaft) versus society (Gesellschaft), Durkheim's mechanical versus organic society, and Simmel's comparison of town and metropolis described a contrast between two types of social organization."[1]

---

1. *From the Small Town to the Great Community* (New Brunswick, N.J.: Rutgers University Press, 1970), p. 18.

Few Americans were familiar with all of these scholars, yet at least three sociologists and a half-dozen other writers were developing similar insights, as Quandt demonstrates, concerning the contrasts between small towns and large cities. But their thinking, as she sees it, was based only in part on that of Europe, and sprang more directly from their experience and interacting development from small town origins into educators and administrators of large communities. Several had by 1910 already played significant urban roles, John Dewey as a creative educator, Jane Addams as an innovative social worker, Frederic C. Howe as an administrator, Charles H. Cooley as a sociologist, but their full contributions to America's awakening consciousness of its urban problems and characteristics would come in later decades.

Table 8.   URBANIZATION AND INDUSTRIALIZATION.*

	1860	1870	1880	1890	1900	1910
Total population *in thousands*	31,443	38,558	50,155	62,947	75,994	91,972
Urban totals *in thousands*	6,212	9,902	14,129	22,106	30,159	41,998
Urban centers	392	663	939	1,348	1,737	2,262
Percent urban	19.8	25.7	28.2	35.1	39.7	45.7
Employed *in thousands*						
in manufacturing	1,930	2,130	3,210	4,620	6,250	82,508
in construction		700	850	1,400	1,640	2,310
in transportation	780	580	850	1,470	2,020	3,200
in trade		850	1,280	2,060	2,870	3,620
Mineral fuels *in trillions of British thermal units*	419	904	1,934	4,225	7,759	15,033
Value of output of finished products *in millions of dollars*		6,732.5	3,472.3	5,116.5	7,296.1	12,731.5
Miles of railroads	30,626	52,922	93,262	166,703	193,346	240,293
Value of imports *in millions of dollars*	363	462	668	789	850	1,557
Value of exports	400	530	836	858	1,394	1,745

*Derived from U.S. Bureau of the Census, *Seventeenth Census: 1950* (Washington, D.C.: U.S. Government Printing Office), *Population* I, Summaries 1–3,5,7,17; U.S. Bureau of the Census, *Historical Statistics of the U.S.* (Washington, D.C.: U.S. Government Printing Office, 1949), pp. 64, 155, 183, 200, 244.

BIBLIOGRAPHY

Cole, Donald B. *Immigrant City: Lawrence, Massachusetts: 1845–1921*. Chapel Hill: University of North Carolina Press, 1963.

Creese, Walter L. *The Search for Environment: The Garden City, Before and After*. New Haven: Yale University Press, 1966.

Cross, Robert D. ed. *The Church and the City: 1865–1910*. Indianapolis: Bobbs-Merrill Co., 1967.

Dean, Warren. *The Industrialization of São Paulo: 1880–1945*. Austin: University of Texas Press, 1969.

Elazar, Daniel J. *Cities of the Prairie*. New York: Basic Books, Inc., 1970.

Kingsbury, Franklin J. "The Tendency of Men to Live in Cities." *U.S. Commissioner of Education Report*, 4 (1894–95), 1282.

Köllmann, Wolfgang. "The Process of Urbanization in Germany at the Height of the Industrialization Period." *Journal of Contemporary History*, 4 (July 1969), 59–76.

McKelvey, Blake. *The Urbanization of America: 1860–1915*. New Brunswick, N.J.: Rutgers University Press, 1963.

Morse, Richard M. "The Lima of Joaquin Capelo: A Latin American Archetype." *Journal of Contemporary History*, 4 (July 1969), 95–110.

Nelli, Humbert S. *The Italians in Chicago: 1880–1930: A Study in Ethnic Mobility*. New York: Oxford University Press, 1970.

Osofsky, Gilbert. *Harlem: The Making of a Ghetto: Negro New York, 1890–1930*. New York: Harper & Row, Publishers, 1965.

Quandt, Jean B. *From the Small Town to the Great Community*. New Brunswick, N.J.: Rutgers University Press, 1970.

Richardson, James F. *The New York Police: Colonial Times to 1901*. New York: Oxford University Press, 1970.

Rischin, Moses. *The Promised City: New York's Jews, 1870–1914*. Cambridge, Mass.: Harvard University Press, 1962.

Schmitt, Peter J. *Back to Nature: The Arcadian Myth in Urban America*. New York: Oxford University Press, 1969.

Thernstrom, Stephan. "Urbanization, Migration, and Social Mobility in Late Nineteenth Century America." In *Towards a New Past*, ed. B. J. Bernstein. New York: Random House, Inc., 1968.

Warner, Sam B., and Colin B. Burke. "Cultural Change and the Ghetto." *Journal of Contemporary History*, 4 (October 1969), 173–87.

PART THREE

Urbanization in an Age of Metropolitanism, 1910 to the Present

The urbanization of America entered a new stage in the second decade of the twentieth century. The frontier and merchant cities scattered across the continent in the course of its settlement had undergone an extensive transformation in response to the new industrial technology introduced from England in the middle 1800s. Many had become industrial specialists, and together they had finally surpassed in number, rate of urbanization, and productivity the older cities of both Britain and the Continent. But the momentum of their growth, the broad and still challenging expanse of their natural environment, and the accelerating innovations of their technology were now combining in the early decades of the twentieth century to effect a breakthrough to a new stage of urbanization on a larger community scale best described as metropolitan regionalism.

Numerous circumstances peculiar to North America contributed to this development, which in its turn brought three important consequences. The century-long migration of newcomers to America, peopling an ever widening network of cities, was finally brought to a virtual halt by World War I and the immigrant restriction acts that followed. Relieved of that pressure but confronted at the same time with the problem of staffing their expanding industries, the cities of the North accepted the task of absorbing new migrants from the rural South and found themselves increasingly engaged during the next four decades in a nationwide realignment of the population. Tied by the race issue to the nation's historic task of redeeming its democratic pledge, the expanding metropolises found themselves increasingly dependent on federal assistance to meet their mounting costs without imposing tax increases that would drive choice functions outside their limits. They also turned to federal authorities for aid in achieving an effective metropolitan polity, a struggle still in process.

These were all slow historical developments. In the twenties an increasingly abundant output of automobiles enabled many urbanites to venture for the first time on exciting trips into the surrounding countryside, and encouraged many of them to move out into new suburban settlements. Pressed to provide improved facilities for travel, communication, and other services, several metropolises launched regional planning programs to supervise their expansion. But these early efforts to organize the emerging metropolitan regions were suddenly halted by the outbreak of the Great Depression in 1929. Disillusioned by the unexpected breakdown of the private economy and denied the authority to enlist the full energies of their regions, many frustrated urban leaders turned for aid and leadership to the federal authorities, who in the long dark years of the depression experimented with new measures to rejuvenate the cities and restore their productive energies. The halting and indecisive character of this effort failed to achieve a full recovery, however, until the outbreak of World War II created a new unity and determination, which prompted and gave sanction to a succession of federal-city programs that produced a burst of productivity and renewed urban and metropolitan growth.

The postwar years brought an increasing recognition of the need for federal-city cooperation and a steady expansion in its application. Both internal and external factors sped these developments. A new flood of migrants from the South displaced the earlier immigrants and transformed their ethnic neighborhoods into black ghettos that hastened the flight of central-city residents to the suburbs. Pleas for federal assistance in the provision of housing and other welfare programs and for federal guarantees of proportionate representation for the cities and federal enforcement of the civil rights of their minorities brought responses that gradually gave birth to a new metropolitan federalism, which has great potentialities for the future course of urbanization in America.

The new metropolitan regionalism contrasted with the earlier era of urban industrialization in several important respects. Most metropolises lost the high degree of specialization they had previously attained as commercial centers or industrial cities and developed instead a wide assortment of functions and activities—commercial, industrial, social, and cultural. All endeavored to expand their civic services and extend their political influence over their metropolitan regions, and into the state and national capitals as well. Although the struggle to secure integrated metropolitan polities made little headway, the precedence of civic interests over private corporate interests became more widely recognized. Citizens as well as municipal leaders began to look to the universities and other groups of scholars not only for technological innovations in industrial production, but also for administrative breakthroughs and social programs that would make possible higher standards of community living. A rising determination to check the pollution of air and water in metropolitan districts reflected a new concern for the urban ecology and represented a realistic approach to the regional setting, as well as to the problems of the city. These multiple developments, plus a quickening interest among social scientists in urban studies, attested to the vitality of metropolitan regionalism.

Although metropolitan developments in the United States were for the most part indigenous, a glance beyond the nation's borders revealed a widespread upsurging of large and expanding cities and many dramatic efforts at their reorganization. Indeed, the forms of government developed by Toronto and numerous other cities surpassed in rational design and often in efficiency those attained by American metropolises, and the contrasts were revealing as to the nature of urbanization in the various countries. As American scholars and other reformers became aware of the larger responsibilities assumed by central governments abroad, they pressed for the development of new urban-federal relationships in the States while endeavoring to retain a larger degree of local initiative.

If the American metropolis lacked some of the structural formality and orderliness of many cities abroad, its dynamic vitality was unabated. While the urbanization of the United States had originally been based in considerable part on the abundant natural resources of a virgin continent, assisted by the settlers' will and talents to develop them, the human factor had finally assumed the major role. In civic matters a democratic and widely participatory tradition had an early origin and gained new force with each generation. The true economic base of a great metropolis, as Wilbur R. Thompson has put it, lies in

"the creativity of its universities and research parks, the sophistication of its engineering firms and financial institutions, the persuasiveness of its public relations and advertising agencies, and the other dimensions of infrastructure that facilitate the quick and orderly transfer from old dying bases to new growing ones."[1]

Other national systems of cities have developed some of these qualities, but few can rival the profusion of energies released in several of America's leading metropolitan regions.

---

1. As quoted by Corinne Gilb in her "Urban History and Comparative National History: Some Common Questions and Points of Congruence" (paper delivered at the AHA meetings in 1970), p. 48.

8

The Growth
of Metropolitan
Regionalism

The vitality of the urbanization process was demonstrated in the 1920s as the mushrooming cities, not content simply to grow in size, acquired a new relationship with their hinterlands. Most of the major metropolises had originally developed as commercial and promotional centers of large frontier districts, and several of them, faced by aggressive rivals, had progressively improved their water and rail facilities in order to defend or extend their territories. To further strengthen their position some had introduced processing and fabricating industries that directly served their districts, and others, such as Boston and New York, had backed the establishment of such industrial ventures at outlying natural power sites within their commercial spheres. These industrial centers had in their turn achieved an independent vitality, based in part on the broader contacts soon formed with technological developments elsewhere, and in part on the search for wider markets. But if some of the industrial cities, such as Lowell and Paterson, had started with slight dependence on their regions, except for the water power of their respective rivers, and if some former merchant cities, such as Rochester, had forgotten their original regional relationships as new industrial activities absorbed their attention, all of those that experienced continued growth were now discovering a new interest in their immediate neighborhoods. Indeed, the distinguishing characteristic of the new metropolitan regionalism was to be the progressive urbanization of entire regions, a process in which American cities took a distinct lead.

THE EXPANDING METROPOLIS

Many forces contributed to the evolution of a new metropolitan regionalism. Increasing demands for fresh food supplies and improved knowledge of the health hazards involved made all growing cities more enterprising in extending highways and other utilities into their regional hinterlands and in applying health regulations and other safeguards throughout their expanding milk and produce basins. As the obnoxious city cowbarns and the suburban truck patches, which in industrial cities had displaced the family cows and backyard gardens of earlier village days, gave way in turn to the more widely scattered and more progressively managed dairies and vegetable farms that brought a new surge of prosperity to the agricultural districts surrounding all emerging metropolises, so the former vacant-lot ballfields and the creek and river fishing and swimming holes appropriated by the expanding cities for other uses were replaced not only by commercial ball diamonds and public parks and playgrounds, but also by suburban amusement resorts and numerous lakeside and riverbank cottages and camps. Urbanites, who since the arrival of the steam trains had seen the neighboring countryside only from a speeding window as they journeyed to distant cities and in some cases to foreign resorts, now were able to ride the suburban electrics on frequent visits to nearby villages. Increasing numbers explored the neighboring valleys in their newly acquired automobiles. Metropolitan auto clubs took the lead in erecting road signs at rural crossings to help their members find their way through the strange territory and pressured the county and state governments to improve and eventually to pave their roads.

Most growing cities had for decades made successive annexations of adjoining tracts to accommodate their overflow. The desire of the suburban migrants for city services—water and sewer mains, transit and electric lines— had generally assured quick passage of such bills in the past, but the development and wide use of economical septic tanks in the early 1900s and the invention of well-drilling machines gave suburban residents a greater sense of self-sufficiency. Privately owned utilities were eager to serve them as soon as their number justified the necessary extensions, and in fact many electric light and telephone companies rushed speculative lines into sparsely settled territories when rival companies from other cities threatened an invasion. Some utility leaders and other promoters acquired large tracts near transit and power lines and laid out speculative subdivisions to accommodate urban migrants seeking a rural retreat. As this process of uncontrolled expansion quickened in the teens with the multiplication of privately owned autombiles, and redoubled as the number of migrants mounted in the twenties when the invention and wide use of radio brought them additional self-sufficiency, suburban resistance to annexation mounted and the need to develop some form of broader metropolitan planning or control became increasingly insistent.

Several of the major metropolises had met this problem in earlier days by absorbing suburban cities, as in the case of Philadelphia in 1854 and New York in 1898, or by the consolidation of city and county functions, as in New Orleans in 1874 and to a limited degree in Boston several times. But most of these solutions were soon outgrown, and Boston, hemmed in by the arms of its bay and by the restraints of its commonwealth, found itself in 1910 a city of 670,000, which, however, was only 43 percent of its metropolitan total—easily the smallest ratio of any central city in the nation. It was little wonder that Boston should have taken the lead that year in an effort to promote areawide planning for community development throughout its metropolitan district. With Edward A. Filene, its leading retail merchant, in the chair and John Nolan as chief planning consultant, the temporary commission appointed by the governor prepared to create a metropolitan regional planning board that would have promoted and coordinated the development of the greater Boston district had it not failed to secure the suburban support necessary for its adoption. Pittsburgh, the eighth city in size that year but with a metropolitan district that was twice its population and fifth in size, would make the next concerted attempt to secure metropolitan organization, though not for another two decades and only after other significant developments had occurred.

The suburban rings about Boston and Pittsburgh, like those about Manhattan and old London, resulted from a combination of geographic and transportation developments. In these and numerous other cities, as ferries and bridges had spanned rivers and other water barriers, and as steamboats and trains had replaced the earlier sailboats and horse-drawn omnibuses, the first ring of suburban settlements had experienced a surge of growth surpassing that of the central cities. D. A. Reeder has described such developments in London in the midnineteenth century and Peter Knights those in Boston in the same decades. With the introduction of electric transit in the nineties, a second and third ring of suburbs developed, and each in turn enjoyed a burst of growth partly at the expense of the inner-city districts. The rings of travel zones were not uniform throughout, for often broad sectors, as Sam Warner tells us of Philadelphia, were mixed industrial and ethnic residential, continuing the functional and other characteristics of adjoining tracts of the older city. The geographic features of the site greatly influenced if they did not determine the special combination of sector and ring patterns for each metropolis. The full potentialities of the outer rings awaited the arrival of the automobile in great numbers in the 1920s.

Yet as the central cities fell behind the suburbs in population growth, they acquired new economic and social functions and undertook a dramatic reconstruction of their business districts. The high-rise office buildings erected in Chicago, New York, and elsewhere in the 1890s multiplied after the turn of the century. As the ninety skyscrapers of ten and more stories in 1910 increased fivefold in the next two decades, New York, and to a lesser degree Chicago, acquired spectacular new skylines that dwarfed the steeples and other institutional towers of the traditional urban landscape. These and a dozen other American metropolises with towering skyscrapers at their cores presented a startling appearance to visitors from abroad, as well as to those from the surrounding countryside. They also presented new transportation problems and a direct challenge to the automobile, which vied with rapid transit for urban priority.

Only New York, Boston, and Chicago had built both elevateds and subways to assure rapid service in their congested downtown districts. Philadelphia had a subway, plus frequent commuter trains on its major rail lines, and several metropolises had commuter service over the interurban electric lines that had begun to fan out from the central cities in the early 1900s. But the rapid increase in the number of automobiles during the twenties checked the development of such transit services. Detroit led the way in 1929 by rejecting the construction of a subway and turning instead to the building of an improved highway system, and Rochester and other hubs of interurban networks saw their suburban lines collapse as the states extended highway improvements out from the ends of the principal urban thoroughfares.

No other physical agent could match the automobile in its influence on the development of the metropolis in America. Based in part on inventions abroad, where the first machines were built, the automobile found its most enthusiastic acceptance and its most congenial habitat in America. As in the case of machine production with steam power, where the factory system and the industrial city were the more significant developments, as Lampard has maintained, so with the automobile it was not the internal combustion engine or even the assembly line system of production perfected by Henry Ford, but the social responses and the new metropolitan patterns fostered by the automobile that constituted the more important innovations. As the number of motor vehicles increased from 25,000 in 1905 to 900,000 in 1915, and to eight million cars and one million trucks by 1920, automobiles were transformed from the mechanical toys of wealthy sportsmen into the horseless carriages of all urbanites who yearned for a home on the city's outskirts, or for an opportunity to visit and enjoy its environs. As the number of automobiles multiplied in the twenties, reaching a peak of 23,000,000 cars, 3,400,000 trucks, and 40,000 buses by 1929, the number of migrants to the suburbs likewise increased and their rate of growth for the first time doubled that of the central cities. Even more significant, as Sam Warner emphasizes, was the development of specialized suburbs as the automobile enabled both the wealthy and those of more modest circumstances to find congenial neighborhoods. Thus some of the melding influences of the old central cities were lost as metropolitan expansion occurred.

The rapidly growing affluent suburbs and urbanized farmsteads of American cities were strikingly absent from most expanding metropolises abroad. In Japan, where a half-dozen mushrooming metropolises were developing in an urban belt linking the tidewater districts along the southern edge of its main island, steam and electric railroads conncected clusters of closely settled industrial satellites, each with narrow, winding pedestrian roads lined with one-family buildings. This sprawling matrix of indigenous towns surrounded the central metropolitan cities, where Western, largely American and German, influences and urban styles predominated. No other nation rivaled the rapidity and intensity of Japan's urban industrial growth in the twenties, when Tokyo and Yokohama grew into a vast conurbation of six million inhabitants, challenging London's claim to second place. Several cities in Germany and Russia were spreading into industrial suburbs linked to the center by electric and steam trains, but most of these districts retained aspects of the rural life that persisted beyond their borders. No period in Russia's history saw as rapid a growth of new and old cities as the Soviets achieved in the thirties largely by virtue of industrial expansion, as Chauncy Harris has shown, but their residential provisions were widely neglected. And in Latin America and Southeast Asia vast settlements comprised of makeshift dwellings were developing on the outskirts of several old primate cities as new migrations of landless natives descended on the cities. Metropolitan growth in the Latin American countries for the first time rivaled in numbers and problems that of the more dynamic cities north of the Rio Grande, but not in productivity or spatial expanse, and the success of the Latin cities in absorbing their rural migrants was minimal.

The impact of the automobile on the structure of the American city was far reaching. It drove private carriages from the avenues of wealthy residents and created an effective demand for the displacement of macadam by asphalt pavement on the principal streets and on the roads to nearby suburbs and resorts. As the number of cars and trucks increased, displacing horses in the downtown streets, the movement of traffic accelerated. The introduction in the late twenties of motorbuses able to use alternate routes relieved congestion on the principal trolley routes. But as the number of vehicles mounted congestion returned and more accidents occurred. Citizen protests prompted the organization of local safety councils and spurred the cities to enact ordinances limiting the speed of automobiles and restricting their parking, and also to erect traffic lights for the control of their movement. The experimental introduction of these and other regulations by one city or another spread rapidly. Shortly after New York installed the first manually controlled traffic lights in 1922, Philadelphia introduced automatic controls, and Cleveland later synchronized them for moving traffic. Numerous cities banned parking on their principal streets, and Boston was the first to collect a fee for standing privileges on side streets, but another decade passed before Oklahoma City produced the first parking meter. Kansas City in 1924 created the pioneer shopping center with an adjoining lot for customer parking, and Detroit built the first ramp garage four years later. A St. Paul planner developed and displayed the first traffic-density map in support of his recommendations in 1923, but the needs of that city were moderate compared with those of Detroit, which a year later first proposed a network of divided highways to serve its suburbs and soon secured the extension beyond its limits of Woodward Avenue, in accordance with that plan, to test its practicability.

The automobile had a special impact on cities actively engaged in its production. Detroit, the motor capital, increased 126 percent during the teens, a ratio second only to that of much smaller Akron, the tire capital, which experienced a growth of 173 percent. Other rapid growers included Los Angeles and Houston, both oil producers. And in the next decade, when the emphasis shifted from car production to the exploitation of its use and to the development of other recreational potentialities, Los Angeles, with its congenial climate, its spacious layout, and its Pacific beaches, took second place in rate of growth only to Miami, the Florida resort center. Both reported exceptionally high ratios of auto registrations to families. Moreover, Los Angeles County, despite the deserved fame of the city's model transit system, embarked in the midtwenties on the planning of a highway system that rivaled even that under construction in Detroit. Both Los Angeles and Detroit annexed additional tracts in these decades, but saw their outlying suburbs grow still more rapidly. Indeed, most of the cities in the 100,000 bracket that enjoyed substantial gains in the twenties saw their suburbs outpace them.

HOUSING AND REGIONAL PLANNING

These growth rates and the shifting directions they took reflected significant changes, too, in the character of the urban population. The flood of immigrants that had for decades supplied the major source of urban growth was sharply checked by World War I, which reduced the number of newcomers from a peak of 1,218,480 in 1914 to 326,700 the next year. American cities had absorbed a million immigrants a year in the early teens, and the sudden reduction to less than 250,000 annually for the rest of the decade forced heavy-industry cities that relied on an influx of workers to seek other sources. St. Louis and Chicago, Cincinnati and Cleveland, Philadelphia and Pittsburgh, all attracted a new stream of blacks from the South to help man their heavy industries. Like the foreign-born before them, most of the poor blacks settled in the old inner-city districts from which the offspring of former immigrants were already moving. Their arrival frequently aroused the hostility of those who remained. Destructive antiblack riots erupted in East St. Louis in 1917 and in Chicago two years later, and lesser disturbances occurred in other cities that drew many newcomers from the South.

The end of the war brought a renewed influx of immigrants. Their numbers mounted to over 800,000 in 1921, more than a fourth of them from Italy. The poverty of these refugees and the radical views some brought from eastern Europe, where the Russian revolution was making startling headway, produced a "Red scare" that disrupted ethnic relations in many cities and hastened the passage of the immigrant restriction acts of 1922 and 1924. These measures sharply reduced the number of foreigners admitted annually and gave preference to those from Britain and western Europe.

The immigration acts dealt the final blow to the old ethnic neighborhoods in many cities. Denied adequate replacements for those who moved out, the high-density districts saw their economy threatened, and landlords with vacant houses and tenements were persuaded to rent to any applicants—a situation that permitted blacks from the South to find lodgings in the inner-city ghettos. Their arrival sped the migration of the foreign-born to the outskirts. Many moved on to the suburbs, achieving a spatial diffusion that marked a triumph of the assimilation process. Industrial suburbs attracted blacks, too, and in the southern cities, notably Memphis and Birmingham, blacks predominated in the outer districts of the metropolis. Their presence there, as that of blacks and Indians on the periphery of Latin American cities, could easily be overlooked, but in the northern cities, where their increasing numbers were transforming old immigrant ghettos into black belts, new problems of housing and welfare were emerging.

The major housing problem, at first principally one of shortages, was not in fact new, nor was it confined to American cities. Many cities in Britain and western Europe had long been afflicted with crowded and antiquated housing and some had assumed the task of building new houses to meet their needs. The acute shortages in several British industrial cities during the war had prompted the government to launch a large-scale housing program, which supplied a precedent for a move by the United States government to build homes for shipbuilders and other workers in several rapidly expanding war-production centers. Several of America's leading architects had helped plan the projects authorized in forty cities. Only a few were completed before the war ended, however, notably a model settlement of permanent housing in Bridgeport, Connecticut, and fifteen "wooden city" temporary projects at scattered war-plant sites. Despite the pleas of urban reformers and planners that America follow Britain's example and create a federal authority to build houses for workingmen in cities faced with a short supply, the Wilson administration, eager to surrender its war powers, hastened to sell its wartime housing projects and turn such problems back to the cities and states.

The wartime experience had alerted an increasing number of officials and other citizens to the housing problem. Several of the men who had met to organize the National Planning Association in 1909 called a separate meeting the next year to form the National Housing Association. Lawrence Veiller, who had led the battle for a revision of the tenement house laws on New York City, became the principal leader of the association and the editor of its journal, *Housing Betterment,* in which he advocated the reform and enforcement of housing codes and a reliance on private enterprise and philanthropy in the construction and management of housing. He applauded the efforts of reformers in other cities who organized better housing associations to promote code revisions and enforcement and to sponsor the construction of limited divided housing projects for workingmen. Veiller commended the garden city movement in England, but noted the difficulties encountered by an effort in Massachusetts to build public housing, and vigorously opposed advocates of such projects elsewhere.

Urban leaders in America continued during the twenties to rely for the most part on private and volunteer efforts in planning and housing. Chambers of commerce and other interested groups in more than a score of cities engaged one or more of the leading planners to draw up comprehensive plans for their communities, which were duly published and circulated as educational guides to prospective developers. In a few cities, most notably Chicago, the city councils gave official sanction to the proposed plans, though the binding power of their provisions remained in doubt. But New York City, confronted with the prospect of a wave of unrestricted new construction, established in 1916 comprehensive zones and standards that at least prescribed height and use restrictions. The New York zoning ordinance, which carried precedents set in Germany and elsewhere a long step forward, served as an incentive for the adoption of zoning regulations in most cities as this negative aspect of planning gained rapid acceptance in the next ten years.

Favorable decisions upholding zoning ordinances encouraged some city planners to undertake more positive measures. Official planning commissions, introduced in Hartford in 1907, appeared in most of the leading metropolises during the next decade, but the limited size of the planning staffs checked their effectiveness. Several of the professional planners—Olmsted, Nolan, Harland Bartholomew, and others—who served as expert consultants to local boards or commissions requested information concerning the economic and social aspects of the city under review, but few staffs could provide it. Some turned for assistance to the bureaus of municipal research established in more than a score of cities by business groups interested in collecting accurate data to assure civic efficiency. A few of these research bodies and the citizen study committees of the more activistic city clubs and independent survey groups stressed the need for more positive planning than that concerned chiefly with street maps, the location of public buildings, and zoning. Several of these local studies recommended plans to promote wholesome residential neighborhoods by the location of schools, playgrounds, parks, and public utilities to serve their inhabitants. A few saw the need for more far-reaching regional planning.

After the defeat of Boston's efforts to achieve a regional organization, a full decade slipped by before a movement started in New York to promote regional planning. Backed by the Russell Sage Foundation and headed by Charles D. Norton, a previous supporter of the Burnham plan for Chicago, the privately organized New York Regional Plan Association engaged the services of Thomas Adams, a distinguished planner from Britain, to supervise the preparation of a master plan for the greater New York region. The announcement of that project and of a list of planners engaged to help develop the economic, physical, social, and legal aspects of the plan spurred leaders in other metropolises to similar efforts, as described in admirable detail by Mell Scott. Chicago planners were busy implementing aspects of the Burnham plan, but its City Club, eager for broader action, pressed for the creation of a private regional planning association to safeguard recreational and other regional resources beyond the city limits. Los Angeles staged regional planning conferences in several suburban cities and secured their aid in persuading the county to organize a regional planning commission to coordinate their planning efforts. Minneapolis and St. Paul, Milwaukee, Buffalo, and Washington saw the start of regional planning efforts in 1924, and the next year brought similar moves by private groups in Cincinnati, San Francisco, and Philadelphia. The City Club of Philadelphia, recalling that William Penn had been the first regional planner, assembled interested officials and business leaders from all localities within a thirty-mile radius to form the Regional Planning Federation of the Philadelphia Tri-State District. Boston continued to rely on its regional park, water, and sewer special-district commissions, appointed by the state, and both Cleveland and Detroit undertook special-district planning.

But in the opinion of Professor Thomas H. Reed of the University of Michigan, regional planning without the power to act would not meet the needs of expanding metropolises. His study of metropolitan organization abroad pointed up the necessity for more positive measures. On his advice Pittsburgh drafted a charter for a metropolitan federation that would unite 124 urban and regional communities into one municipality with full responsibility for planning and other mutual functions, while the cities and boroughs retained jurisdiction over local matters. However, the state legislature, dominated by rural representatives, amended the bill authorizing this action to require a two-thirds vote in a majority of the communities involved, with the result that an intransigent minority was able to block its adoption.

Meanwhile, the New York Regional Plan had finally reached completion after the expenditure, over a period of seven years, of the million-dollar subsidy granted by the Russell Sage Foundation. In addition to wide praise, it drew criticism from some who were dissatisfied with its centralizing tendencies. A few objected specifically to the priorities it gave to rail and highway improvements designed to make it convenient to enter and leave Manhattan from suburbs within a fifty-mile radius. Others protested the densities permitted and actually encouraged by the plan, which some maintained should instead have checked the growth of the great metropolis by encouraging the development of new, independent communities beyond the New York region. Lewis Mumford, champion of a regional plan recently drafted for Governor Smith by Henry Wright which proposed the development of a chain of urban communities stretching across the state, deplored the efforts of New York to plan for its own continued growth. Thomas Adams, in reply, noted Mumford's endorsement of the model community under development by Wright and Clarence Stein in Radburn, New Jersey, located well within the New York region to assure its success. He defended his attempt to make the great metropolis more agreeable to the many millions who wanted to live and work there.

A similar debate as to the proper size and structure of large metropolitan cities was underway in Europe. Few cities abroad had yet experienced the traffic problems or the densities of high-rise office buildings that already confronted the leading metropolises in America, but several were troubled by a shroud of smoke similar to that which darkened Pittsburgh, Chicago, and several other industrial cities in the States, prompting the creation of boards to deal with "atmospheric sanitation." Numerous cities on the Continent, experiencing new growth after the return of peace—Dusseldorf and Stuttgart in Germany, Lyons in France, and Stockholm in Sweden—were making new advances in planning and housing, in some cases on a regional basis. But in England the two garden cities of Letchworth and Welwyn were making only slow progress because of their failure to attract local industry, while London continued to expand. Nowhere had the planners clearly demonstrated a capacity to check the growth of the great metropolises.

Planners in England and on the Continent had both municipal and national authority behind them—a great advantage over most planners in the States—but they lacked the economic power available only to socialist planners in Russia and other authoritarian countries. American cities relied almost wholly on private enterprise in the commercial and industrial fields, and although by the 1920s the nation's economy was being increasingly drawn into large corporate organizations, many were intercity in scope, with plants in several places, and felt little incentive to establish and control large company towns. Diversified commercial and industrial interests supplied most cities with a booming economy, and their competitive goals assured an animated civic dialogue which, however, seriously handicapped American city planners in comparison with many abroad.

BOOM AND DEPRESSION

Unlike urban trends in Europe, planning in America continued to rely in large part on private efforts. Private enterprise could, for example, promote the development of a specialized industrial city into a regional metropolis and engender a sense of communitywide identity and loyalty, but it could not, as we have seen, achieve civic unity throughout that area. Some corporate groups helped determine the extent and define the boundaries of each metropolis. Gas and electric, telephone, and transit companies, by extending their services beyond the city limits, bound an inner ring of suburbs to the central city. The metropolitan dailies, which after the development of trucking service reached out to distribute their more voluminous editions into outlying hamlets, helped capture a wider regional market for their urban advertisers. Radio and later TV stations readily dispatched their programs across political boundaries, but except in cases of closely spaced rival cities generally confined their broadcasting to the metropolitan district. Each of the leading metropolises endeavored to maintain a major league ball club with which sports fans throughout the area could identify while they supported the efforts of local teams to win regional contests. The wide distribution of the country's natural resources and the diffusion of enterprise had in the course of the preceding two centuries produced a network of cities clustered around the more dynamic metropolitan giants. Each urban center performed a variety of economic and other functions depending on the size and character of its hinterland and on the channels of trade and communication it had developed with other major and minor centers. All were bound by various economic ties in a national system centered at New York.

But New York's economic sway was no longer clear-cut and undisputed. Not only had foreign trade been vastly overshadowed by local industry and internal trade, but by the late twenties even the flood of immigrants through its portals had been reduced to a trickle. New York's metropolitan population continued to mount, but after 1930 it barely equaled the total of its closest two rather than three rivals. Only in the fields of banking and communications was it still supreme, and even there, especially in banking, challengers were arising. Neither Boston nor Philadelphia had ever quite surrendered their original status in the early national period as independent banking centers, and as Chicago and St. Louis grew to become dominant centers of internal trade in the 1880s, their bankers, too, were granted central reserve auxiliary status. Mounting complaints among urban bankers throughout the country against the weaknesses of the National Banking System finally brought a drastic reorganization by the Wilson administration, which in 1914 created the Federal Reserve System, with twelve theoretically equal reserve centers scattered in regional cities across the country. Although the boundaries of these reserve districts included a far larger area than any of the designated centers could claim as its proper hinterland, the naming of one or more additional cities within each district as subcenters was further recognition of the emerging pattern of metropolitan regions.

Except for New York, which still retained its luster as the principal banking center, and the two rising metropolises in the South, Atlanta and Dallas, few of the reserve centers or their subbranches relied heavily on banking for their regional influence. Each had a special combination of functions of regional or national importance, and some shared New York's other specialty as a communication center. But New York, with its newspapers and publishing companies, was also the nerve center of the press bureaus and the new radio networks, and the combined storehouse and creative studio of both audio and visual arts. Thus retaining its vitality as the nation's leading metropolis, it eagerly pressed mounting claims to world leadership. Like greater London, which it finally surpassed in population in the midtwenties, New York was a rapid-transit metropolis. Yet the dramatic technological changes brought by the automobile, the airplane, and the radio did not stall its development, though they more actively promoted the fortunes of some regional metropolises.

But New York, along with the other American metropolises, lacked the political and civic integration with its region that many metropolises abroad enjoyed. That deficiency had appeared marginal in view of the marvelous economic productivity that the widely extended system of cities, each with more or less specialized functions, seemed to make possible. Technological advances promoted by competitive innovators in many rival cities, each endeavoring to improve its industrial proficiency in order to fulfill its regional functions and to reach out to national markets, had achieved unprecedented increases in output. Although the nation's industrial workers had increased only from thirty-seven to forty-seven million from 1914 to 1929, the value of its exports, according to Colin Clark, had mounted more than twice as rapidly as that of its imports, which were now overshadowed. Unfortunately, the surging productivity required responsive markets, and in spite of the tremendous strides made in advertising, a field in which American cities, according to Wilbert Moore, exceeded all others, fears of the inadequacy of the demand began to grow in the late twenties. Whether because of the curtailment of local markets resulting from declining real wages, or the restriction of foreign markets produced by unfavorable exchange rates, or for totally different causes that economic historians have yet to elucidate, the confidence displayed by the industrial leaders of most American cities in the twenties suddenly disappeared following the stock market crash of 1929, and the loss of nerve precipitated a worldwide depression.

An intriguing question for urban economists is the possible causal relationship to the depression of the transition from the industrial to the metropolitan stage of urbanization. Most of the industrial cities were in fact becoming less exclusively industrial and more service oriented, but were they devoting sufficient energies to their new function to make it a sustaining market? Had privatism, as Sam Warner argues, sapped the capacity of cities to master their problems, or was their inability to enlist the full resources of their regions, including those of migrants to the suburbs, in a cooperative effort at balanced metropolitan development proving to be an economic as well as a civic liability? Whether as cause or result, the urbanization process experienced a sudden jolt and assumed a new direction with the onset of the depression.

Yet at the start American cities faced the crisis with a self-confidence born of the Progressive era. The research bureaus, city clubs, and good government leagues had promoted a number of charter reforms designed to safeguard the honesty and increase the efficiency of municipal government. Many cities had followed the leads of Galveston, Texas, and Dayton, Ohio, which under dramatic circumstances had substituted the commission and the council-manager forms of government, respectively, for the politically dominated boards of aldermen to achieve more effective administrations. The prominent citizens willing to serve for a term or two as commissioners with large powers, or as members of a small council to work with a professionally trained manager, had brought many improvements in the tone and performance of municipal affairs to such cities as Cleveland, Cincinnati, Kansas City, Rochester, and a hundred others that adopted these reform charters. Some of their leaders maintained that science and technology, not politics, were needed for the solution of traffic problems, road and sewer construction, water purification, and garbage reduction. Many European, particularly German, cities had long relied on expert administrators chosen by councils on which business leaders enjoyed a heavy representation. But in the large metropolises in the States, where new decisions were also called for in housing and planning, among other matters, the nonpartisan approach offered little advantage, and Cleveland, unable because of its nonpartisan administration to exert political pressure in the state legislature in behalf of its proposed regional planning board, abandoned the manager form after a brief trial for the strong-mayor system.

Cleveland's difficulty was not so much the fault of its nonpartisan government as of its underrepresentation at the state capital. As was the case with most metropolises, its citizens had an inadequate voice in the legislature, where ten Cleveland voters were outweighed by one from Ohio's smallest county. Cleveland readopted a strong mayor charter and secured authority to develop a county park system, but it failed to win reapportionment. Boston, Pittsburgh, Chicago, and several other metropolises got the power to create regional authorities to develop area parks, water and sewer systems, and port and bridge improvements beyond their limits, but their repeated requests for increased taxing powers were blocked in the rural-dominated state legislatures, and every move for reapportionment in the late twenties was defeated. The only course open to expanding cities seeking improvements was to float bonds. And when a tax league in mushrooming Detroit attacked that policy, the Detroit Bureau of Governmental Research defended it in a report revealing that the city's accumulating debts were overbalanced by the value of the improvements for which they had been appropriated. Several other bureaus compiled similar reports in the late twenties, and the cities appeared in a sound position until the faltering bankers closed all sources of credit in 1929 and plunged the nation into a deep depression.

The cities of America had developed still another important agency during the twenties, the local community chests, to which many now turned for assistance. These volunteer bodies had assumed the task of raising the funds needed to meet the annual budgets of charitable institutions in cities across the land. The enthusiasm and community spirit they generated had strengthened the confidence of many cities, and at the onset of the depression some chests, such as that in Rochester, hastily scheduled a second drive in 1930 to meet the needs of relief agencies for a supplementary budget. A Citizens' Committee on Employment formed in Cincinnati the year before supplied the model for similar committees in Detroit, Cleveland, Rochester, and elsewhere that rallied the forces of the local community to meet the depression. Their efforts to tabulate the number of the unemployed, to round up temporary jobs for them, to establish training programs, to promote and finance home improvements, and to organize and administer relief programs represented an assumption of community responsibility on a scale unprecedented in America's urban history. But the inability of private agencies to meet the challenges of a great depression were clearly revealed when the community chests of America, at President Hoover's request, conducted a united drive in the fall of 1931 that raised a total of nearly eighty-five million dollars, which quickly proved hopelessly inadequate to meet the needs of the unemployed in the 380 cities and towns that had participated.

Faced with shrinking revenues because of the widespread economic slowdown, municipal authorities, like the state governments, hastened to cut expenditures. As the numbers of the unemployed mounted, a few cities and at least two states launched work-relief programs, but fears for their credit soon brought most of these remedial efforts to an end. Many cities abroad, battling the worldwide effects of the depression, enjoyed the benefits of home building and highway construction projects launched and financed by their national governments. In America, where the states had direct jurisdiction over the cities, several were developing regulatory restraints on urban utilities, but otherwise their reliance on free enterprise was unswerving. The federal government under President Hoover, after considerable pressure, launched a program to relieve unemployment by extending federal credit to revenue-producing ventures and other self-liquidating projects, but the hard-pressed cities had to await the election of Franklin Roosevelt for the development of a more positive federal program.

Several precedents for the development of closer federal-city relationships had appeared during World War I. Not only had the federal government built houses in certain war-industry centers, but it had designated twenty-one leading industrial cities as the centers for its ordinance districts and had delegated to their business groups the management of this vital activity. It had also named thirty-two widely scattered cities as the sites for airmail stops and was soon involved in the maintenance of their airfield services. The federal government had a longer record of support for port developments, weather bureau stations, and numerous other matters, but the problems of the depression were to bring a dramatic change in federal-city relations.

RESPONSES TO THE DEPRESSION

Indeed, the desperate needs of the major cities, as S. J. Eldersveld has shown, played a dramatic role in the political overturn in the fall of 1932. Of twelve leading metropolises that voted Democratic for the first time in many years that November, ten carried their states into Roosevelt's column, and the mayors of these and a few other cities gathered at Washington the next February to organize the United States Conference of Mayors to press their needs on the new administration. Roosevelt had promised federal economies, but he had also promised a "new deal," and the national emergency in which he found himself soon prompted the launching of a series of work-relief experiments and other measures that reached in an increasing number of ways into the cities and towns and called for their direct collaboration with federal efforts. Some of the relief programs initiated by the cities were soon placed under state administrators, but urban leaders had for the first time active relations with the federal government, and Mayor La Guardia of New York, who served for years as the chairman of the United States Conference of Mayors, was more influential than any governor in shaping New Deal policies.

Although the combined relief efforts of the cities and the federal government reduced the hardships of many thousands of unemployed urbanites and averted a more serious crisis, they failed to restore the economy. Public works projects were not, after all, major aspects of the nation's economy, and as sources of pump-priming funds they were generally cut off before a steady output was attained. But if recurrent pressures for economy checked the moves of several cities to secure federal backing for major local projects, some bold new plans were formulated for future action, and a recognition of federal responsibility for the nation's economy was fostered.

Federal action in the housing field had a more direct effect on the urban structure. A provision in the Industrial Recovery Act of 1933 permitted the funding of housing projects as a means of promoting employment, and Secretary Ickes approved a number of such projects in cities that assumed the initiative in creating local housing authorites. While a debate raged over the launching of a more aggressive housing program, as proposed by Senator Wagner of New York, other New Deal measures funded the previously established Federal Home Loan Bank, enabling it to extend credit to private builders, and created the Resettlement Administration to develop a number of "green-belt" towns in the suburban districts of expanding metropolises. Jealous real-estate interests checked all but three of these imaginatively planned new towns, but welcomed the easy credits supplied under the Home Loan Bank, which was amended and greatly expanded under the National Housing Act of 1934. These provisions made funds available for the completion of several subsistence homestead projects launched as limited-dividend ventures on the outskirts of several growing cities, and encouraged central-city residents to seek new homes built with FHA loans in the suburbs, but they did little for the rehabilitation of the inner-city districts.

The early New Deal measures raised heated controversies between various groups. Some wanted the federal government to assume full responsibility for restoring the economy by launching great national projects, others wanted the federal government to supply the funds or the credits for locally sponsored and administered projects, and still others wanted the federal government to limit its efforts to banking reforms and tariff restraints and to give the free enterprise system full sway. Many who had at first advocated generous outlays for federal relief became alarmed as the national administrators began to take charge of projects in the field. Most of the volunteer groups that had backed varied causes in the cities in previous decades had organized national associations, as we have noted above, and several of these now joined forces to open a headquarters in Chicago where they could collaborate in the collection of data on urban problems and in the promotion of mutual interests through associational efforts. While they busied themselves in assembling material for the annual *Municipal Year Books,* the National Planning Board created by Ickes in one of his relief agencies transformed itself into the National Resources Committee and undertook a series of probing studies, one of *Our Cities and Their Role in the National Economy.*

Neither Wagner nor the responsible mayors of the big cities could await the completion of these and other studies. The needs of the unemployed became more desperate as the depression continued. Many who had relied on their savings to tide them over had now exhausted their resources. Artists and professional people whose jobs had been abolished in the interest of economy were forced to join the unemployed factory workers and other applicants for relief. Fortunately the WPA and other federal agencies helped revive and reinvigorate public recreation staffs and finance white-collar relief programs and construction projects. Thus unemployed professionals and other tertiary workers won the support of agency directors who recognized that, to restore a healthy urban society even in industrial cities, jobs had to be supplied to many nonproductive workers. As a result, numerous unemployed actors, musicians, writers, and other professionals worked for modest sums at cultural projects in cities across the land, helping to revive the nation's morale.

Both the cities and the federal government were thus discovering a new interdependence, for if industrial cities could not function and prosper without a healthy national economy, neither could the nation's free enterprise economy survive in a democracy without the political support of the cities, which now contained a majority of the population. To assure such support the

New Dealers not only moved ahead with their housing programs, but also adopted the Wagner Labor Relations Act assuring workers the right of collective bargaining to safeguard their interests in the expanding corporate structure of American industry. The Labor Charter, as the Wagner Act was popularly called, served the additional purpose of recognizing union activity as a civic right, and thus brought workingmen into fuller participation in community affairs. Newly established industrial unions sought and secured recognition in several of the major industrial fields and assumed more positive roles in the politics as well as the economy of many industrial metropolises.

Workingmen and urbanists had already won recognition as members of the national and local polities in Britain and on the Continent. Most public works abroad—highways, railroads, waterworks, and the like—were nationally constructed or subsidized before the onset of the depression made the expansion of these programs a natural corrective. Public housing had gained acceptance as a national program in many European countries after the war, and labor-dominated or influenced governments were active promoters of these programs. Indeed, in contrast with the American cities, which were underrepresented in and generally constrained by their state governments, the major European cities exerted a powerful influence over their national governments. The great city was in most countries also the capital, and while ancient towns and small cities located far from the metropolis frequently developed a strong sense of their independent identity and traditions, they welcomed and often contended for national improvements within their borders and, as the Andersons discovered at Wissous near Paris, eagerly took advantage of the opening of new arteries of communication with the capital.

Because of the active relationship of the cities to the national governments of Europe, the leading social scientists and philosophers of France and Germany and the humanitarians and planners of Britain were already alert to the problems and the significance of the cities when their fellows in the States were first awakening to the new situation. We have already noted how British humanitarian precedents stimulated the formation of societies for organized charity and the establishment of settlement houses in the leading metropolises of the Northeast, and how probing studies of housing conditions and poverty in London and elsewhere in Europe prompted similar investigations in America. So it was not surprising that, when American sociologists and geographers began to study the city, they found the European scholars ahead of them.

Yet the pioneer studies of the city in America were more a product of an increased consciousness of its urbanization than a result of the international transit of ideas. Both Robert E. Park and Ernest W. Burgess, the sociologists at the University of Chicago who launched their famous field studies in that city in 1918, had themselves pursued advanced study in Europe, where they became aware of the writings of Simmel and Durkheim, but the early phase of their work in Chicago was less theoretical than problem oriented. They were close to the settlement houses, where several of their students served as residents. Yet if the early books of these students revealed a continued concern with urban problems—*The Hobo, The Gang, The Gold Coast and the Slum*— their contents disclosed the development of new research techniques and a regard for objectivity that marked a scholarly advance.

The wide interest stirred by Park's original essay, "The City: Suggestions for the Investigation of Human Behavior in the Urban Environment," first published in the *American Journal of Sociology* in 1915, marked an increased awareness of the city and spurred numerous other studies in Chicago and elsewhere. Louis Wirth, Park's student and later colleague, produced a pioneer study of *The Ghetto* and then compiled a *Local Community Fact Book* for Chicago that proved so informative and useful that it inspired similar efforts in other cities and made Professor Wirth the leading Chicago authority on cities. His major contribution was made in a paper on "Urbanism as a Way of Life," published in the *American Journal of Sociology* in 1938. Here the contributions of other scholars were recognized and assimilated in the first attempt in America to formulate a sociological theory of urbanization.

Possibly because of the central location and predominant position of Paris in the urban development of France, its geographers displayed an early interest in urbanization. Their studies, chiefly of the external geography and location of cities, were known to the Americans who again took a new tack and specialized in the internal geography of the metropolis. Park's central thesis emphasized the importance of natural areas for community development within Chicago, as did the concept of concentric zones of growth developed by Burgess and MacKenzie. The opposing theory advanced by Homer Hoyt, whose intensive study of changing property values in Chicago led him to depict urban growth as moving outward in broadening wedges or sectors of poverty, affluence, and ethnic residential concentration, also shared this emphasis. Clarence Perry, among others, observed the importance of neighborhoods in urban planning and housing and emphasized the vital relation of local schools, playgrounds, and other social and cultural facilities to each subcommunity.

Most of the early studies by sociologists, geographers, humanitarians, and other scholars were of metropolitan cities beset by ethnic complexities, but the Lynds chose instead a small and largely old-American city in the first throes of industrialization. Their study of Muncie, Indiana, which they called Middletown, disclosed the urbanizing effects of industrial growth on the transformation over the course of two decades of a small regional center of 10,000 inhabitants into a one-industry town of 35,000. The two central themes of their first book, *Middletown*—the impact of industrialization on community patterns and the varied evidences of social mobility that survived it—prompted the Lynds to make a second study of the same community, *Middletown in Transition*, after the onset of the depression had confronted it with a new set of problems. Their work, with that of others at Columbia and elsewhere, revealed that the scholarly awakening to the city that had begun at Chicago a decade before was now spreading to other leading universities.

When the National Resources Committee, chaired by Harold Ickes, created the Committee on Urbanism to study the problems of cities in 1936, these and numerous other more pragmatic appraisals of the urban situation found their way into the most comprehensive analysis of urban problems yet made in America, the previously mentioned *Our Cities and Their Role in the National Economy*. Headed by Clarence Dykstra, former city manager of Cincinnati and soon-to-be-named president of the University of Wisconsin, the committee included a presidential adviser, Louis Brownlow, and Professor Wirth among its active members, with Harold S. Buttenheim of the *American City* magazine as a collaborator, and L. Segoe, a scholarly city planner, as research director. The serious character of the study was recognized in its foreword: "As America pitches back and forth between . . . depression and . . . prosperity, it is in the Nation's cities that the shadow of economic insecurity is darkest. For in the city will be found the workshop of our industrial society and the nerve center of our vast and delicate commercial mechanism. . . . "[1] In the pages that followed the committee analyzed population and economic trends, wages and their effect on the standard of living of various groups in the community, health problems and other aspects of municipal service, education, welfare, delinquency and crime, and a host of other problems, including water and air pollution. It considered the nature of the urbanization process and recognized its potential contribution to the nation's welfare.

The committee also recognized the gravity of unsolved urban problems in a country whose urban ratio now exceeded that of western Europe or any other comparable expanse of territory. In all other major regions, even Latin America, the rural population vastly exceeded that of the United States and

---

1. Washington, D.C.: U.S. Government Printing Office, 1937, p. v.

Table 9. METROPOLITAN POPULATION INCREASES.*

	1910	1920	1930	1940	1950	1960
Number of Districts	97	112	143	150	191	212
Population of Districts	42,012	52,508	66,712	72,576	88,964	112,385
White Population	38,985	48,779	61,470	66,487	80,249	99,509
Black Population	2,820	3,547	4,991	5,840	8,360	12,194
Percent in Central Cities	64.6	66.0	64.6	62.7	58.6	51.4
Percent in Central Cities that are White	93.2	92.6	91.2	90.1	87.2	82.4
Percent in Central Cities that are Black	6.3	6.9	8.4	9.6	12.4	16.8
Percent of Whites in Central Cities	64.9	65.9	63.9	61.6	56.6	47.8
Percent of Blacks in Central Cities	60.4	67.2	72.8	74.6	77.2	79.6

*Derived from U.S. Census Office, *Eighteenth Census: 1960* (Washington, D.C.: U.S. Government Printing Office), Standard Metropolitan Statistical Areas, PC 3, 1DI.

provided a cushion to absorb the shock of widespread industrial unemployment. Only in Britain and the Low Countries had urbanization reached a higher level of concentration, but an official concern for the cities was widely apparent in many countries. With over 60 percent of America's population urban by 1940 and nearly 48 percent resident in the 140 leading metropolises, it was highly appropriate that the federal government should seek a fuller understanding of its cities.

BIBLIOGRAPHY

Anderson, Robert T., and Barbara G. Anderson. *Bus Stop for Paris: The Transformation of a French Village.* New York: Doubleday & Co., Inc., 1965.

Bedarida, Francois. "The Growth of Urban History and Geography in France." In *The Study of Urban History,* ed. H. J. Dyos. New York: St. Martin's Press, Inc., 1968.

Burgess, Ernest W., and Donald J. Bogue, eds. *Contributions to Urban Sociology.* Chicago: University of Chicago Press, 1964.

Griffith, Ernest S. *The Modern Development of City Government in the United Kingdom and the United States.* College Park, Md.: McGrath Publishing Co., 1969.

Harris, Chauncy D. *Cities in the Soviet Union.* Chicago: Rand McNally & Co., 1970.

Kulski, Julian E. *Land of Urban Promise: Continuing the Great Tradition: A Search for Significant Urban Space in the Urbanized Northeast.* Notre Dame, Ind.: University of Notre Dame Press, 1967.

Lampard, Eric E. "The Evolving System of Cities in the United States: Urbanization and Economic Development." In *Issues in Urban Economics,* ed. H. S. Perloff and L. Wingo, Jr. Baltimore: The Johns Hopkins Press, 1968.

McKelvey, Blake. *Rochester: An Emerging Metropolis: 1925–1961.* Rochester: Christopher Press, Inc., 1962.

Miller, Robert M. *American Protestantism and Social Issues.* Chapel Hill: University of North Carolina Press, 1958.

National Resources Committee. *Our Cities and Their Role in the National Economy.* Washington, D.C.: U.S. Government Printing Office, 1937.

Reeder, D. A. "A Theatre of Suburbs: Some Patterns of Development in West London." In *The Study of Urban History,* ed. H. J. Dyos.

Schnore, Leo F., and Peter R. Knights. "Residence and Social Structure: Boston in the Ante-Bellum Period." In *Nineteenth-Century Cities,* ed. Stephen Thernstrom and Richard Sennett. New Haven: Yale University Press, 1969.

Scott, Mell. *American City Planning Since 1890.* Berkeley: University of California Press, 1969.

Stein, Maurice. *The Eclipse of Community: An Interpretation of American Studies.* Princeton: Princeton University Press, 1960.

Trewarta, Glenn T. "Japanese Cities: Distribution and Morphology." *Geographical Review,* 24 (1934), 404–17.

Warner, Sam Bass, Jr. *The Private City: Philadelphia in Three Periods of Its Growth.* Philadelphia: University of Pennsylvania Press, 1968.

9

The Development
of Metropolitan
Federalism

World War II, with its defense orders, revitalized the American economy and brought a resurgence in the cities that obliterated the last traces of the depression. Despite fears of a collapse at the close of the war, the resurgence continued and confronted municipal authorities with unexpected demands for increased services, as well as renewed pressures for more and better housing and, in the larger cities, for equal rights for all. Unable as in the twenties to satisfy these demands single handedly and again rebuffed by the states, the cities turned increasingly to the federal government for assistance. A growing number of federal aid programs resulted and helped sustain the urbanization trend, which reached a new stage of population diffusion that presented baffling problems to many old central cities.

Indeed, despite their marvelous achievements in production and the widespread affluence enjoyed by most urban residents, the cities of America eventually found themselves cast in the role of despoilers rather than benefactors or promoters of the nation's well-being. While the urbanization process continued, its rate of increase was declining, as in England and other highly urbanized countries, in contrast with the more rapid growth of cities in underdeveloped nations. The slowdown was not as disturbing, however, as the failure of the cities to maintain the essential unity of their expanding communities. It was the reorganization and restructuring of the metropolis, rather than its rate of growth, that constituted the most important aspect of urbanization in these decades, and mounting difficulties in the sixties created an atmosphere of crisis.

The sense of alarm deepened as the suburban sprawl grew. Sped by the multiplication of automobiles, which by the fifties exceeded one for every urban family, the mushrooming suburbs dispatched thousands of workers into central-city traffic jams every morning, and cast clouds of pollution over metropolitan regions that challenged their shiny pretenses. Yet these physical difficulties were overshadowed by the dilemmas created by the vast reshuffling of the population as the first suburban migrants left a vacuum in the inner city that attracted a mounting flood of poor blacks from the South and spurred a more rapid flight from the central cities, threatening the creation of sharply divided communities and the defeat of the American dream. Fortunately, a resurgent and democratically inspired federalism offered hope for an escape from these dilemmas, but the outcome would remain uncertain as the sixties drew to a close.

The course of urbanization in the States attracted increased attention from university scholars, some of whom began to view it against the background of urban developments in other parts of the world. Rapidly declining death rates were producing a surplus of births in every land, causing an unprecedented surge of urban growth. Although, according to a United Nations-sponsored study of world urbanization trends (1966), as quoted by Professor Gerald Breese, America north of the Rio Grande maintained a clear lead in its percentage of the total population in urban centers of twenty thousand and more, its rate of urbanization was now surpassed by all major regions except Europe; moreover, both East and South Asia had surged ahead in the numbers residing in cities. Yet the urban growth in these Asian lands resulted from huge increases in their total populations and except for Japan exerted but a moderate urbanizing impact on their development. In contrast, the United States was experiencing a qualitative as well as a quantitative increase in urbanization, with gains in output that brought not only unprecedented abundance but also new problems of distribution priorities.

HOUSING AND RACIAL PROBLEMS

In the forties and fifties, at least, the contrasts all seemed favorable to urban developments in the States. The profusion of private investors and the volunteer groups that had hastened urbanization in the twenties had learned to cooperate with the federal authorities during the depression and rallied with such enthusiasm in support of defense programs that many private urban leaders were ready at the return of peace to join hands within each community in postwar planning efforts that deviated sharply from earlier concepts of private enterprise. And many were prepared, when confronted by urgent needs, to call for the support and leadership of the federal government.

The problem that brought the cities and the federal government into most active collaboration was housing. Experience with wartime housing programs during the world wars, and with WPA housing during the depression, prepared the way for joint action in the late forties to supply housing for returning veterans and to launch programs for urban redevelopment both to clear blighted areas and to ward off the threat of a postwar slump. Laudatory reports of the housing projects appearing in wartorn British and European cities, some backed by generous Marshall Plan aid from the States, spurred movements for the redevelopment of blighted areas in Pittsburgh and Milwaukee and a host of other enterprising cities. Local redevelopment and housing authorities assumed the initiative in these efforts, and with the passage of the National Housing Act of 1949 the federal government finally accepted the subsidizing of low-income housing in cities as a national responsibility and pledged funds to back slum clearance and to support urban redevelopment.

The U.S. Conference of Mayors and other groups that backed the housing program carefully safeguarded local initiative in the application of the program. They were less successful in maintaining local direction in some other fields of joint city-federal collaboration—notably in the planning and construction of a new system of interstate highways and in the operation of airports. Nationwide interests held precedence there and national authorities generally determined the routes of the superhighways and the favored stops on the airways, but the federal government finally agreed in 1956 to pay the cost for extending the superhighways into and through the cities—an action that soon proved a mixed blessing, however, as the land acquisition and demolition of houses and shops fractured old communities and spread hardships and benefits unequally over the urban residents.

The incessant building activities that repeatedly reconstructed the central districts of most American cities, greatly astonishing many foreign visitors, acquired a significant new element as public authorities assumed a major share in these operations. Private investors had made the decisions and paid the bills for most of the earlier rebuilding operations, and individuals who suffered losses or dislocations could exact a higher price or protest the heartless operations of the capitalist system. When a public housing or redevelopment authority entered the picture, however, its professed commitment to the public good invited vocal protests and political opposition from all who felt abused or threatened by the project. Thus the various local and national housing programs not only established a new bond between city and federal authorities, but also brought their efforts at collaboration into the forefront of postwar politics.

Urban redevelopment funds, as provided by the federal government in 1949, were promptly applied in several cities by business leaders eager to clear the blighted districts near the business center for more profitable use. As these projects cleared out clusters of wretched tenements and decaying stores and shops, many poor families and struggling merchants were dislodged and forced to find accommodations elsewhere. Their protests mounted as the projects increased, and prompted Congress in 1954 to require an adequate recompense for their losses and the submission of a "workable program" for their relocation before additional projects could be funded. These provisions, which satisfied the ethical standards of the nation's majority, permitted the removal of some marginal householders, such as the group of Boston Sicilians graphically described by Herbert Gans in *The Urban Villagers,* but required adequate provision for their resettlement, which in many cases called for the construction of public housing projects at other sites in the city. That requirement provoked even more intense battles over the selection of public housing sites and stalled the program in many cities.

The opposition to the location of public housing in various neighborhoods became more frantic as the possibility that it would bring in destitute blacks and other impoverished minorities became apparent. Even a strongly entrenched political leader such as Mayor Daley of Chicago, determined not to sacrifice the interests of his black supporters or those of the national Democratic party, had great difficulty siting new housing projects, as Meyerson and Banfield tell us. The grudging assignment of sites and their limited dimensions forced the erection of high-rise and often densely clustered apartment blocks, which soon acquired an institutional character that contrasted sharply with the row housing prevailing in Britain. There the projects, called estates, were frequently built on the city's outskirts, generally with small patches in the front or rear for flower gardens for each family, who often made it a lifetime home. Few housing authorities in American cities had the option widely used in Europe of locating projects in the suburbs, and the fears of many opponents of public housing were, as a result, quickly realized as many of the poorly located slabs became modernized slums. But public housing in most European cities was relatively the only new middle-class housing in the postwar years, and those who gained admittance felt privileged rather than, as in the States, domiciled temporarily in welfare quarters until they could afford a free-standing house in the suburbs where most of the American middle class resided. The distinction in the States was so sharp that it stigmatized the residents of all identifiable projects.

In an effort to escape these dilemmas the housing reformers pressed for the adoption of a new urban renewal program. The new measure, adopted by Congress in 1954, supplied funds for the rehabilitation of old neighborhoods as an alternative to slum clearance, and a new volunteer body, the American Council to Improve our Neighborhoods (ACTION), rallied civic support for such projects in many cities. The new act provided funds to promote the practice of regional planning, but it also called for "the maximum feasible participation" of the affected residents in the planning of renewal programs. This last provision soon brought into the open the long smoldering conflict between planning groups, such as ACTION and its local counterparts, and the less prestigious neighborhood associations.

That emerging conflict also revealed the unexpected dimensions of some demographic trends that were transforming the character of many American metropolises in these postwar decades. As the migration of southern blacks to northern cities resumed during the war, spurred by the need for manpower, the nine cities north of the Ohio River that were over 10 percent black in 1940 increased to eighteen within a decade and doubled again in the postwar years, and by 1960 nonwhites exceeded 20 percent of the population in thirteen of these northern cities. Although the number of newcomers from abroad had likewise doubled in the forties despite the war, and again in the fifties, at least a third of them now hailed from the West Indies and other parts of Latin America. Moreover, the number of European-born residents even in the northern cities continued to drop and by 1950 exceeded the nonwhites in only thirteen of the twenty standard metropolitan statistical areas over 500,000 in that region. Within another decade the ratio was reversed in five of the thirteen, and the nonwhites exceeded the foreign-born in thirty-five of the country's fifty-three standard metropolitan statistical areas of 1960. Not only were the earlier foreign-born inhabitants and their offspring, regardless of whether they continued to reside in ethnic neighborhoods, now essentially urbanized, but the blacks, too, were beginning in large numbers to undergo that transforming process.

Yet the number of in-migrating blacks, though considerable in a great industrial metropolis such as Chicago, where 227,000 arrived during the forties, was not always out of proportion to other gains. In Kansas City, for example, which increased by 100,000 during that decade, only 15,000 of its newcomers were nonwhites. The growing cities of the North needed and could have absorbed these eager migrants had they been able to distribute them more evenly. But in many places the only quarters open to them were located in deteriorating portions of old immigrant districts from which so many former residents had migrated that the remaining property owners were ready to accept any applicants. And as the influx of blacks overflowed these available inner-city districts, spilling into adjoining areas, friction developed and occasionally produced serious outbreaks.

In Detroit, where jobs in the motor industry had attracted an influx of fifty thousand blacks in the first year of the war, the mounting hostilities erupted on a hot Sunday in June, 1943, in a race riot similar to the violent outbreaks in East St. Louis and Chicago over two decades before. Lesser riots occurred in several other cities that had experienced a sudden influx, but in Chicago a Mayor's Committee on Race Relations had launched a number of programs which, in the opinion of the black author St. Clair Drake, helped relieve tensions. Similar committees in a score of other metropolises, in the South as well as in the North, worked earnestly for moderation. Indeed, a survey of southern police departments in 1948 disclosed that forty-three had a total of 228 blacks in uniform, and several of these communities boasted of the "separate but equal" high schools and swimming pools they were providing their black residents.

"Separate but equal," however, no longer satisfied many black Americans, more than half of them metropolitan residents by 1950. Even in southern cities, as Vance and Demerath have observed, blacks had broken loose from the old rural pattern of submissiveness and had acquired a limited choice of jobs and activities. As the number of black ministers, teachers, and businessmen increased, many joined local units of the NAACP, the Urban League, and various other bodies, some of which in 1944 formed the Southern Regional Council. Black voters' leagues appeared in several cities and increased their registration to 900,000 in the South by 1950. Numerous cases protesting discrimination in employment and in public services, especially in the schools, appeared in the lower courts. And while most of these were summarily dismissed as contrary to the statutes, the mounting concern for equal treatment in the South stirred agitation in several northern cities and brought the adoption of fair employment practices ordinances in Milwaukee, Cleveland, Philadelphia, and Chicago. Under pressure from its great metropolis, New York State adopted the first antidiscrimination law for public-aided housing. The groundswell of black discontent and upper-middle-class white disquiet over discrimination in housing, in public parks, on public buses, and at restaurant counters continued to mount in northern and southern cities in the early fifties. The final breakthrough came in May, 1954, when the Supreme Court handed down its historic decision, *Brown* v. *the Topeka Board of Education,* in which it declared that separate but equal schooling was not equal under the Constitution.

By its decision the Supreme Court called again on the cities to rectify a national deficiency. Numerous cities and towns in the border states, among them Washington and Baltimore, soon began to comply by admitting blacks who applied to white schools. Several southern governors protested the violation of state rights, however, and the issue came to a head when the school board of Little Rock, Arkansas, prepared to admit a few blacks to its Central High School in the fall of 1957, and the governor called out the National Guard to prevent it. A federal judge enjoined the governor from obstructing the order, but when the troops were withdrawn a mob replaced them, and President Eisenhower, appalled by the spectacle, dispatched paratroopers to Little Rock to reopen the school on an integrated basis.

Although these actions did not solve the problem of integrating the schools, they set a pattern of cooperation between the cities and the federal government that progressively extended the principal of the black man's equal civil rights to cover his treatment on public buses in Montgomery, in the public parks in Memphis, and in a public housing project in San Francisco. And if these court and administrative actions, even when backed by volunteer pressure groups organized by vigorous new leaders such as Dr. Martin Luther King, Jr., did not suddenly change the social practices of the South, let alone those of the entire nation, the confrontations did achieve some accommodations and represented a sufficient innovation in societal aspects of the urbanization process to merit scholarly attention.

NEW STUDIES AND STRATEGIES

Many scholars were in fact probing various aspects of the city, seeking a theory of urbanism. Perhaps the dominant concept of the late forties and early fifties was the power-structure thesis of C. Wright Mills, who found a small elite located in a few dominant metropolises in control of the nation, with subordinate elites apparently applying their directives to the lesser cities. However, most students of the power structure of individual cities failed to detect the guidelines coming down from above. None of these studies was concerned with decision making on such complex matters as race relations. In fresh approaches, free of power-structure concepts, Morton Grodzins warned of the development of a "great schism" or widening cleavage between whites, especially lower-middle-class whites, and blacks in American cities, and Morris Janowitz deplored the fact that the flight to the suburbs was creating a ring of "communities of limited liability" around the central cities that threatened the cities' capacity to solve their problems.

Although some scholars were becoming skeptical about man's capacity to master the problems of the city, others saw a chance for improvement through the creation of effective metropolitan units large and powerful enough to meet all their basic needs. When the numerous local bodies endeavoring to formulate and promote such developments again saw their proposals blocked by hostile rural and suburban interests in the state legislatures, some of the more optimistic urbanists appealed to federal authorities for support in their struggle for reapportionment and for assistance in the development of metropolitan regionalism. No state was yet ready to follow the Province of Ontario, which in 1954 authorized the organization of a metropolitan government for Toronto and its twelve adjoining suburbs, but the example presented a challenging goal to many cities and the next year helped persuade the newly formed President's Advisory Commission on Intergovernmental Relations to include a recognition of the needs and functions of metropolitan communities in its first report. Since the federal census had previously been the only official agency to recognize the existence of the metropolis, this was a step forward. But two years later, when Dade County in Florida secured the creation of the first metropolitan government in the States in order to frustrate Miami's attempt to absorb its suburbs, its action absorbed Miami instead and left it burdened with its old inner-city problems.

Apparently the solution did not lie in the form but in the substance or spirit of the American communities, and although many observers were becoming increasingly gloomy in the late fifties. some who were studying the course of urbanization abroad were viewing the American cities in a different perspective. Few of their articles and books would appear before the middle sixties, but already some of the contrasts between American cities and those in the newly developing countries were becoming evident. The more rapid numerical growth of many of these emerging cities was the first surprising discovery, which seemed the more baffling as their failure to develop an industrial base was noted. The ebb and flow of the rural-urban migrations that peopled Asian cities contrasted sharply with the one-direction movement in America. Striking contrasts were expected between the physical structure or morphology of the cities of America and of Asia, though many were surprised by the extent of Western influences on the Eastern metropolises. Striking contrasts also appeared between the authoritarian, bureaucratic governments of most Asian cities and the regimes in American cities, regardless of whether one described the latter as essentially democratic or as dominated by power-structure elites. A new sense of the greater depth of the urbanization process in America began to emerge from these comparative studies, as we shall see below.

The urbanization process, which was still primarily a centrally administered phenomenon throughout most of the world, had been acquiring politically conscious social action characteristics on the local level in American cities since the 1890s, a development that had occurred still earlier in several British cities and in scattered capital cities elsewhere. But the first outspoken recognition of, and commitment of support to, the process on a national level in the United States came with the election of President Kennedy in November, 1960. All but eleven of the ninety principal cities supported his candidacy and several of their mayors soon became frequent visitors to the White House. His urban-oriented administration not only pledged and soon provided additional funds for housing for moderate- as well as low-income families, but also opened the door for support on the local level of libraries and other cultural activities, as well as public health and sanitation programs. To supervise the development of these efforts the President proposed the formation of a Department of Housing and Urban Affairs, but he repeatedly declared his intention of leaving the actual decisions on local projects to the cities involved. To this end the Housing Act of 1961 not only supplied increased funds for housing and urban renewal, but also provided grants in support of city and even metropolitan planning, for open space acquisition, and for aid to historic preservation programs.

The tragic end of the Kennedy administration in 1963 left the implementation of most of its urban programs to President Johnson, but Kennedy had made several significant contributions to the urbanization process. His interest in the arts had a metropolitan slant and served to bring culture into the federal-city relationship, as it had long been in most cities in Europe. His appointment of a Committee on Juvenile Delinquency not only gave official recognition to the mounting problems of youths in the cities, but also focused neighborhood and scholarly attention on the search for solutions. The need for an assumption of local responsibility in this and other urban fields finally prompted the Supreme Court to reverse itself in March, 1962, and call in *Baker* v. *Carr* for a fair redistricting of the states' electoral divisions. In the reapportionment battles that followed, many cities for the first time secured an equitable vote in their state legislatures, and although the results were not as significant as expected, chiefly because of the more dramatic growth of the suburbs during the fifties, the city representatives acquired added prestige in many state capitals and were able to support urban-oriented governors in promoting local cooperative efforts on a metropolitan basis.

Most of the major metropolises were in fact reviving earlier regional planning schemes or establishing new ones. The Regional Plan Association of New York completed a series of planning studies that served as a model for other volunteer efforts, while Philadelphia took the lead in organizing an official Pennsylvania-New Jersey-Delaware Metropolitan Project as the successor to its earlier volunteer federation. The San Francisco Bay Area Association promoted the formation of the Association of Bay Area Governments, and similar official bodies appeared in a dozen other leading metropolitan areas, though none of them as yet had more than consultative functions. At the recommendation of the President's Advisory Commission on Intergovernmental Relations, several governors appointed aids to work with these regional bodies, but only the Coordinating Council on Urban Policy created by Governor Brown in California in 1963 acquired legislative status.

Several metropolises made a renewed effort in the sixties to organize metropolitan area governments. Suburban opposition again defeated such attempts in Seattle and St. Louis, among other places, but Nashville and Davidson County in Tennessee achieved a partial metropolitan government similar to that of Miami and Dade County, Florida, and with somewhat the same objective of preventing the central city from absorbing its immediate suburbs and burdening them with its problems. Los Angeles County expanded its functions to offer a variety of urban services to the city's suburbs, some on a contractual basis. The practical success of this system prompted the research director of the Seattle Metropolitan Council to propose the adoption of a municipal services market model in lieu of a formal organization. That system offered numerous efficiencies and economies, as well as an escape from political involvement. But it was for just this reason that Professor Norton E. Long attacked the proposal, declaring that what the metropolitan areas needed was new citizenship, not consumership.

THE RACIAL CRISIS

The debate over the degree of central-city and suburban participation in and responsibility for metropolitan decisions neglected an issue that finally burst into the open and pushed all other questions aside. The civil rights campaign, which had focused attention in the late fifties on discriminatory practices in southern cities, and which in 1962 delayed the enactment of several of Kennedy's urban reform measures, suddenly took a new turn the next year when, in connection with a drive for a new civil rights bill in Congress, organized protests against "de facto segregation" spread to the northern cities. The freedom marchers and black boycotters who had opened the white schools and parks of the South to blacks now reappeared in northern metropolises protesting the service and hiring practices of department stores and restaurants and the rental practices of hotels and apartment houses. Before President Johnson was able to complete his dramatic campaign for the enactment of Kennedy's civil rights and other urban legislation, including the creation of a cabinet-level Department of Housing and Urban Development, the black protests in northern cities had erupted into violence.

Most residents of northern cities were astonished at the furor of the outbursts that began in the summer of 1964. Many white leaders, aware of numerous inequalities, were attempting to correct them by launching programs designed to stop discrimination in housing and to help black renters and buyers find the homes they sought, to eliminate racial screening in job placements, to supply educational and recreational facilities that would make up for the deficiencies suffered by children in slum areas, and to assure fair treatment by the police and in the courts. But few whites were aware of the extent of the grievances that persisted in these and other situations. And despite the many demographic studies that were being made of the cities, none had foreseen the impact that the rapid influx of newcomers would have on the existing social system. Perhaps the rigid restraints of the statistical approach, seeking only to understand the basic trends, and the neglect of such data by the humanists, who concentrated their attention on the institutional activity and remedial programs, explain the failure even of conscientious leaders to see the gaps in their awareness of the problem.

Regardless of whether the riots could have been prevented, they represented a violent phase of the urbanization process that called for analysis and understanding. Waves of blacks had crowded, since the midfifties, into Bedford-Stuyvesant, a neglected district in Brooklyn, into upstate Rochester, previously 95 percent white, and into Watts, a modest but pleasant Los Angeles neighborhood, and these newcomers, like their fellows in other cities, were inundating the black institutions and swamping some community services while overlooking others. Relatively minor police incidents triggered the outbreaks in each case after a protracted period of excessive heat had driven the teeming inhabitants into the streets. The rioting generally continued for several nights, with residents shattering windows and pillaging stores and shops throughout the affected slum areas and defying all police efforts to restore order. Astonished by the violence that had erupted in their midst, the leaders of these and a score of other cities that soon experienced similar outbreaks began to seek possible explanations and hopeful remedies. Comparisons with earlier instances of mass violence in American cities quickly revealed that most outbreaks had occurred during or shortly after a huge influx of newcomers whose problems had proven overwhelming. The riots, in other words, represented a breakdown in the normal process of urban growth.

But when one accepted this causal explanation and sought for solutions, the differences between the successive breakdowns became more important than the similarities. The black riots of 1964 and 1965 were not bloody race wars, as in Chicago and Detroit in earlier decades, nor did they arouse fanati-

cal religious and ethnic hostilities comparable to those produced by the great
Irish migrations before and after the Civil War. Despite their violence, the
black riots were related to the civil rights marches in southern cities. They
were chaotic demonstrations against the system—the affluent society symbol-
ized by the well-stocked stores in their midst and the police who protected
that society. Insofar as the riot leaders could be identified, they were most
frequently young adults and teen-age dropouts who had grown up without
hope in the community, while the uprooted newcomers supplied the looters
and frenzied crowds who roamed the streets. Graphic accounts over the air-
waves and in the press incited similar outbreaks in other troubled cities,
leaving few unscathed.

The urban response produced many changes but no sure remedies. Fear of
a white backlash proved exaggerated as many now sophisticated urban institutions sought to accommodate the newcomers and relieve their hardships. Although the police in many cities were intent on tightening their controls, in
some metropolises they recruited additional black officers and endeavored in
other ways to reduce the hostility to the police that had developed in slum
areas. Factory managers and department store heads began to increase the
number of their black trainees and hastily placed a few in conspicuous posts to
publicize their compliance with the antidiscrimination laws. Social workers
opened new nursery schools and health clinics in the slum districts. The
public schools, baffled by the problem of educating poor youngsters whose
families were constantly on the move, began to experiment, particularly in
New York State cities, with busing and other methods of scattering the disadvantaged among the more stable city schools where they could learn from
their more fortunate classmates. Prodded by the returning freedom marchers,
many urban churches assumed the championship of the underprivileged and
backed efforts such as TWO in Chicago and FIGHT in Rochester to organize
blacks into neighborhood associations that could achieve an effective voice in
community affairs. Some of the leaders of these groups, convinced that there
was a power structure that could right the black man's wrongs, pressured
successive executives and occasionally won pledges of jobs and other equities
including some that the officials could not deliver or the underprivileged could
not use. Other leaders of inner-city groups were able to express the longings
and defend the interests of their followers, and in some cases became the
political leaders of their neighborhoods and won positions of power in the
larger community. Like the Irish, the Germans, the Italians, and other newcomers before them, the blacks acquired a new dignity and sense of belonging
with the election of such men as Mayor Carl B. Stokes in Cleveland and
Mayor Richard Hatcher in Gary, but they also soon learned something about
the limits and responsibilities of power.

One of the first black administrators to discover the limits of power was
Robert C. Weaver, named by President Johnson as Secretary of the new Department of Housing and Urban Development. A close adviser to the President
in his War on Poverty and Great Society programs, Weaver contributed to the
development of the Community Action Program approach to the allotment of
federal relief grants and urged that neighborhood groups participate in the
planning of renewal projects. He insisted that adequate "workable programs"
for the relocation of residents be submitted before slum clearance could be

authorized. He also took a keen interest in the efforts of some of the more active neighborhood groups in blighted areas to rehabilitate their districts and achieve an effective voice in politics. But Weaver soon discovered that efforts to secure neighborhood agreement on proposed renewal plans were time consuming, and that every delay brought added hardship to some householders and residential shifts that sometimes required new polls of local opinion and further delays. Moreover, the pledged objective of integration in housing was becoming harder to reach as some participating groups in the inner city insisted on exclusive black control and occupancy of housing projects, while most participating residents of outlying neighborhoods loudly protested the location of such projects in their districts. Urban redevelopment in democratic cities, even when directed by a popular leader like Mayor Richard Lee of New Haven and supported by minority-group administrators such as Secretary Weaver, was a difficult operation and stirred vocal protests, as Lee discovered in New Haven, and the able black mayor Kenneth A. Gibson in Newark fared no better.

THE NATIONAL RESPONSE

The federal government was likewise discovering some of the limitations of power. President Johnson's dramatic success in pressing his urban measures through Congress launched a larger number of ambitious programs than any predecessor had sought, but with limited results. Bills passed in 1964 and 1965 supplied funds for many additional housing units, for new urban renewal projects, and for increased assistance to urban and metropolitan planning. But the opposition of most urban neighborhoods outside the inner city to the location of housing projects in their midst delayed construction, while the difficulties in relocating inner-city residents without a supply of such housing stymied slum clearance efforts. Rapid developments occurred in the planning field, however, and numerous research projects documented the more urgent needs. New legislation resulted, authorizing experiments in mass transit, the acquisition of urban and suburban lands for open space use, and the granting of federal aid for sewage treatment plants and other antipollution programs.

The vast dimensions of these urban problems, which extended far beyond the boundaries, as well as the capacities, of individual cities, called for federal action. Even in cultural matters, the outward migration of the city's more affluent residents to exclusive suburbs dissipated support for such central city institutions as the libraries, museums, symphonies, music halls, and theaters that had been the pride of many cities a few decades earlier. The central city libraries, which provided numerous services for many town and village libraries, clearly merited wider support, and in the absence of responsible metropolitan governments, Congress accepted a part of the burden. Aid for local orchestras and galleries, traditionally assumed by the national authorities in Europe, was tentatively added to the list of urban grants-in-aid. But the measures that passed authorizing assistance to the cities for the battle against pollution, for the struggle with traffic jams, and for the support of cultural institutions represented little more than a token recognition of these problems.

To some, baffled by the mounting problems of old cities, the easiest and best solution appeared to lie in the establishment of new cities, as Britain and several other countries were doing. This, of course, was a traditional aspect of the urbanization process in America, where the number of urban places increased from 3464 to 7061 between 1940 and 1970, and the number of standard metropolitan districts from 140 to 243. But the new-town movement was radically different and called for the planning and controlled development of whole new cities. The "green-belt" towns of the New Deal were distant predecessors, though none had acquired more than a suburban residential character. Of the several bold schemes projected by large private developers, Reston and Columbia in the Washington area achieved the most tangible results. These and some of the more striking accomplishments in Europe provided an incentive for the inclusion of a provision of federal funds for new towns in the Housing Act of 1965. But the United States Conference of Mayors and other groups representing the existing cities, fearful that such funds would be cut from the limited grants made to the cities, successfully deferred action on this proposal and held the provision for new towns in later legislation to token proportions.

Federal outlays for the War on Poverty were not, of course, confined to the cities, but the problems of the ghettos and of youths in the streets were becoming increasingly absorbing. Most of the larger metropolises soon had Neighborhood Youth Corps and job training courses, and four hundred cities organized Community Action Programs, while local educators cooperated in launching Project Head Start classes in over two thousand communities. The efforts to achieve a consensus among neighborhood groups and to involve as many of the relief recipients as possible in the operation of the programs slowed progress but added to the experience and status of those who participated. The Model City Demonstration Program, devised in 1966 to assure a coordinated application of antipoverty and urban renewal funds to the rehabilitation of entire inner-city communities, accepted the additional objective of enlisting the residents as participants in the planning and developing of their neighborhoods. And although planners and other professionals, eager to achieve attractive designs and try out innovative residential patterns, often felt frustrated when commonplace structures and arrangements were preferred, if the brick and mortar produced lacked some of the charm achieved in a few European redevelopment projects, the major objective of building a sense of self-reliance and community among the residents seemed nearer to accomplishment.

Possibly the most dramatic evidence of progress in the urbanization of the new black residents of the northern cities appeared in their shifting attitudes toward the schools. From a position of widespread indifference and apathy, they moved quickly in the midsixties to vocal support for integration and for an end to de facto segregation. But as the scattered attempts to achieve that goal developed and generally only black children were bused out of their neighborhoods, many of their parents began to protest this new form of discrimination. With the growth of a new sense of pride in their identity as blacks, many inner-city residents rejected the principle of integration and demanded control of their own neighborhood schools. Other residents of the inner-city opposed such efforts, and heated disputes occurred. The issue remained unresolved as the decade drew to a close, but observers could no longer complain of the indifference and stupor of slum residents in America. Even the last of the city's minorities, the Puerto Ricans in the Northeast, the Chicanos in the Southwest, and the Indians throughout the country were, with the more numerous blacks, asserting their right and will to share in the political, economic, and cultural life of their communities.

The black man's increasing role in the life of American cities was reflected in the impact of his problems on urban studies. Few students of America's urbanization had taken more than passing note of the nonwhites before the late fifties. That faceless term was in itself revealing of the attitude that screened blacks out of most of the more meaningful studies, statistical or otherwise, of urban trends. Morton Grodzins was, as we have seen, the first to note the "great schism" that was developing in American cities, separating the blacks from the whites, and a few years later Constance Green, the historian of Washington, in describing the growing black community in the capital, characterized it as a "secret city." The blacks did not fit neatly into either Warner's six-layered stratification of the thirties or Mills' power-structure thesis of the forties. In fact the civil rights issue they posed in the fifties created havoc with the current version of the latter thesis by pitting one "establishment" against another and demonstrating the limits of legislative, executive, judicial, and even religious power. By the late sixties many blacks, disillusioned with the concept of a power structure that could, if pressured, grant them their demands, were beginning to attain a new level of urban sophistication.

Most urban scholars had likewise moved on to other concepts of the nature of the city. Professor Dahl's *Who Governs?* emphasized the plural character of urban society, which he saw as comprised of many interrelated but vertical, rather than horizontal, special-interest groups. Other political scientists, with the geographers, were interested in studying the boundaries, structures, and functions of subcommunities, within and on the edges of cities, and of the larger metropolitan regions they formed. Sociologists were turning from their earlier absorption with stratification and mass-society studies to an analysis of a variety of urban social systems, a reappraisal of the nature and values of local communities, and measurement of the mobility within them. Psychiatrists and social workers were searching for processes by which urban residents, particularly the young and the underprivileged, could be involved as constructive participants in urban society. Planners now recognized the need to devise not simply more efficient and pleasing urban designs, but designs that would meet the desires of the inhabitants and win their effective backing. Economists were seeking more reliable data on the productivity of various commercial and industrial activities and the interrelationships in their development and that of service occupations; they were devising models and formulae and employing computers to help project guidelines and formulate programs for urban and regional development. Historians were assuming the joint tasks of gathering the empirical evidence on the growth of cities and interpreting it with the aid of the best insights provided by the social scientists. With the political scientists they were discovering that urbanization was not an experience limited to those residing within the city's legal boundaries, but rather, in its broader sense, a process of social change throughout the entire ecology of the urban resident, which encompassed the central city with its

Table 10. COMPARATIVE METROPOLITAN URBANIZATION AROUND 1950.*

Country	Percentage of Population in Metropolitan Areas[1]	Measure of Industrial Diversification (MID)[2]	Measure of Technological Development (MTD)[3]	Measure of External Dispersion (MED)[4]
Argentina, 1947	44.6	.8147	0.76	604
Australia, 1947	55.4	.8348	3.12	1457
Austria, 1951	37.7	.7911	1.54	237
Belgium, 1947	41.4	.7969	0.28	793
Canada, 1951	42.7	.8197	6.47	1373
Ceylon, 1946	9.5	.6723	0.08	197
Colombia, 1951	19.3	.6624	0.27	119
Costa Rica, 1950	19.9	.6565	0.24	224
Cuba, 1953	26.1	.7420	0.48	248
Denmark, 1950	37.3	.8007	2.09	464
Dominican Republic, 1950	11.2	.6293	0.09	100
Ecuador, 1950	14.9	.6793	0.12	81
Egypt, 1947	19.6	.6394	0.22	143
El Salvador, 1950	11.9	.5689	0.09	134
Finland, 1950	17.0	.7193	1.17	509
France, 1954	34.7	.8100	2.03	360
Greece, 1951	22.0	.7114	0.22	235
Guatemala, 1950	10.5	.5086	0.14	82
Haiti, 1950	6.0	.3010	0.02	46
Honduras, 1950	7.3	.3029	0.15	73
India, 1951	7.8	.4788	0.10	34
Ireland, 1951	27.5	.7631	1.10	504
Israel, 1948–52	55.8	.8187	0.80	919
Japan, 1950	36.6	.7055	0.78	164
Malaya, 1947	12.7	.5500	0.28	846
Mexico, 1950	20.6	.6303	0.60	95
Netherlands, 1947	45.5	.8132	1.96	655
New Zealand, 1951	43.6	.8256	2.43	3310
Nicaragua, 1950	13.3	.5140	0.09	51
Norway, 1950	21.8	.8098	4.37	738
Pakistan, 1951	5.1	.4033	0.04	42
Panama, 1950	23.9	.6956	0.30	234
Paraguay, 1950	15.6	.6549	0.02	104
Peru, 1940	11.0	.5816	0.19	58
Philippines, 1948	10.3	.5418	0.09	235
Portugal, 1950	19.6	.7073	0.26	129
Spain, 1950	25.5	.7014	0.57	41
Sweden, 1950	22.4	.8007	3.22	873
Switzerland, 1950	28.9	.7762	2.15	882
Thailand, 1947	6.8	.2735	0.02	35
Turkey, 1950	9.5	.4082	0.26	82
Union of South Africa, 1951	29.9	.7059	1.89	796
United Kingdom, 1951	71.5	.7687	4.42	1188
United States, 1950	55.9	.8130	7.74	381
Venezuela, 1950	25.2	.7597	0.77	420

1. Source: Data prepared by International Urban Research. These percentages supersede earlier provisional figures reported by Gibbs and Davis in the *American Sociological Review*, 23 (October 1958), 504–14.
2. Source: *Demographic Yearbook.*
3. Source: *Statistical Yearbook.* Commercial consumption of energy expressed in metric tons of coal per capita.
4. Source: United Nations, *Statistical Papers*, Series T, 6, no. 10.
*From Jack P. Gibbs and Walter Martin, "Urbanization, Technology, and the Division of Labor: International Patterns," *American Sociological Review* 27 (October 1962), 672. Reproduced with permission of the *American Sociological Review.*

varied districts, its suburban overflow, its supplying and consuming hinterlands, and, as time progressed and communications developed, the entire national system of cities and the federal polity as well. Local and national foundations were supporting these studies and organizing institutes and conferences to promote a cooperative approach to an understanding of urbanization. Universities were creating departments of urban studies, and numerous local and national journals and publishers were helping to bring the cities and their problems into the forefront of the nation's consciousness. Finally, politicians in increasing numbers, on both the local and the national level, were responding to the plight of their cities.

BIBLIOGRAPHY

Abrams, Charles. *The City Is the Frontier.* New York: Harper & Row, Publishers, 1965.

Breese. Gerald, ed. *The City in Newly Developing Countries.* Englewood Cliffs, N.J.: Prentice-Hall, Inc., 1969.

Clark, Kenneth B. *Dark Ghetto: Dilemmas of Social Power.* New York: Harper & Row, Publishers, 1965.

Dahl, Robert. *Who Governs?* New Haven: Yale University Press, 1961.

Gans, Herbert J. *The Urban Villagers.* New York: Free Press, 1962.

Green, Constance McLaughlin. *Washington, Capital City: 1879–1950.* Princeton: Princeton University Press, 1963.

Grodzins, Morton. *The American System: A New View of Government in the United States.* Chicago: Rand McNally & Co., 1966.

Harris, Walter D., Jr. *The Growth of Latin American Cities.* Athens, Ohio: The Ohio University Press, 1971.

Hauser, Philip M., ed. *Urbanization in Asia and the Far East.* Calcutta: UNESCO Research Center on the Social Implications of Industrialization in Southern Asia, 1957.

Hauser, Philip M., and Leo F. Schnore, eds. *The Study of Urbanization.* New York: John Wiley & Sons, Inc., 1965.

McKelvey, Blake. *The Emergence of Metropolitan America: 1915–1966.* New Brunswick, N.J.: Rutgers University Press, 1968.

Mills, C. Wright. *The Power Elite.* New York: Oxford University Press, 1956.

Report of the National Advisory Commission on Civil Disorders. New York: E. P. Dutton & Co., Inc., 1968.

Vance, Rupert B., and Nicholas J. Demerath, eds. *The Urban South.* Freeport, N.Y.: Books for Libraries, Inc., 1954.

Weaver, Robert C. *The Urban Complex: Human Values in Urban Life.* New York: Doubleday & Co., Inc., 1960.

Williams, Oliver P., and Charles Press, eds. *Democracy in Urban America: Readings on Government and Politics.* Chicago: Rand McNally & Co., 1961.

10

American Urbanization, Past and Future, Viewed Comparatively

In less than three and a half centuries the urbanization of the United States has reached a stage of development surpassing that of all other continental areas. Both South and East Asia have long had more urban residents, but these have comprised a smaller portion of their total populations. All the major continents have older cities, and several of their great cities have, as capitals, played a more dominant role in their country's history than any individual cities north of the Rio Grande, but only one principal nation, Great Britain, is more completely urbanized, and even there more and stronger traces of an earlier rural tradition have persisted than in the States.

COLONIZATION, EXPANSION, AND INDUSTRIALIZATION

But other aspects of the urbanization of America are more noteworthy than its pervasiveness. The fact that the Atlantic ports had from the start exerted a generative or urbanizing influence on the British colonial settlements, in contrast with the parasitic or exploitative effect of the cities of Latin America and most other colonial areas, gave the cities of British North America a tradition of close integrality with their hinterlands that few attained elsewhere. In their advance into the virgin continent, the urban and rural pioneers faced the hardships and challenges of the frontier together. They shared the same heritage, part of it acquired in older settlements to the east and part imported from Europe, but the long ocean voyage and the stopover in the East had freed them from most of the medieval traditions that still marked cities and towns in Europe. Because of their development in advance of the organization of strong state and national authorities, they enjoyed greater scope for initiative than provincial cities in Europe, and much greater freedom than the closely planned and controlled cities of the more truly colonial world, which continued to rely on the home fleet for protection. Moreover, the federal character of the new American nation, with the cities chartered as subordinate divisions of the states and unrelated until recently to the national government, enhanced the diverstiy of their development. And the somewhat novel location of the federal capital at a fresh site, far from the dominant urban centers of the new nation, increased their independence.

So urbanization in British North America took a special course. Many colonial ports of the seventeenth century had enjoyed rapid development as outposts of spreading mercantile empires. As cities they had performed subordinate commercial and administrative roles for the mother country. With the emergence in the British colonies during the eighteenth century of thriving settlements of Englishmen and other Europeans, their cities not only acquired a closer relationship with their hinterlands, both demographically and culturally, than Latin American cities achieved, but also developed an economic partnership that made them increasingly independent of Great Britain. The principal Atlantic ports, with links already established to the commercial centers of Europe, were thus in the early years of the nineteenth century ready to take the lead in developing the flow of exports and imports that sped the growth of the older trading cities and promoted the construction of water and rail highways into the interior, where new towns were arising. Despite the contributions of a few state governments to internal improvements, the new system of cities that emerged was more firmly and exclusively based on private enterprise than was the case in any contemporary society, and the urbanizing influences permeated the entire nation.

A mounting stream of newcomers from abroad contributed to the growth of the new nation, particularly to that of its cities. Migrants from the British Isles, especially from Scotland and Ireland, crowded the Atlantic ports and, with many immigrants from Germany and other parts of the Continent, swelled the population of the new inland cities and gave them an ethnic diversity unrivaled in any of the other developing urban societies of the period. Large contingents of blacks, most of them slaves descendent from blacks brought from Africa in the late colonial period, added to the heterogeneity of the southern cities and checked the growth of immigrant colonies there. Lesser numbers of free blacks appeared in the northern cities, but nowhere in the States did blacks comprise as large a portion of the urban population as in several cities in the West Indies and a few in other parts of Latin America where, with the Indians, they formed the great majority of the population.

Yet the chief contrast, demographically, between the cities north and south of the Rio Grande in the nineteenth century was not in their ethnic diversity, though that was much greater in the north, but in the urbanizing process that contributed to the progressive assimilation of most minorities in the States, while rigid inhibitions obstructed it further south. Even after the Latin American countries had acquired their independence, largely because of the collapse of the empires that had founded them, the traditional division between the Latin American elites and the masses of Indians and blacks persisted and prolonged the parasitic blight on their economies. The situation to the north stood in sharp contrast. While in the case of the poor refugees from famine-stricken Ireland, as of some unskilled German peasants, the process of assimilation often proved long and painful, with the exception of the slaves (and in practice of most free blacks as well) all newcomers were officially accepted as potentially equal citizens and soon joined in the absorbing task of developing prosperous cities.

Closely linked with the mounting tide of immigration was the flood of technological innovations known as the industrial revolution. Likewise originally imported from England, where its early development helped set the stream of human migrants in motion, the new industrial technology was eagerly welcomed by the enterprising promoters of the cities of the Northeast and Midwest, where most of the immigrants found lodgment. Skilled craftsmen among the newcomers helped construct the machines and develop the manufacturing procedures that so increased the productivity of cities at water power sites and those enjoying easy access to coal for steam power that they increasingly absorbed rural handicrafts and enjoyed a rapid growth. By the midcentury the cities of the North, which was already 20 percent urban as against 6 percent in the South, had given the leaders of northern states sufficient power to halt the extension of slavery into the West, and a decade later they would prompt the nation to abolish it throughout the South. In that titanic struggle the cities of the North, whose adults, half native and half foreign-born, attained a new common identity as Yankees, not only preserved the Union but laid the foundations for a dynamic industrial society. The generation of the sixties abolished slavery but assumed no responsibility for the assimilation of the freed blacks, though many blacks crowded into makeshift settlements on the outskirts of some of the cities of the South. Almost a century would pass before American cities would begin to come to grips with this problem.

America's continued urbanization in the age of industrialism invited comparison with developments in Europe, not Latin America. The industrial revolution, which had its origins in the Midland cities of Britain in the early 1800s, exerted an early impact in several places on the Continent, as well as in New England and Pennsylvania. By the midcentury at least a dozen cities in western Europe and almost as many in the States had acquired manufacturing enterprises that combined the use of water or steam power with machine production in specialized factories. As the decades advanced and limited-dividend corporations took over from earlier partnerships, and trade unions from craft guilds, old commercial cities acquired factories and new industrial cities sprang up on both sides of the Atlantic, especially in districts where coal was readily available.

Specialized production and the efficiencies it achieved were the key features of the new system. In Europe this development was usually tied closely to the technological innovations achieved in each city. In America, on the other hand, industrial specialization was more frequently based on the natural resources and expanding needs of the area. The British textile and metallurgical innovations also responded to the natural and manpower resources and world-trade potentialities of the Midlands, but the British cities lacked the large regional setting enjoyed by American cities, whose industrialists generally had great quantities of local produce to process and a sufficient demand for manufactured goods to keep many fabricating firms busy. Even the Continental cities, with larger regional hinterlands, lacked the promotional incentives enjoyed in the western cities in America, where the industrial cities such as St. Louis and Chicago prospered by exploiting the potentialities of their developing regions. As a result, the bright prospects of the inland cities and their vast hinterlands attracted a flood of newcomers from abroad—from northern, southern, and eastern, as well as western, Europe. Some came to till the fields and work the mines of adjoining districts, others to man the mills and factories in town or move the increasing supplies of merchandise in and out of the city's busy stores and warehouses. Skilled craftsmen among the newcomers vied with Yankees in launching new enterprises, which readily attracted support from the numerous private, state, and national banks that made their appearance in every city.

DEMOGRAPHIC AND POLITICAL CONTRASTS

The progressive settlement and development of the western states, vigorously promoted by their cities, reduced somewhat the ratio of urbanization as compared with that of growing cities in Europe located in fully developed regions, but in some other aspects of urbanization the American cities quickly took the lead. Their greater heterogeneity gave rise to a diversity of churches and other social and cultural institutions that fostered a cosmopolitan atmosphere. Each minority group had its own social club and welfare society, as well as its own native church, and migrants who had never before participated in such activities took pride in their support. Many groups established their own schools and newspapers or supported such ventures in the larger cities. The recognition their activities received in the urban dailies helped bring them into the mainstream of the city's affairs. Thus the minority groups helped give the associational life of the American cities a diversity unrivaled elsewhere.

But the great influx of immigrants of varied backgrounds and skills added to the complexities of urban growth and accentuated many problems. The newcomers were jealously eager to master their own difficulties and generally took steps to that end, but many Yankees were equally concerned for the good name of their cities and hastened to found a variety of welfare societies and other volunteer organizations to care for the needy and safeguard the weak in body and spirit. Indeed, the volunteer societies, matching the enterprise of private ventures in industry and trade, took over the support of culture as well and gave every thriving city not only an athenaeum, library, music hall, and opera house—institutions often publicly supported in European cities— but generally in the larger cities an art gallery, science museum, and symphony orchestra as well.

The free enterprise and voluntarism that characterized the American cities fostered an exhilarating growth in good times, but also suffered and perhaps contributed to the outbreak of repeated depressions. When hard times struck in the seventies and nineties and many factories shut down to avoid bankruptcy, thousands of workers lost their jobs, exhausting the resources of the old relief agencies. New charity organization societies made their appearance, determined to head off the creation of a pauper class similar to that said to infest many European cities, and a new social gospel animated some old urban churches. Together these movements and the numerous educators working to develop schools adequate to the needs of their heterogeneous student bodies acquired a new awareness of the city as a vital community—a challenge to a citizen's understanding and talents for leadership.

Industrial cities, in England and on the Continent, even without the problem of absorbing a work force of foreigners, also faced periodic economic

crises, but with different results. Because of the more stable national populations, the old distinctions between owners and managers on the one hand and
craftsmen and workmen on the other persisted as workers moved from village
to town to city, and helped produce a sharper class division than American
cities, except in the Deep South, experienced. Labor leaders in Europe were
consequently more responsive to the class struggle doctrines of Karl Marx and
the radical socialists. To reduce their challenge, Bismarck and other national
leaders promoted a form of municipal socialism that not only supplied many
city services left to corporate groups in the States, but also performed the
cultural and welfare functions supplied by volunteer associations in American
cities.

In the still more difficult task of providing sufficient housing to accommodate their mounting populations, neither the European nor the American cities
made much progress. Philanthropists on both sides of the Atlantic built a few
model projects, but exerted little influence on the speculative builders who
crowded the land with endless rows of mean little houses in the industrial
cities of Europe, and with tightly packed four- and five-story dumbbell tenements and flimsy three-deckers in the States. Societies of workingmen built
housing cooperatives in several British and Continental cities, but their resources were too limited to make a real response to the problem. The pioneer
attempts of some of these cities to build houses with governmental backing
also proved disappointing. Radical protests erupted against the poor housing
and other afflictions of the poor, but national authorities hastened to suppress
them. Only the relatively moderate growth of most European cities, which
enabled realtors to build rows and blocks of rental quarters for middle-class
occupants, forestalled more serious outbreaks.

In American cities, partly because of their many volunteer agencies and
the rapid spread of home ownership among the middle and working classes,
urban reform efforts took an opposite and more moderate course. The wide
adoption of manhood suffrage before the Civil War, in contrast with the property requirements prevailing abroad, and the generous grant of full citizenship
to immigrants after brief periods of residence, had drawn many newcomers
into active politics and enabled varied ethnic factions to seize control in some
cities. One object of their activity was to liberalize the granting of liquor
licenses and to remove other restraints, but as these developments occurred a
reaction appeared seeking a restoration of the traditional mores. Civic officials
also had the responsibility for letting contracts for municipal improvements
and issuing franchises for public utilities, more generally provided by public
agencies abroad. These decisions involved huge sums and conferred great benefits on the recipients, many of whom were ready to share their bounty with
the officials or party involved. Evidence of corruption appeared in many cities,
strengthening the demands for reform.

The urban aspect of the Progressive movement, promoted by good government clubs in many cities, had numerous, sometimes divergent, objectives.
Moral reformers, attacking the saloons, vice, and gambling, took the lead in
some places, educational reformers in others, but after the turn of the century
the corrupting influence of predatory interests became the major concern. Unlike the situation in the industrial cities of England and Europe, where an
earlier civic revival had sought a broader local franchise and greater scope for

municipal initiative in the development of utility services, in late-nineteenth-century America the franchise was already widely shared and services too had been freely parceled out to eager applicants. Among the new solutions proposed in the States, immigration restriction attracted little support in cities already dominated by the foreign-born and their children, but pleas for better schools to assure the adequate training of future workers and voters won a quick response. Advocates of municipal ownership of utilities were generally rebuffed, but a widespread move for local and finally for state regulation of urban utility rates and services represented a partial break with the old *laissez-faire* doctrine and pointed towards a wider public control of municipal developments. A rebirth of thg city planning movement in America after the turn of the century provided another indication of the same trend.

The progressives, charity organizers, and spokesmen for the social gospel were not alone in their new awareness of the city as a primary societal unit. Recreational and cultural leaders, formerly organized under societies and churches, regrouped in these years into city teams, orchestras, and federations and won a new and enthusiastic community following. Chambers of commerce and central trades councils, formerly the agents respectively of business and labor interests, acquired a new solicitude for citywide concerns. University scholars, too, particularly in Chicago, were awaking to the challenge of the city as a fascinating research subject conveniently located at their very doorstep. Perhaps never before in America had the opportunity to enlarge and test man's knowledge of his society appeared so promising and inviting as in Chicago in the early 1920s.

But the American city was not standing still for its portrait. Long before the sociologists in Chicago and elsewhere had progressed very far with their analysis of the internal structure of the great industrial city, the horseless carriage and other ingenious devices had enabled the city to spread beyond its limits and assume the new structural character of a regional metropolis. So rapid was the wider community's growth that it created an urgent need for reorganization. But political scientists who conducted surveys and drafted charters for new metropolitan federations were rebuffed in America by rural-dominated state legislatures. While many great cities abroad, with considerable support from their national administrations if not their actual direction, generally kept pace with their territorial expansion and maintained a reasonable political unity, the expansive cities in the States had to be content with the development of a new economic and social regionalism. The earlier industrial cities, in addition to providing the sinews for such units, in the form of automobiles, telephones, radios, and the like, and producing machines to operate the farms, had drawn displaced farmers into their factories and partially urbanized those who remained behind. But the continued growth of the central cities and their absorption, if not assimilation, of many new ethnic strands had created tumultuous communities that not only stimulated the outward migration of many old residents to quieter and more exclusive suburbs, but also prompted the dwindling rural population to cling more tenaciously to its political control of the state legislatures.

The outbreak of the Great Depression at this point may have had no causal connection with this organizational impasse, but it presented the cities with problems they could not master and turned them increasingly to the federal government for help. New federal-city relationships, gradually developed during the long depression, were further strengthened during World War II and its aftermath. In the postwar decades the American cities, now supported by many federal grants-in-aid, have undertaken extensive urban renewal projects, public housing for the poor and the aged, and vast highway and downtown redevelopment programs. Again with federal support they have launched regional planning studies and attempted to rejuvenate some of their cultural traditions weakened by the flight to the suburbs. But even with a few partial successes in merging city and county functions, American cities have nowhere achieved the metropolitan organization successfully developed in Toronto and a number of other great cities abroad, though the decisive action in most of these cases was taken at the national rather than the local or regional level.

THE BLACK REVOLUTION

Yet the organizational impasse of the American metropolis has been overshadowed and greatly influenced by still another challenge, the migration of southern blacks to the cities. World War I and the immigration curbs that followed it had brought the great flood of newcomers to a halt and forced northern cities to turn for their accustomed fresh supplies of heavy labor to the South, where new machinery was releasing many blacks from the cotton fields. These simultaneous developments started a new migration to the cities, created new frictions in old immigrant districts, and raised fresh doubts as to the city's capacity to assimilate its heterogeneous inhabitants. Difficulties encountered in the several heavy-industry cities that drew the first large contingents of blacks during World War I were partially forgotten during the depression and the war that followed, but renewed migration in the forties made the black man's struggle for civil rights the key issue in southern cities in the fifties and in northern cities in the sixties.

Although at its height the black revolution, as it has sometimes been called, appeared to threaten the continued existence of the North American city, it can now be seen as a forward step in America's urbanization. Not only have most southern blacks finally left the rural South, where their services have been replaced by the employment of machinery, but in their migration to the cities they have acquired a new purpose and a new hope of attaining full American citizenship. And as the migration has progressed black Americans, who were 73 percent rural in 1910 and 73 percent urban in 1960, have vastly improved their economic circumstances, acquired new opportunities for education and advancement, and attained such a wealth of experience that they are now able to make their voices heard in city councils and national assemblies, and to win an increasing place in the affairs of the city.

Yet this phase of America's urbanization has been beset by much violence. Forced by poverty to cluster in the poorest districts from which the latest immigrants were already migrating, the blacks seemed about to repeat the residential cycle of earlier newcomers when new circumstances intervened. The federal-city programs for urban redevelopment, barely launched before the black migration became pronounced, competed for some of the more deteriorated inner-city tracts, adding to the house-hunting difficulties of the black migrants. The migrants' color presented another difficulty with which they were only too familiar, but in the new urban situation that difficulty was compounded. Despite the pervasive racial prejudice, the national pledge of equality reaffirmed by the Supreme Court prompted federal authorities to require the submission of "workable programs" for the relocation of any persons displaced by renewal projects. To fulfill this requirement it was often necessary first to erect public housing on another site, and the search for such sites brought demonstrations of prejudice from white neighborhoods that aggravated the sores first opened by the sight of federal bulldozers crumbling the homes of those displaced. Although the outbursts of rage that erupted in many cities in the hot summers of the midsixties were generally directed at the police charged with the preservation of order in a highly volatile situation, and although the fires and destruction they wrought proved more damaging to black than to white residents, the blacks at least registered a dramatic protest and awakened many white citizens to the seriousness of their complaints. In the long and troubled aftermath of the riots, groups of black and white residents have endeavored in many cities to open new opportunities for employment, housing, and education. And as the participation of blacks in urban renewal programs and other civic activities has increased, a few of their leaders have won election as councilmen, even as mayors, and the hope for equality if not full integration has brightened.

As contrasting types of urbanization, the migration of the rural blacks of the South to the cities, North and South, invites comparison with the recent mass movement of displaced rural natives into the great cities of Latin America, Southeast Asia, and Africa. As several scholarly studies have shown, these migrations have rapidly swelled the populations of several of the major cities, accentuating their primacy and giving them growth rates that exceed any previously attained by cities of a comparable size in the Western world. In contrast with the situation in the States, where the black migrants to the northern cities have settled in the inner-city ghettos, the migrants to Latin American, Asian, and African cities have settled in makeshift *barrios* or other temporary communities on the outskirts. Pushed upon the cities by an overpopulated countryside, these unskilled native refugees have created rings of poverty around many giant cities, stirring fears of overurbanization among some officials, while others have argued that the poor urban squatters are less wretched than before, when they were an excess burden on the land. In the cities they are at least learning new urban ways, and some are performing service functions while others are increasing the value of the lands they now occupy by adding improvements. With limited needs for shelter because of the climate, and with modest expectations, the migrants have formed self-regulating communities that require and receive little attention from the authorities. But if they pose no immediate threat to the inhabitants of the central cities comparable to that presented by the blacks pressing out from the inner-city districts of northern cities, neither do they pose a challenge to creative innovation comparable to that experienced in the States.

The urbanization of the black Americans has already achieved striking results. Not only has it prompted the nation to reaffirm in clearer and more positive terms its dedication to the principle of equal rights for all, but it has also brought formal acceptance of and legislative backing for the traditional American practice of wide citizen participation in public affairs, particularly on local community levels. The wider application of these two principles has already had its effect on the two major urbanizing trends of the last half-century—the transformation of specialized industrial cities into more diversified metropolitan regions and the development of new city-federal relationships. Moreover, the black American's determination to achieve equal civil rights and equal privileges in the cities has reinforced an earlier urbanizing trend toward self-conscious communities.

A LOOK AHEAD

Of course, the prospects of self-conscious cities are far different from those facing towns still bound in the natural processes of unplanned growth and decay. Urban prognosticators in the States no longer need to be content with extending trend lines into the future, though they still must keep at least one foot planted on solid ground. Although few if any American cities have yet developed planning authorities with real powers comparable to those of some governments abroad, many have achieved a community consciousness that is both more democratic and more widely shared than in most cities elsewhere. And although the ties that bind the various segments of each metropolis together lack the hereditary and legalistic elements prevalent in many great cities of Europe, for example, the voluntary nature of American urban cohesiveness supplies a vitality that can rectify most deficiencies. The deficiencies, as many commentators have noted, are legion, and the material forms of the American city are especially disappointing and growing worse, but the energies and talents to remedy these structural flaws are present and can do the job when the inhabitants will it.

Prominent among other deficiencies is the lack of a metropolitan polity to assume responsibility for effective communitywide action. Local neighborhood and suburban jealousies and desires to retain exclusive privileges have obstructed repeated efforts toward consolidation or federation, and recent fears on the part of blacks and other minorities of a loss of hard-won local representation have checked efforts to achieve a wider polity. Nevertheless, the probable economies of a more centralized and effective organization of metropolitan services supply a continuing incentive for a consolidation of functions, though, as Professor Norton C. Long has put it, the great need of the metropolis is for concerned citizenship, not consumership. Professor Kenneth E. Boulding recently emphasized the same point when he declared that the cities need not more technological innovations in the material sphere, but more creative ideas or inventions in the social and moral spheres, in order to restore a sense of community.

But it helps to have specific goals, and as it happens one of the city's most chilling threats—water and air pollution—presents a challenge that may supply a compelling drive for the development of a new sense of metropolitan intradependence. And once the interest engendered in the restoration of the region's natural ecology is extended to include a concern for its entire human ecology, the prospects for the metropolis and all its member neighborhoods will brighten. Indeed, as Lampard has hinted, the magic term "ecology" may at long last dispel the old urban-rural dichotomy as the city and its hinterland are recognized as ecologically one urbanizing community.

But the metropolitan region, if less specialized than the industrial city, and if better able to encompass a number of diversified neighborhoods as well as dissimilar economic and social functions, can even when effectively organized never aspire to economic self-sufficiency or political independence. Indeed, in America it will continue to need more rather than less federal economic backing, for in a competitive economy when those able to pay large taxes are free to dodge them by moving to a low-tax area, the low-service metropolises drive out the high-income communities. American cities have escaped the stultifying influences of the centralism that still afflicts some European cities, especially in Russia, but they can no longer depend so heavily on real estate taxes, especially not in the central cities, where property values are tending to decline, nor on foundations and other voluntary resources, and they will need increasing federal tax support. Fortunately this need, as in the case of the threat of pollution, presents an opportunity to promote the formation of responsible metropolitan regional units, as the Advisory Commission on Intergovernmental Relations has repeatedly emphasized.

If the American city's major economic problem is the fiscal one of taxing its productive capacities without driving them beyond its borders, and if the productive capacity of this urbanized nation promises, as Lyle C. Fitch calculates, to meet most of its projected urban goals before the close of the century, responsible leaders of the prosperous and affluent metropolitan regions and of the powerful federal union they comprise will also have to reach a satisfactory working and cooperative relationship with many national systems of cities that are in some cases beset with severe poverty and in others torn by internal and perhaps external strife. America's urbanization, in other words, has reached a stage, like that of Britain many decades earlier, at which the productivity or lack of it of distant centers beyond the nation's borders becomes an integral part of its ecosystem. International credits and outright grants to underdeveloped countries, reciprocal trade agreements with those enjoying an economic upsurge, and scientific, technological, and cultural exchanges may help avoid another holocaust, but the major need is for a broadly based agreement on national birth quotas and a more equitable distribution of the world's inhabitants and productive resources.

Such an outlook raises again the prospect of the resumption of large-scale international migration. Certainly the cities of the United States, with or without cooperative international understandings, will receive an increasing flow of newcomers from beyond the Rio Grande. No cities in the world are growing more rapidly than several in South America, and whether or not their economies can keep pace, the increasing contacts between the cities of North and South America made possible by improved air lines and other communications will bring more and more immigrants to the States. Hopefully the long experience of North American cities in absorbing new ethnic minorities, though seriously tested in the sixties by the blacks, will continue to hold out sufficient opportunities for newcomers to realize their capacities and to contribute to the metropolitan and national well-being. This basic aspect of the urbanization process in the States continues to provide a firm basis for progress and to assure its future promise.

As America's self-conscious communities achieve a metropolitan polity able to utilize their fair share of the nation's productive energies, and as they maintain their ecological and demographic vitality by promoting the full capacities of their mounting populations, they may also be able at last to achieve a more satisfactory physical setting. In this connection, the current bogey of an all-absorbing and crushing megalopolis can be discarded as the troubled nightmare of scholars who poured too long over their data and never got out to drive leisurely "through the great city" with Anthony Bailey or some other knowledgeable guide to discover the charms of nature and the open spaces that still encompass and separate even the closely dotted cities on the map of the eastern seaboard. Residents of the dozen or so metropolises in that cluster will probably long continue to regard themselves as Bostonians, Hartfordians, and the like, rather than as Megalopolitans, but they will have to bestir themselves and vote funds for the acquisition and maintenance of adequate open areas to assure the preservation of their separate status. And as their numbers increase they can and in time will spawn new urban centers nearby, such as Reston near Washington, or in the vast open spaces that make North America the envy of the residents of all other continents.

Numerous technological developments appear to support the continued development of individually integrated metropolitan regions. While the automobile during the early decades of the century promoted a sprawling urban growth which was further extended as the progressive channeling of traffic into limited-access highways promoted the development of widely spaced suburbs, the resulting metropolitan regions seemed for a time boundless. But as the scale of urban growth promoted by the superhighway produced vast conurbations, such as Los Angeles, held together by the need to provide regional water supplies and similar urban services, other technological requirements developed to check their spread. Rapid-transit undergrounds, long essential to the development of densely settled metropolises such as New York, London, and Paris, are now making a comeback as more great cities turn to this alternative to the multiplication of superhighways, which have proven destructive to the old central cities. But subways, as New York has discovered, can also become too congested at the center, and too extended on the outskirts, where their successful operation requires a greater density of settlement than that provided by automobile suburbs. San Francisco is preparing to experiment with a rapid-transit line to service a string of suburbs, such as is already used in Stockholm. The wide distance between stops required to attain the desired speed will permit a sufficient development at each place not only to supply a paying load, but also to create a viable urban community with a distinctive identity and a responsible polity.

The technology of air transport also promises support for metropolitan regions. Although the increased speed and size of planes have in recent years drawn most of the business into the major airports and handicapped many smaller cities, New York and other great terminals already have as much traffic as they can bear, so transoceanic flights will land more frequently at Boston and other alternate ports. Nearby metropolises will be connected by rapid-transit rail lines, but air service will abandon most linear hookups for multiple direct connections, and even neighboring cities will continue to develop their special characteristics and distant contacts rather than merge into a seamless mass.

Some of the other current problems of modern metropolises will be eased as leaders learn to encourage and direct rather than buck several long-term trends. The progressive decline in central city populations, which began in London in the late eighteenth century and reached Manhattan in the early twentieth century, and which has since spread to most large central cities, can be accepted as an improvement rather than a setback in urban living provided the metropolis attains a polity and a tax base that enable it to maintain open space in the center in proper splendor, rather than as boarded-up wasteland.

North American cities in the pioneer, industrial, and metropolitan eras have generally attracted newcomers with offers of productive jobs, in contrast to the many cities in underdeveloped countries which have been inundated with refugees from an overpopulated hinterland. Yet despite their failure to develop productive industries, these more tropical cities have continued to maintain an orderly economy by a proliferation of tertiary or service functions. The warm climate most of these cities enjoy has freed their inhabitants from the more insistent demands in northern cities for shelter and clothing. Their geographic situation, among other circumstances, has encouraged a low regard for material goods and enabled many to survive on a relatively limited output. As a result, their residents have become accustomed to long periods of idleness. In contrast, the great metropolises farther north, because of the increasing productivity of their industrial sectors, have faced repeated crises due to the limits of their markets. It is now possible that current advocates of the counter-culture, with low material demands but high leisure-time needs, will point the way for the development of a more permissive and less job-oriented metropolitan society in the future.

Much indeed appears possible even with the present potential of the North American metropolis. Professor Sorokin, who recently predicted the end of "sensate" man, with his obsession with material wealth, has envisaged the dawn within another century or two of an "integral" age that will merge the supersensory or spiritual qualities of the East with the rational and technological contributions of the West. He assumes, among other matters, the continued creativity of mankind and the avoidance of a major war, but his time span of three to six generations places his projections far beyond present horizons. It may, however, be permissible, with the same assumptions, to forecast the continued concentration during the next three decades of an increasing number of residents, mostly native but many of foreign birth, in larger and more spaciously designed and safely mobile metropolises where, with the aid of fresh insights provided by varied social scientists and the new authority achieved through a widely participatory democracy, they will endeavor to increase opportunities for creative expression for those who desire it and to assure comfortable living facilities for all residents.

But it should be recognized that the continued urbanization of the United States, now that it has virtually exhausted the possibility of additional population concentration, will have to occur in other dimensions of urbanism. And as at former turning points, when new mechanical and social inventions and new

Table 11.   WORLD URBANIZATION TRENDS, 1920 TO 1960.
(From An Interim Report by the Population Division of the United Nations Bureau of Social Affairs). *

Urban Population (Localities of 20,000 or More Inhabitants) in Major Areas of the World, 1920 to 1960 *(rough estimates, in millions)*

Major Area	1920	1930	1940	1950	1960
World Total	252.9	328.1	427.0	531.5	753.4
Europe (ex. USSR)	104.4	123.3	140.1	147.6	173.8
Northern America	43.5	58.0	64.3	83.2	112.5
East Asia	39.1	56.6	81.6	105.8	160.5
South Asia	27.0	34.6	50.5	77.0	116.1
Soviet Union	16.0	24.0	47.0	50.0	78.0
Latin America	12.9	18.1	25.2	40.6	67.8
Africa	6.9	9.7	13.8	21.5	36.4
Oceania	3.1	3.8	4.5	5.8	8.3

Urban Population (20,000 and Over) as a Percentage of Total Population in Major Areas of the World, 1920 to 1960 *(rough estimates)*

Major Area	1920	1930	1940	1950	1960
World Total	14	16	19	21	25
Europe (ex. USSR)	32	35	37	38	41
Northern America	38	43	45	50	57
East Asia	7	10	13	15	20
South Asia	6	7	8	11	14
Soviet Union	10	13	24	28	36
Latin America	14	17	19	25	32
Africa	5	6	7	10	13
Oceania	34	35	38	42	50

Big-City Population (500,000 and Over) as a Percentage of Total Population in Major Areas of the World, 1920 to 1960 *(rough estimates)*

Major Area	1920	1930	1940	1950	1960
World Total	5	6	8	9	12
Europe (ex. USSR)	14	15	16	16	17
Northern America	19	23	25	30	36
East Asia	3	4	5	6	11
South Asia	1	1	2	4	5
Soviet Union	1	3	7	7	13
Latin America	6	8	9	12	17
Africa	1	1	2	3	4
Oceania†	18	19	21	22	31

†Percentages computed with unrounded data.

*From Gerald Breese, ed., *The City in Newly Developing Countries: Readings on Urbanism and Urbanization* (Englewood Cliffs, N.J.: Prentice-Hall, Inc., 1969), pp. 28, 32. Reprinted with permission of Prentice-Hall, Inc., and the United Nations.

forms of power joined to produce the industrial city in the 1800s, and a
century later the metropolis, so the prospect of a similar combination of fresh
technological and sociopolitical developments with new atomic energies presents at least a possible alternative to the holocaust many fear or the progressive urban decay most expect. Despite its many hazards, continued urbanization appears to offer the brighter prospect.

BIBLIOGRAPHY

Bailey, Anthony. *Through the Great City.* New York: The Macmillan Co., 1968.
Beyer, Glenn H., ed. *The Urban Explosion in Latin America: A Continent in the
Process of Modernization.* Ithaca, N.Y.: Cornell University Press, 1967.
Bollens, John C., and Henry J. Schmandt. *The Metropolis: Its People, Politics
and Economic Life.* New York: Harper & Row, Publishers, 1965.
Breese, Gerald, ed. *The City in Newly Developing Countries: Readings on Urban-
ism and Urbanization.* Englewood Cliffs, N.J.: Prentice-Hall, Inc., 1969.
Gulick, Luther H. *The Metropolitan Problem and American Ideas.* New York:
Alfred A. Knopf, Inc., 1962.
Lampard, Eric E. "The Dimensions of Urban History: A Footnote to the
'Urban Crisis.' " *Pacific Historical Review,* 39 (August 1970), 261–78.
McKelvey, Blake. "Cities as Nurseries of Self-Conscious Minorities." *Pacific
Historical Review,* 39 (August 1970), 367–81.
Meyerson, Martin, ed. *The Conscience of the City.* New York: George Braziller,
Inc., 1970.
Pickard, Jerome P. *Dimensions of Metropolitanism.* Research Monograph 14.
Washington, D.C.: Urban Land Institute, 1967.
Popenoe, David, ed. *The Urban Industrial Frontier.* New Brunswick, N.J.:
Rutgers University Press, 1969. See essays by Kenneth E. Boulding, Lyle
C. Fitch, and Norton E. Long.
Walsh, Annmarie H., ed. *The Urban Challenge to Government: An International
Comparison of Thirteen Cities.* New York: Praeger Publishers, 1969.

Index